FREE Test Taking Tips DVD Offer

To help us better serve you, we have developed a Test Taking Tips DVD that we would like to give you for FREE. **This DVD covers world-class test taking tips that you can use to be even more successful when you are taking your test.**

All that we ask is that you email us your feedback about your study guide. Please let us know what you thought about it – whether that is good, bad or indifferent.

To get your **FREE Test Taking Tips DVD**, email freedvd@studyguideteam.com with "FREE DVD" in the subject line and the following information in the body of the email:

a. The title of your study guide.

b. Your product rating on a scale of 1-5, with 5 being the highest rating.

c. Your feedback about the study guide. What did you think of it?

d. Your full name and shipping address to send your free DVD.

If you have any questions or concerns, please don't hesitate to contact us at freedvd@studyguideteam.com.

Thanks again!

Praxis Core Study Guide 2018

Academic Skills for Educators 5712, 5722, 5732 Math, Writing, and Reading

Test Prep Books Teaching Test Prep Team

Table of Contents

Quick Overview

As you draw closer to taking your exam, effective preparation becomes more and more important. Thankfully, you have this study guide to help you get ready. Use this guide to help keep your studying on track and refer to it often.

This study guide contains several key sections that will help you be successful on your exam. The guide contains tips for what you should do the night before and the day of the test. Also included are test-taking tips. Knowing the right information is not always enough. Many well-prepared test takers struggle with exams. These tips will help equip you to accurately read, assess, and answer test questions.

A large part of the guide is devoted to showing you what content to expect on the exam and to helping you better understand that content. In this guide are practice test questions so that you can see how well you have grasped the content. Then, answer explanations are provided so that you can understand why you missed certain questions.

Don't try to cram the night before you take your exam. This is not a wise strategy for a few reasons. First, your retention of the information will be low. Your time would be better used by reviewing information you already know rather than trying to learn a lot of new information. Second, you will likely become stressed as you try to gain a large amount of knowledge in a short amount of time. Third, you will be depriving yourself of sleep. So be sure to go to bed at a reasonable time the night before. Being well-rested helps you focus and remain calm.

Be sure to eat a substantial breakfast the morning of the exam. If you are taking the exam in the afternoon, be sure to have a good lunch as well. Being hungry is distracting and can make it difficult to focus. You have hopefully spent lots of time preparing for the exam. Don't let an empty stomach get in the way of success!

When travelling to the testing center, leave earlier than needed. That way, you have a buffer in case you experience any delays. This will help you remain calm and will keep you from missing your appointment time at the testing center.

Be sure to pace yourself during the exam. Don't try to rush through the exam. There is no need to risk performing poorly on the exam just so you can leave the testing center early. Allow yourself to use all of the allotted time if needed.

Remain positive while taking the exam even if you feel like you are performing poorly. Thinking about the content you should have mastered will not help you perform better on the exam.

Once the exam is complete, take some time to relax. Even if you feel that you need to take the exam again, you will be well served by some down time before you begin studying again. It's often easier to convince yourself to study if you know that it will come with a reward!

Test-Taking Strategies

1. Predicting the Answer

When you feel confident in your preparation for a multiple-choice test, try predicting the answer before reading the answer choices. This is especially useful on questions that test objective factual knowledge. By predicting the answer before reading the available choices, you eliminate the possibility that you will be distracted or led astray by an incorrect answer choice. You will feel more confident in your selection if you read the question, predict the answer, and then find your prediction among the answer choices. After using this strategy, be sure to still read all of the answer choices carefully and completely. If you feel unprepared, you should not attempt to predict the answers. This would be a waste of time and an opportunity for your mind to wander in the wrong direction.

2. Reading the Whole Question

Too often, test takers scan a multiple-choice question, recognize a few familiar words, and immediately jump to the answer choices. Test authors are aware of this common impatience, and they will sometimes prey upon it. For instance, a test author might subtly turn the question into a negative, or he or she might redirect the focus of the question right at the end. The only way to avoid falling into these traps is to read the entirety of the question carefully before reading the answer choices.

3. Looking for Wrong Answers

Long and complicated multiple-choice questions can be intimidating. One way to simplify a difficult multiple-choice question is to eliminate all of the answer choices that are clearly wrong. In most sets of answers, there will be at least one selection that can be dismissed right away. If the test is administered on paper, the test taker could draw a line through it to indicate that it may be ignored; otherwise, the test taker will have to perform this operation mentally or on scratch paper. In either case, once the obviously incorrect answers have been eliminated, the remaining choices may be considered. Sometimes identifying the clearly wrong answers will give the test taker some information about the correct answer. For instance, if one of the remaining answer choices is a direct opposite of one of the eliminated answer choices, it may well be the correct answer. The opposite of obviously wrong is obviously right! Of course, this is not always the case. Some answers are obviously incorrect simply because they are irrelevant to the question being asked. Still, identifying and eliminating some incorrect answer choices is a good way to simplify a multiple-choice question.

4. Don't Overanalyze

Anxious test takers often overanalyze questions. When you are nervous, your brain will often run wild, causing you to make associations and discover clues that don't actually exist. If you feel that this may be a problem for you, do whatever you can to slow down during the test. Try taking a deep breath or counting to ten. As you read and consider the question, restrict yourself to the particular words used by the author. Avoid thought tangents about what the author *really* meant, or what he or she was *trying* to say. The only things that matter on a multiple-choice test are the words that are actually in the question. You must avoid reading too much into a multiple-choice question, or supposing that the writer meant something other than what he or she wrote.

5. No Need for Panic

It is wise to learn as many strategies as possible before taking a multiple-choice test, but it is likely that you will come across a few questions for which you simply don't know the answer. In this situation, avoid panicking. Because most multiple-choice tests include dozens of questions, the relative value of a single wrong answer is small. As much as possible, you should compartmentalize each question on a multiple-choice test. In other words, you should not allow your feelings about one question to affect your success on the others. When you find a question that you either don't understand or don't know how to answer, just take a deep breath and do your best. Read the entire question slowly and carefully. Try rephrasing the question a couple of different ways. Then, read all of the answer choices carefully. After eliminating obviously wrong answers, make a selection and move on to the next question.

6. Confusing Answer Choices

When working on a difficult multiple-choice question, there may be a tendency to focus on the answer choices that are the easiest to understand. Many people, whether consciously or not, gravitate to the answer choices that require the least concentration, knowledge, and memory. This is a mistake. When you come across an answer choice that is confusing, you should give it extra attention. A question might be confusing because you do not know the subject matter to which it refers. If this is the case, don't eliminate the answer before you have affirmatively settled on another. When you come across an answer choice of this type, set it aside as you look at the remaining choices. If you can confidently assert that one of the other choices is correct, you can leave the confusing answer aside. Otherwise, you will need to take a moment to try to better understand the confusing answer choice. Rephrasing is one way to tease out the sense of a confusing answer choice.

7. Your First Instinct

Many people struggle with multiple-choice tests because they overthink the questions. If you have studied sufficiently for the test, you should be prepared to trust your first instinct once you have carefully and completely read the question and all of the answer choices. There is a great deal of research suggesting that the mind can come to the correct conclusion very quickly once it has obtained all of the relevant information. At times, it may seem to you as if your intuition is working faster even than your reasoning mind. This may in fact be true. The knowledge you obtain while studying may be retrieved from your subconscious before you have a chance to work out the associations that support it. Verify your instinct by working out the reasons that it should be trusted.

8. Key Words

Many test takers struggle with multiple-choice questions because they have poor reading comprehension skills. Quickly reading and understanding a multiple-choice question requires a mixture of skill and experience. To help with this, try jotting down a few key words and phrases on a piece of scrap paper. Doing this concentrates the process of reading and forces the mind to weigh the relative importance of the question's parts. In selecting words and phrases to write down, the test taker thinks about the question more deeply and carefully. This is especially true for multiple-choice questions that are preceded by a long prompt.

9. Subtle Negatives

One of the oldest tricks in the multiple-choice test writer's book is to subtly reverse the meaning of a question with a word like *not* or *except*. If you are not paying attention to each word in the question, you can easily be led astray by this trick. For instance, a common question format is, "Which of the following is...?" Obviously, if the question instead is, "Which of the following is not...?," then the answer will be quite different. Even worse, the test makers are aware of the potential for this mistake and will include one answer choice that would be correct if the question were not negated or reversed. A test taker who misses the reversal will find what he or she believes to be a correct answer and will be so confident that he or she will fail to reread the question and discover the original error. The only way to avoid this is to practice a wide variety of multiple-choice questions and to pay close attention to each and every word.

10. Reading Every Answer Choice

It may seem obvious, but you should always read every one of the answer choices! Too many test takers fall into the habit of scanning the question and assuming that they understand the question because they recognize a few key words. From there, they pick the first answer choice that answers the question they believe they have read. Test takers who read all of the answer choices might discover that one of the latter answer choices is actually *more* correct. Moreover, reading all of the answer choices can remind you of facts related to the question that can help you arrive at the correct answer. Sometimes, a misstatement or incorrect detail in one of the latter answer choices will trigger your memory of the subject and will enable you to find the right answer. Failing to read all of the answer choices is like not reading all of the items on a restaurant menu: you might miss out on the perfect choice.

11. Spot the Hedges

One of the keys to success on multiple-choice tests is paying close attention to every word. This is never truer than with words like almost, most, some, and sometimes. These words are called "hedges" because they indicate that a statement is not totally true or not true in every place and time. An absolute statement will contain no hedges, but in many subjects, the answers are not always straightforward or absolute. There are always exceptions to the rules in these subjects. For this reason, you should favor those multiple-choice questions that contain hedging language. The presence of qualifying words indicates that the author is taking special care with his or her words, which is certainly important when composing the right answer. After all, there are many ways to be wrong, but there is only one way to be right! For this reason, it is wise to avoid answers that are absolute when taking a multiple-choice test. An absolute answer is one that says things are either all one way or all another. They often include words like *every*, *always*, *best*, and *never*. If you are taking a multiple-choice test in a subject that doesn't lend itself to absolute answers, be on your guard if you see any of these words.

12. Long Answers

In many subject areas, the answers are not simple. As already mentioned, the right answer often requires hedges. Another common feature of the answers to a complex or subjective question are qualifying clauses, which are groups of words that subtly modify the meaning of the sentence. If the question or answer choice describes a rule to which there are exceptions or the subject matter is complicated, ambiguous, or confusing, the correct answer will require many words in order to be expressed clearly and accurately. In essence, you should not be deterred by answer choices that seem excessively long. Oftentimes, the author of the text will not be able to write the correct answer without offering some qualifications and modifications. Your job is to read the answer choices thoroughly and completely and to select the one that most accurately and precisely answers the question.

13. Restating to Understand

Sometimes, a question on a multiple-choice test is difficult not because of what it asks but because of how it is written. If this is the case, restate the question or answer choice in different words. This process serves a couple of important purposes. First, it forces you to concentrate on the core of the question. In order to rephrase the question accurately, you have to understand it well. Rephrasing the question will concentrate your mind on the key words and ideas. Second, it will present the information to your mind in a fresh way. This process may trigger your memory and render some useful scrap of information picked up while studying.

14. True Statements

Sometimes an answer choice will be true in itself, but it does not answer the question. This is one of the main reasons why it is essential to read the question carefully and completely before proceeding to the answer choices. Too often, test takers skip ahead to the answer choices and look for true statements. Having found one of these, they are content to select it without reference to the question above. Obviously, this provides an easy way for test makers to play tricks. The savvy test taker will always read the entire question before turning to the answer choices. Then, having settled on a correct answer choice, he or she will refer to the original question and ensure that the selected answer is relevant. The mistake of choosing a correct-but-irrelevant answer choice is especially common on questions related to specific pieces of objective knowledge. A prepared test taker will have a wealth of factual knowledge at his or her disposal, and should not be careless in its application.

15. No Patterns

One of the more dangerous ideas that circulates about multiple-choice tests is that the correct answers tend to fall into patterns. These erroneous ideas range from a belief that B and C are the most common right answers, to the idea that an unprepared test-taker should answer "A-B-A-C-A-D-A-B-A." It cannot be emphasized enough that pattern-seeking of this type is exactly the WRONG way to approach a multiple-choice test. To begin with, it is highly unlikely that the test maker will plot the correct answers according to some predetermined pattern. The questions are scrambled and delivered in a random order. Furthermore, even if the test maker was following a pattern in the assignation of correct answers, there is no reason why the test taker would know which pattern he or she was using. Any attempt to discern a pattern in the answer choices is a waste of time and a distraction from the real work of taking the test. A test taker would be much better served by extra preparation before the test than by reliance on a pattern in the answers.

FREE DVD OFFER

Don't forget that doing well on your exam includes both understanding the test content and understanding how to use what you know to do well on the test. We offer a completely FREE Test Taking Tips DVD that covers world class test taking tips that you can use to be even more successful when you are taking your test.

All that we ask is that you email us your feedback about your study guide. To get your **FREE Test Taking Tips DVD**, email freedvd@studyguideteam.com with "FREE DVD" in the subject line and the following information in the body of the email:

- The title of your study guide.
- Your product rating on a scale of 1-5, with 5 being the highest rating.
- Your feedback about the study guide. What did you think of it?
- Your full name and shipping address to send your free DVD.

Introduction to the Praxis Core Tests

Function of the Test

The **Praxis Core** tests are taken by college students or professionals who wish to apply to teacher preparation programs. There are three separate tests involved in the Praxis Core: the Reading Test, Writing Test, and Mathematics Test. These tests are designed to measure the skills of teaching candidates and assess their overall knowledge in certain subject areas.

Evaluation of test scores depends on the particular program candidates are interested in. Some universities use test scores to determine admission into teacher education programs, while some states look at test scores for their teacher licensing process.

The Praxis Core tests are computer-based tests that can be taken internationally. If taken outside the United States, they must be taken for either entrance or certification into a teacher education program or employment inside the United States.

Test Administration

To find test dates and centers, go to https://www.ets.org/praxis/register/centers_dates/. This has information about where and when tests are offered. The core tests all have a "continuous testing" window. Note that all three tests can be taken at the same time; this option is called **Combined Test**.

Retesting is an option if a test taker feels they did not perform well on the test; however, the retest must be taken twenty-one days after the initial test was taken.

Those who have need of accommodation in the testing environment will need to apply to have their accommodation approved by ETS Disability Services. Note that this process may take up to six weeks to review. Additional documentation can take up to another six weeks, so be sure and begin the process well in advance of the testing date. Once approved, ETS will send instructions on how to register for the test. Don't register for the test until documentation has been approved and sent back to you.

Test Format

On the day of the test, a photo ID as well as the admission ticket should be brought with you to the testing center. Test takers should arrive at least half an hour before the test starts to ensure they are on time and have all the resources available to them. Scientific, graphic, and four-function calculators are allowed in the testing area for *some* praxis tests. The ETS website will provide information to determine if the test being taken permits the use of a calculator. Food and drink are not permitted in the testing area.

There are three different tests that can be taken for the Praxis Core: Reading, Writing, and Math. The Combined Test offers all three of these tests at the same time. Here is the breakdown of each test:

Test	Questions	Time
Reading	56	85 minutes
Mathematics	56	85 minutes
Writing (2 sections)	40 + 2 essays	40 minutes + 60 minutes

Scoring

Score information on the score report will be available 10 to 16 business days after the test. Test takers can find online scores through an account set up with the Praxis website, and they have the option to send scores to up to four agencies when they first register for the test. Test scores are downloadable for ten years from the reporting date.

To determine what score is considered a passing one, test takers will have to check with the state, institution, or association that requires the test. On the ETS website, there is a link that provides information on every state that requires the Praxis Core. The information will lead to the agency's website where it can be determined what the passing score will be for a specific agency or institution.

Recent/Future Developments

The ETS updates the Praxis website annually to show how states or agencies have altered their requirements for passing the test. Check with the state or agency on the ETS website to get detailed information about passing scores and requirements.

Praxis Core Reading

Key Ideas and Details

Directly Stated Information vs. Implications

Engaged readers should constantly self-question while reviewing texts to help them form conclusions. Self-questioning is when readers review a paragraph, page, passage, or chapter and ask themselves, "Did I understand what I read?," "What was the main event in this section?," "Where is this taking place?," and so on. Authors can provide clues or pieces of evidence throughout a text or passage to guide readers toward a conclusion. This is why active and engaged readers should read the text or passage in its entirety before forming a definitive conclusion. If readers do not gather all the pieces of evidence needed, then they may jump to an illogical conclusion.

At times, authors **directly state** conclusions while others simply **imply** them. Of course, it is easier if authors outwardly provide conclusions to readers because it does not leave any information open to interpretation. On the other hand, implications are things that authors do not directly state but can be assumed based off of information they provided. If authors only imply what may have happened, readers can form a menagerie of ideas for conclusions. For example, look at the following statement: "Once we heard the sirens, we hunkered down in the storm shelter." In this statement, the author does not directly state that there was a tornado, but clues such as "sirens" and "storm shelter" provide insight to the reader to help form that conclusion.

Drawing Inferences and Implications from a Text

Readers should be able to make inferences. Making an **inference** requires the reader to read between the lines and look for what is implied rather than what is directly stated. That is, using information that is known from the text, the reader is able to make a logical assumption about information that is *not* directly stated but is probably true. Read the following passage:

> "Hey, do you wanna meet my new puppy?" Jonathan asked.
>
> "Oh, I'm sorry but please don't—" Jacinta began to protest, but before she could finish, Jonathan had already opened the passenger side door of his car and a perfect white ball of fur came bouncing towards Jacinta.
>
> "Isn't he the cutest?" beamed Jonathan.
>
> "Yes—achoo!—he's pretty—aaaachooo!!—adora—aaa—aaaachoo!" Jacinta managed to say in between sneezes. "But if you don't mind, I—I—achoo!—need to go inside."

Which of the following can be inferred from Jacinta's reaction to the puppy?

a. She hates animals
b. She is allergic to dogs
c. She prefers cats to dogs
d. She is angry at Jonathan

An inference requires the reader to consider the information presented and then form their own idea about what is probably true. Based on the details in the passage, what is the best answer to the question? Important details to pay attention to include the tone of Jacinta's dialogue, which is overall polite and apologetic, as well as her reaction itself, which is a long string of sneezes. Choices *A* and *D* both express strong emotions ("hates" and "angry") that are not evident in Jacinta's speech or actions. Choice *C* mentions cats, but there is nothing in the passage to indicate Jacinta's feelings about cats. Choice *B*, "she is allergic to dogs," is the most logical choice—based on the fact that she began sneezing as soon as a fluffy dog approached her, it makes sense to guess that Jacinta might be allergic to dogs. So even though Jacinta never directly states, "Sorry, I'm allergic to dogs!," using the clues in the passage, it is still reasonable to guess that this is true.

Making inferences is crucial for readers of literature because literary texts often avoid presenting complete and direct information to readers about characters' thoughts or feelings, or they present this information in an unclear way, leaving it up to the reader to interpret clues given in the text. In order to make inferences while reading, readers should ask themselves:

- What details are being presented in the text?
- Is there any important information that seems to be missing?
- Based on the information that the author does include, what else is probably true?
- Is this inference reasonable based on what is already known?

Bias and Stereotypes

Not only can authors state facts or opinions in their writing, they sometimes intentionally or unintentionally show bias or portray a stereotype. A **bias** is when someone demonstrates a prejudice in favor of or against something or someone in an unfair manner. When an author is biased in his or her writing, readers should be skeptical despite the fact that the author's bias may be correct. For example, two athletes competed for the same position. One athlete is related to the coach and is a mediocre athlete, while the other player excels and deserves the position. The coach chose the less talented player who is related to him for the position. This is a biased decision because it favors someone in an unfair way.

Similar to a bias, a **stereotype** shows favoritism or opposition but toward a specific group or place. Stereotypes create an oversimplified or overgeneralized idea about a certain group, person, or place. For example:

> Women are horrible drivers.

This statement basically labels *all* women as horrible drivers. While there may be some terrible female drivers, the stereotype implies that *all* women are bad drivers when, in fact, not *all* women are. While many readers are aware of several vile ethnic, religious, and cultural stereotypes, audiences should be cautious of authors' flawed assumptions because they can be less obvious than the despicable examples that are pervasive in society.

Determining Central Ideas or Themes of a Text

Identifying Theme or Central Message

The **theme** is the central message of a fictional work, whether that work is structured as prose, drama, or poetry. It is the heart of what an author is trying to say to readers through the writing, and theme is largely conveyed through literary elements and techniques.

In literature, a theme can often be determined by considering the over-arching narrative conflict within the work. Though there are several types of conflicts and several potential themes within them, the following are the most common:

- Individual against the self—relevant to themes of self-awareness, internal struggles, pride, coming of age, facing reality, fate, free will, vanity, loss of innocence, loneliness, isolation, fulfillment, failure, and disillusionment
- Individual against nature—relevant to themes of knowledge vs. ignorance, nature as beauty, quest for discovery, self-preservation, chaos and order, circle of life, death, and destruction of beauty
- Individual against society—relevant to themes of power, beauty, good, evil, war, class struggle, totalitarianism, role of men/women, wealth, corruption, change vs. tradition, capitalism, destruction, heroism, injustice, and racism
- Individual against another individual—relevant to themes of hope, loss of love or hope, sacrifice, power, revenge, betrayal, and honor

For example, in Hawthorne's *The Scarlet Letter*, one possible narrative conflict could be the individual against the self, with a relevant theme of internal struggles. This theme is alluded to through characterization—Dimmesdale's moral struggle with his love for Hester and Hester's internal struggles with the truth and her daughter, Pearl. It's also alluded to through plot—Dimmesdale's suicide and Hester helping the very townspeople who initially condemned her.

Sometimes, a text can convey a **message** or **universal lesson**—a truth or insight that the reader infers from the text, based on analysis of the literary and/or poetic elements. This message is often presented as a statement. For example, a potential message in Shakespeare's *Hamlet* could be "Revenge is what ultimately drives the human soul." This message can be immediately determined through plot and characterization in numerous ways, but it can also be determined through the setting of Norway, which is bordering on war.

<u>How Authors Develop Theme</u>

Authors employ a variety of techniques to present a theme. They may compare or contrast characters, events, places, ideas, or historical or invented settings to speak thematically. They may use analogies, metaphors, similes, allusions, or other literary devices to convey the theme. An author's use of diction, syntax, and tone can also help convey the theme. Authors will often develop themes through the development of characters, use of the setting, repetition of ideas, use of symbols, and through contrasting value systems. Authors of both fiction and nonfiction genres will use a variety of these techniques to develop one or more themes.

Regardless of the literary genre, there are commonalities in how authors, playwrights, and poets develop themes or central ideas.

Authors often do research, the results of which contribute to theme. In prose fiction and drama, this research may include real historical information about the setting the author has chosen or include elements that make fictional characters, settings, and plots seem realistic to the reader. In nonfiction, research is critical since the information contained within this literature must be accurate and, moreover, accurately represented.

In fiction, authors present a narrative conflict that will contribute to the overall theme. In fiction, this conflict may involve the storyline itself and some trouble within characters that needs resolution. In nonfiction, this conflict may be an explanation or commentary on factual people and events.

Authors will sometimes use character motivation to convey theme, such as in the example from *Hamlet* regarding revenge. In fiction, the characters an author creates will think, speak, and act in ways that effectively convey the theme to readers. In nonfiction, the characters are factual, as in a biography, but authors pay particular attention to presenting those motivations to make them clear to readers.

Authors also use literary devices as a means of conveying theme. For example, the use of moon symbolism in Shelley's *Frankenstein* is significant as its phases can be compared to the phases that the Creature undergoes as he struggles with his identity.

The selected point of view can also contribute to a work's theme. The use of first person point of view in a fiction or non-fiction work engages the reader's response differently than third person point of view. The central idea or theme from a first-person narrative may differ from a third-person limited text.

In literary nonfiction, authors usually identify the purpose of their writing, which differs from fiction, where the general purpose is to entertain. The purpose of nonfiction is usually to inform, persuade, or entertain the audience. The stated purpose of a non-fiction text will drive how the central message or theme, if applicable, is presented.

Authors identify an audience for their writing, which is critical in shaping the theme of the work. For example, the audience for J.K. Rowling's *Harry Potter* series would be different than the audience for a biography of George Washington. The audience an author chooses to address is closely tied to the purpose of the work. The choice of an audience also drives the choice of language and level of diction an author uses. Ultimately, the intended audience determines the level to which that subject matter is presented and the complexity of the theme.

Central Ideas in Informational Texts

Informational text is specifically designed to relate factual information, and although it is open to a reader's interpretation and application of the facts, the structure of the presentation is carefully designed to lead the reader to a particular conclusion or central idea. When reading informational text, it is important that readers are able to understand its organizational structure as the structure often directly relates to an author's intent to inform and/or persuade the reader.

The first step in identifying the text's structure is to determine the thesis or main idea. The thesis statement and organization of a work are closely intertwined. A **thesis statement** indicates the writer's purpose and may include the scope and direction of the text. It may be presented at the beginning of a text or at the end, and it may be explicit or implicit.

Once a reader has a grasp of the thesis or main idea of the text, he or she can better determine its organizational structure. Test takers are advised to read informational text passages more than once in order to comprehend the material fully. It is also helpful to examine any text features present in the text including the table of contents, index, glossary, headings, footnotes, and visuals. The analysis of these features and the information presented within them can offer additional clues about the central idea and structure of a text.

The following questions should be asked when considering structure:

- How does the author assemble the parts to make an effective whole argument?
- Is the passage linear in nature and if so, what is the timeline or thread of logic?
- What is the presented order of events, facts, or arguments? Are these effective in contributing to the author's thesis?
- How can the passage be divided into sections? How are they related to each other and to the main idea or thesis?
- What key terms are used to indicate the organization?

Next, test takers should skim the passage, noting the first line or two of each body paragraph—the **topic sentences**—and the conclusion. Key **transitional terms**, such as *on the other hand, also, because, however, therefore, most importantly*, and *first*, within the text can also signal organizational structure. Based on these clues, readers should then be able to identify what type of organizational structure is being used. The following organizational structures are most common:

- **Problem/solution**: organized by an analysis/overview of a problem, followed by potential solution(s)
- **Cause/effect**: organized by the effects resulting from a cause or the cause(s) of a particular effect
- **Spatial order**: organized by points that suggest location or direction—e.g., top to bottom, right to left, outside to inside
- **Chronological/sequence order**: organized by points presented to indicate a passage of time or through purposeful steps/stages
- **Comparison/contrast**: organized by points that indicate similarities and/or differences between two things or concepts
- **Order of importance**: organized by priority of points, often most significant to least significant or vice versa

Summaries of Main Points and Supporting Details

Creating an outline that identifies the **main ideas** of a passage as well as the **supporting details** is a helpful tool in effectively summarizing a text. Most outlines will include a title that reveals the topic of the text and is usually a single phrase or word, such as "whales." If the passage is divided up into paragraphs, or the paragraphs into sections, each paragraph or section will have its own main idea. These "main ideas" are usually depicted in outlines as roman numerals. Next, writers use supporting details in order to support or prove the main ideas. The supporting details should be listed underneath each main idea in the outline.

For example:

Title: Whales
I. Killer whales
    a. Highly social
    b. Apex predator
II. Humpback whales
    a. Males produce "song"
    b. Targeted for whaling industry
III. Beluga whales
    a. Complex sense of hearing
    b. Slow swimmers

Making an outline is a useful method of summarization because it forces the reader to deconstruct the text as a whole and to identify only the most important parts of the text.

Ideas from a text can also be organized using graphic organizers. A **graphic organizer** is a way to simplify information and take key points from the text. A graphic organizer such as a timeline may have an event listed for a corresponding date on the timeline while an outline may have an event listed under a key point that occurs in the text. Each reader needs to create the type of graphic organizer that works the best for him or her in terms of being able to recall information from a story. Examples include a **spider-map**, which takes a main idea from the story and places it in a bubble with supporting points branching off the main idea. An **outline** is useful for diagramming the main and supporting points of the entire story, and a **Venn diagram** classifies information as separate or overlapping.

Writing a summary is similar to creating an outline. In both instances, the reader wants to relay the most important parts of the text without being too verbose. A **summary** of a text should begin with stating the main idea of that text. Then, the reader must decide which supporting details are absolutely essential to the main idea of the text and leave any irrelevant information out of the summary. A summary shouldn't be too brief—readers should include important details depicted in the text—but it also shouldn't be too long either. The appeal of a summary to an audience is that they are able to receive the message of the text without being distracted by the style or detours of the author.

Another effective reading comprehension strategy is paraphrasing. Paraphrasing is usually longer than a summary. **Paraphrasing** is taking the author's text and rewriting, or "translating," it into their own words. A tip for paraphrasing is to read a passage over three times. Once you read the passage and understand what the author is saying, cover the original passage and begin to write everything you remember from that passage into your own words. Usually, if you understand the content well enough, you will have translated the main idea of the author into your own words with your own writing style. An effective paraphrase will be as long as the original passage but will have a different writing structure.

Summaries of Informational Texts

Informational text is written material that has the primary function of imparting information about a topic. It is often written by someone with expertise in the topic and directed at an audience that has less knowledge of the topic. Informational texts are written in a different fashion from storytelling or narrative texts. Typically, this type of text has several organizational and structural differences from narrative text. In informational texts, there are features such as charts, graphs, photographs, headings and subheadings, glossaries, indexes, bibliographies, or other guidance features. With the aid of technology, embedded hyperlinks and video content are also sometimes included. Informational material may be written to compare and contrast, be explanatory, link cause and effect, provide opinion, persuade the reader, or serve a number of other purposes. Finally, informational texts typically use a different style of language than narrative texts, which instead, focus more on storytelling. Historically, informational texts were not introduced until students were ready to read to learn versus still learning to read. However, research is now suggesting that informational text can be developmentally appropriate for students at a much younger age.

One very effective strategy for increasing comprehension of informational text is reciprocal teaching. **Reciprocal teaching** is a method of small group teaching that relies on students assuming different roles to practice four reading strategies particularly helpful for readers of informational texts. Predicting, summarizing, questioning, and clarifying will lead students to understand and apply what they read. Skilled readers have acquired a set of techniques that make informational reading effective for them. They begin by previewing text selections and making educated guesses as to what the content will include. They then identify the purpose for reading the text and can explain why the content will be important to know. They are able to filter the reading selection to screen out the trivial points and focus on the most important facts. Using critical thinking skills, they monitor their own understanding of the information by asking themselves questions about what they have read. They use multiple methods to determine the meaning of unknown vocabulary. Finally, they can concisely and succinctly form an overall summary of what they have learned from the text.

Predicting

Predicting requires thinking ahead and, after reading, verifying whether predictions were correct. This method engages students with the text and gets them to pay attention to details that tell them whether their predictions might be coming true. The goal is to help students learn to base their predictions on clues from the text. They should not only state what they predict but also be able to comment on the specifics of the text that lead them to make those predictions.

Summarizing

Through **summarizing**, students learn to identify the main ideas and differentiate them from the less important information in the text. It helps them remember what they read and retell the central concepts in their own words. As students learn to break down larger chunks of information into more concise sentences, they use analytical thinking skills and hone their critical reading capabilities.

Questioning Techniques

Questioning has immeasurable value in the reading process. Answering questions about a text gives purpose for reading to students and focuses them on reading to learn information. Similarly, generating questions about a text for others to answer enables a student to analyze what is important to learn in the text and glean summarizing skills. Keeping Bloom's Taxonomy in mind, teachers can scaffold students toward increased critical thinking capabilities. **Bloom's Taxonomy** shows the hierarchy of learning progressing through the following stages:

- Remembering
- Understanding
- Applying
- Analyzing
- Evaluating
- Creating

Clarifying

Clarifying is the post-reading phase where students learn to clear up any misunderstandings and unanswered questions. Strategies for clarifying include defining any unknown words, rereading at a slower pace, reviewing previous segments of the text, referring to their summaries, and skimming future portions of the text.

Topic Versus Main Idea

It is very important to know the difference between the topic and the main idea of the text. Even though these two are similar because they both present the central point of a text, they have distinctive differences. A **topic** is the subject of the text; it can usually be described in a one- to two-word phrase and appears in the simplest form. On the other hand, the **main idea** is more detailed and provides the author's central point of the text. It can be expressed through a complete sentence and is often found in the beginning, middle, or end of a paragraph. In most nonfiction books, the first sentence of the passage usually (but not always) states the main idea. Review the passage below to explore the topic versus the main idea.

> Cheetahs are one of the fastest mammals on the land, reaching up to 70 miles an hour over short distances. Even though cheetahs can run as fast as 70 miles an hour, they usually only have to run half that speed to catch up with their choice of prey. Cheetahs cannot maintain a fast pace over long periods of time because their bodies will overheat. After a chase, cheetahs need to rest for approximately 30 minutes prior to eating or returning to any other activity.

In the example above, the topic of the passage is "Cheetahs" simply because that is the subject of the text. The main idea of the text is "Cheetahs are one of the fastest mammals on the land but can only maintain a fast pace for shorter distances." While it covers the topic, it is more detailed and refers to the text in its entirety. The text continues to provide additional details called supporting details, which will be discussed in the next section.

Supporting Details

Supporting details help readers better develop and understand the main idea. Supporting details answer questions like *who, what, where, when, why,* and *how*. Different types of supporting details include examples, facts and statistics, anecdotes, and sensory details.

Persuasive and informative texts often use supporting details. In persuasive texts, authors attempt to make readers agree with their points of view, and supporting details are often used as "selling points." If authors make a statement, they need to support the statement with evidence in order to adequately persuade readers. Informative texts use supporting details such as examples and facts to inform readers. Review the previous "Cheetahs" passage to find examples of supporting details.

> Cheetahs are one of the fastest mammals on the land, reaching up to 70 miles an hour over short distances. Even though cheetahs can run as fast as 70 miles an hour, they usually only have to run half that speed to catch up with their choice of prey. Cheetahs cannot maintain a fast pace over long periods of time because their bodies will overheat. After a chase, cheetahs need to rest for approximately 30 minutes prior to eating or returning to any other activity.

In the example, supporting details include:

- Cheetahs reach up to 70 miles per hour over short distances.
- They usually only have to run half that speed to catch up with their prey.
- Cheetahs will overheat if they exert a high speed over longer distances.
- Cheetahs need to rest for 30 minutes after a chase.

Look at the diagram below (applying the cheetah example) to help determine the hierarchy of topic, main idea, and supporting details.

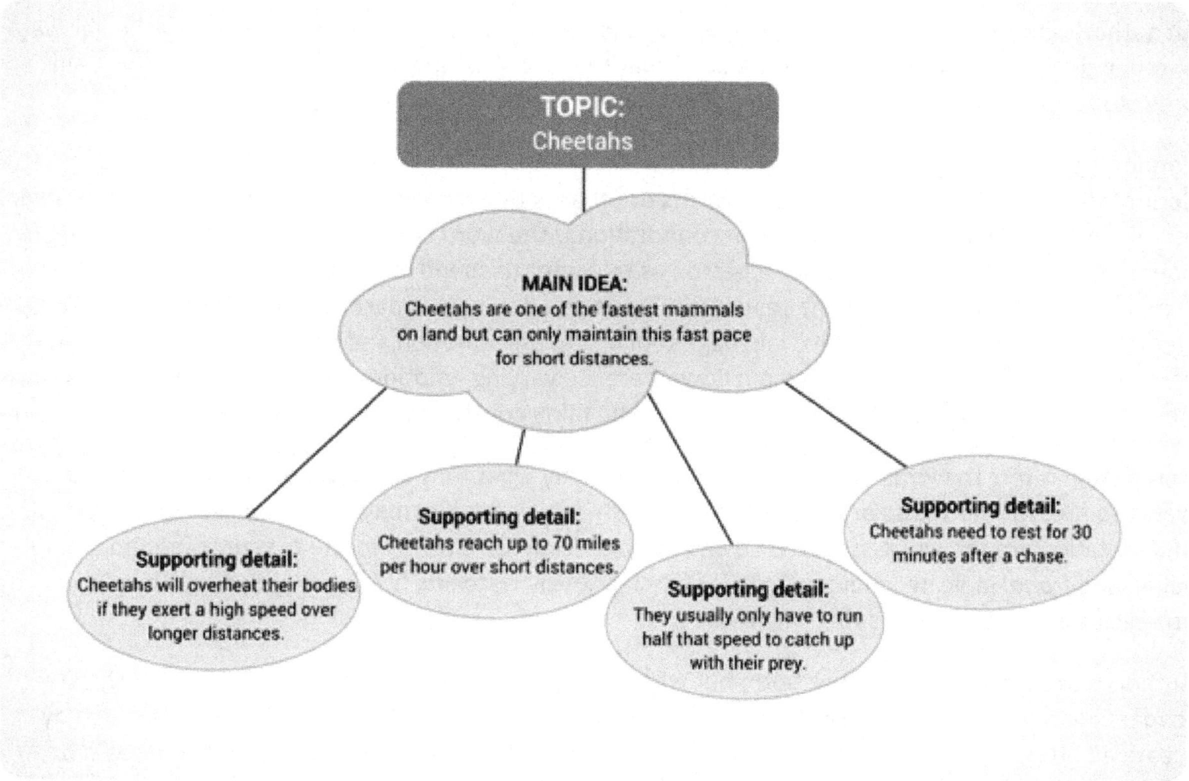

Determining How Ideas or Details Inform the Author's Argument

Once a reader has determined an author's thesis or main idea, he or she will need to understand how textual evidence supports interpretation of that thesis or main idea. Test takers will be asked direct questions regarding an author's main idea and may be asked to identify evidence that would support those ideas. This will require test takers to comprehend literal and figurative meanings within the text passage, be able to draw inferences from provided information, and be able to separate important evidence from minor supporting details. It's often helpful to skim test questions and answer options prior to critically reading informational text; however, test takers should avoid the temptation to solely look for the correct answers. Just trying to find the "right answer" may cause test takers to miss important supporting textual evidence. Making mental note of test questions is only helpful as a guide when reading.

After identifying an author's thesis or main idea, a test taker should look at the supporting details that the author provides to back up his or her assertions, identifying those additional pieces of information that help expand the thesis. From there, test takers should examine the additional information and related details for credibility, the author's use of outside sources, and be able to point to direct evidence that supports the author's claims. It's also imperative that test takers be able to identify what is strong support and what is merely additional information that is nice to know but not necessary. Being able to make this differentiation will help test takers effectively answer questions regarding an author's use of supporting evidence within informational text.

Craft, Structure, and Language Skills

Understanding the Effect of Word Choice

An author's choice of words—also referred to as **diction**—helps to convey meaning in a particular way. Through diction, an author can convey a particular tone—e.g., a humorous tone, a serious tone—in order to support the thesis in a meaningful way to the reader.

Connotation and Denotation

Connotation is when an author chooses words or phrases that invoke ideas or feelings other than their literal meaning. An example of the use of connotation is the word *cheap*, which suggests something is poor in value or negatively describes a person as reluctant to spend money. When something or someone is described this way, the reader is more inclined to have a particular image or feeling. Thus, connotation can be a very effective language tool in creating emotion and swaying opinion. However, connotations are sometimes hard to pin down because varying emotions can be associated with a word. Generally, though, connotative meanings tend to be fairly consistent within a specific cultural group.

Denotation refers to words or phrases that mean exactly what they say. It is helpful when a writer wants to present hard facts or vocabulary terms with which readers may be unfamiliar. Some examples of denotation are the words *inexpensive* and *frugal*. *Inexpensive* refers to the cost of something, not its value, and *frugal* indicates that a person is conscientiously watching his or her spending. These terms do not elicit the same emotions that *cheap* does.

Authors sometimes choose to use both, but what they choose and when they use it is what critical readers need to differentiate. One method isn't inherently better than the other; however, one may create a better effect, depending upon an author's intent. If, for example, an author's purpose is to inform, to instruct, and to familiarize readers with a difficult subject, his or her use of connotation may be helpful. However, it may also undermine credibility and confuse readers. An author who wants to create a credible, scholarly effect in his or her text would most likely use denotation, which emphasizes literal, factual meaning and examples.

Technical Language

Test takers and critical readers alike should be very aware of technical language used within informational text. **Technical language** refers to terminology that is specific to a particular industry and is best understood by those specializing in that industry. This language is fairly easy to differentiate since it will most likely be unfamiliar to readers. It's critical to be able to define technical language either by the author's written definition, through the use of an included glossary—if offered—or through context clues that help readers clarify word meaning.

How an Author's Word Choice Conveys Attitude and Shapes Meaning, Style, and Tone

Authors choose their words carefully in order to artfully depict meaning, style, and tone, which is most commonly inferred through the use of adjectives and verbs. The **tone** is the predominant emotion present in the text and represents the attitude or feelings that an author has towards a character or event.

To review, an **adjective** is a word used to describe something, and usually precedes the **noun**, a person, place, or object. A **verb** is a word describing an action. For example, the sentence "The scary woodpecker ate the spider" includes the adjective "scary," the noun "woodpecker," and the verb "ate." Reading this sentence may rouse some negative feelings, as the word "scary" carries a negative charge. The **charge** is the emotional connotation that can be derived from the adjectives and verbs and is either positive or negative. Recognizing the charge of a particular sentence or passage is an effective way to understand the meaning and tone the author is trying to convey.

Many authors have conflicting charges within the same text, but a definitive tone can be inferred by understanding the meaning of the charges relative to each other. It's important to recognize key **conjunctions**, or words that link sentences or clauses together. There are several types and subtypes of conjunctions. Three are most important for reading comprehension:

- **Cumulative conjunctions** add one statement to another.
    - Examples: *and, both, also, as well as, not only*
    - I.e. The juice is sweet *and* sour.
- **Adversative conjunctions** are used to contrast two clauses.
    - Examples: *but, while, still, yet, nevertheless*
    - I.e. She was tired *but* she was happy.
- **Alternative conjunctions** express two alternatives.
    - Examples: *or, either, neither, nor, else, otherwise*
    - I.e. He must eat *or* he will die.

Identifying the meaning and tone of a text can be accomplished with the following techniques:

- Identify the adjectives and verbs.
- Recognize any important conjunctions.
- Label the adjectives and verbs as positive or negative.
- Understand what the charge means about the text.

To demonstrate these steps, examine the following passage from the classic children's poem, "The Sheep":

> Lazy sheep, pray tell me why
>
> In the pleasant fields you lie,
>
> Eating grass, and daisies white,
>
> From the morning till the night?
>
> Everything can something do,
>
> But what kind of use are you?

–Taylor, Jane and Ann. "The Sheep."

This selection is a good example of conflicting charges that work together to express an overall tone. Following the first two steps, identify the adjectives, verbs, and conjunctions within the passage. For this example, the adjectives are <u>underlined</u>, the verbs are in **bold**, and the conjunctions *italicized*:

> <u>Lazy</u> sheep, pray **tell** me why
>
> In the <u>pleasant</u> fields you **lie**,
>
> **Eating** grass, and daisies <u>white,</u>
>
> From the morning till the night?
>
> Everything can something do,
>
> *But* what kind of use are you?

For step three, read the passage and judge whether feelings of positivity or negativity arose. Then assign a charge to each of the words that were outlined. This can be done in a table format, or simply by writing a + or – next to the word.

The word <u>lazy</u> carries a negative connotation; it usually denotes somebody unwilling to work. To **tell** someone something has an exclusively neutral connotation, as it depends on what's being told, which has not yet been revealed at this point, so a charge can be assigned later. The word <u>pleasant</u> is an inherently positive word. To **lie** could be positive or negative depending on the context, but as the subject (the sheep) is lying in a pleasant field, then this is a positive experience. **Eating** is also generally positive.

After labeling the charges for each word, it might be inferred that the tone of this poem is happy and maybe even admiring or innocuously envious. However, notice the adversative conjunction, "but" and what follows. The author has listed all the pleasant things this sheep gets to do all day, but the tone changes when the author asks, "What kind of use are you?" Asking someone to prove their value is a rather hurtful thing to do, as it implies that the person asking the question doesn't believe the subject has any value, so this could be listed under negative charges. Referring back to the verb **tell**, after reading the whole passage, it can be deduced that the author is asking the sheep to tell what use the sheep is, so this has a negative charge.

+	–
• Pleasant • Lie in fields • From morning to night	• Lazy • Tell me • What kind of use are you

Upon examining the charges, it might seem like there's an even amount of positive and negative emotion in this selection, and that's where the conjunction "but" becomes crucial to identifying the tone. The conjunction "but" indicates there's a contrasting view to the pleasantness of the sheep's daily life, and this view is that the sheep is lazy and useless, which is also indicated by the first line, "lazy sheep, pray tell me why."

It might be helpful to look at questions pertaining to tone. For this selection, consider the following question:

The author of the poem regards the sheep with a feeling of what?

a. Respect
b. Disgust
c. Apprehension
d. Intrigue

Considering the author views the sheep as lazy with nothing to offer, Choice *A* appears to reflect the opposite of what the author is feeling.

Choice *B* seems to mirror the author's feelings towards the sheep, as laziness is considered a disreputable trait, and people (or personified animals, in this case) with unfavorable traits might be viewed with disgust.

Choice *C* doesn't make sense within context, as laziness isn't usually feared.

Choice *D* is tricky, as it may be tempting to argue that the author is intrigued with the sheep because they ask, "pray tell me why." This is another out-of-scope answer choice as it doesn't *quite* describe the feelings the author experiences and there's also a much better fit in Choice *B*.

An Author's Tone, Message, and Effect

<u>Tone</u>

An author's **tone** is the use of particular words, phrases, and writing style to convey an overall meaning. Tone expresses the author's attitude towards a particular topic. For example, a historical reading passage may begin like the following:

> The presidential election of 1960 ushered in a new era, a new Camelot, a new phase of forward thinking in U.S. politics that embraced brash action, unrest, and responded with admirable leadership.

From this opening statement, a reader can draw some conclusions about the author's attitude towards President John F. Kennedy. Furthermore, the reader can make additional, educated guesses about the state of the Union during the 1960 presidential election. By close reading, the test taker can determine that the repeated use of the word *new* and words such as *admirable leadership* indicate the author's tone of admiration regarding the President's boldness. In addition, the author assesses that the era during President Kennedy's administration was problematic through the use of the words *brash action* and *unrest.* Therefore, if a test taker encountered a test question asking about the author's use of tone and their assessment of the Kennedy administration, the test taker should be able to identify an answer indicating admiration. Similarly, if asked about the state of the Union during the 1960s, a test taker should be able to correctly identify an answer indicating political unrest.

When identifying an author's tone, the following list of words may be helpful. This is not an inclusive list. Generally, parts of speech that indicate attitude will also indicate tone:

- Comical
- Angry
- Ambivalent
- Scary
- Lyrical
- Matter-of-fact

- Judgmental
- Sarcastic
- Malicious
- Objective
- Pessimistic
- Patronizing
- Gloomy
- Instructional
- Satirical
- Formal
- Casual

<u>Message</u>
An author's **message** is the same as the overall meaning of a passage. It is the main idea, or the main concept the author wishes to convey. An author's message may be stated outright or it may be implied. Regardless, the test taker will need to use careful reading skills to identify an author's message or purpose.

Often, the message of a particular passage can be determined by thinking about why the author wrote the information. Many historical passages are written to inform and to teach readers established, factual information. However, many historical works are also written to convey biased ideas to readers. Gleaning bias from an author's message in a historical passage can be difficult, especially if the reader is presented with a variety of established facts as well. Readers tend to accept historical writing as factual. This is not always the case. Any discerning reader who has tackled historical information on topics such as United States political party agendas can attest that two or more works on the same topic may have completely different messages supporting or refuting the value of the identical policies. Therefore, it is important to critically assess an author's message separate from factual information. One author, for example, may point to the rise of unorthodox political candidates in an election year based on the failures of the political party in office while another may point to the rise of the same candidates in the same election year based on the current party's successes. The historical facts of what has occurred leading up to an election year are not in refute. Labeling those facts as a failure or a success is a bias within an author's overall message, as is excluding factual information in order to further a particular point. In a standardized testing situation, a reader must be able to critically assess what the author is trying to say separate from the historical facts that surround their message.

Using the example of Lincoln's Gettysburg Address, a test question may ask the following:

> What is the message the author is trying to convey through this address?

Then they will ask the test taker to select an answer that best expresses Lincoln's message to his audience. Based on the options given, a test taker should be able to select the answer expressing the idea that Lincoln's audience should recognize the efforts of those who died in the war as a sacrifice to preserving human equality and self-government.

<u>Effect</u>
The **effect** an author wants to convey is when an author wants to impart a particular mood in their message. An author may want to challenge a reader's intellect, inspire imagination, or spur emotion. An author may present information to appeal to a physical, aesthetic, or transformational sense.

Take the following text as an example:

> In 1963, Martin Luther King stated "I have a dream." The gathering at the Lincoln Memorial was the beginning of the Civil Rights movement and, with its reference to the Emancipation Proclamation, electrified those who wanted freedom and equality while rising from hatred and slavery. It was the beginning of radical change.

The test taker may be asked about the effect this statement might have on King's audience. Through careful reading of the passage, the test taker should be able to choose an answer that best identifies an effect of grabbing the audience's attention. The historical facts are in place: King made the speech in 1963 at the Lincoln Memorial, kicked off the civil rights movement, and referenced the Emancipation Proclamation. The words *electrified* and *radical change* indicate the effect the author wants the reader to understand as a result of King's speech. In this historical passage, facts are facts. However, the author's message goes above the facts to indicate the effect the message had on the audience and, in addition, the effect the event should have on the reader.

Analyzing the Structure of a Text

Good writing is not merely a random collection of sentences. No matter how well written, sentences must relate and coordinate appropriately with one another. If not, the writing seems random, haphazard, and disorganized. Therefore, good writing must be organized, where each sentence fits a larger context and relates to the sentences around it.

<u>Transition Words</u>

The writer should act as a guide, showing the reader how all the sentences fit together. Consider this seat belt example:

> Seat belts save more lives than any other automobile safety feature. Many studies show that airbags save lives as well. Not all cars have airbags. Many older cars don't. Air bags aren't entirely reliable. Studies show that in 15% of accidents, airbags don't deploy as designed. Seat belt malfunctions are extremely rare.

There's nothing wrong with any of these sentences individually, but together they're disjointed and difficult to follow. The best way for the writer to communicate information is through the use of transition words. Here are examples of transition words and phrases that tie sentences together, enabling a more natural flow:

> To show causality: *as a result, therefore*, and *consequently*
> To compare and contrast: *however, but,* and *on the other hand*
> To introduce examples: *for instance, namely,* and *including*
> To show order of importance: *foremost, primarily, secondly,* and *lastly*

Note that this is not a complete list of transitions. There are many more that can be used; however, most fit into these or similar categories. The important point is that the words should clearly show the relationship between sentences, supporting information, and the main idea.

Here is an update to the previous example using transition words. These changes make it easier to read and bring clarity to the writer's points:

> Seat belts save more lives than any other automobile safety feature. Many studies show that airbags save lives as well; however, not all cars have airbags. For instance, some older cars don't.

> Furthermore, air bags aren't entirely reliable. For example, studies show that in 15% of accidents, airbags don't deploy as designed, but, on the other hand, seat belt malfunctions are extremely rare.

Also, test takers should be prepared to analyze whether the writer is using the best transition word or phrase for the situation. For example, the sentence: "As a result, seat belt malfunctions are extremely rare" doesn't make sense in the context above because the writer is trying to show the contrast between seat belts and airbags, not the causality.

Logical Sequence

Even if the writer includes plenty of information to support their point, the writing is only coherent when the information is in a logical order. First, the writer should introduce the main idea, whether for a paragraph, a section, or the entire piece. Then they should present evidence to support the main idea by using transitional language. This shows the reader how the information relates to the main idea and to the sentences around it. The writer should then take time to interpret the information, making sure necessary connections are obvious to the reader. Finally, the writer can summarize the information in a closing section.

Though most writing follows this pattern, it isn't a set rule. Sometimes writers change the order for effect. For example, the writer can begin with a surprising piece of supporting information to grab the reader's attention, and then transition to the main idea. Thus, if a passage doesn't follow the logical order, don't immediately assume it's wrong. However, most writing usually settles into a logical sequence after a nontraditional beginning.

Introductions and Conclusions

Examining the writer's strategies for introductions and conclusions puts the reader in the right mindset to interpret the rest of the text. Look for methods the writer might use for introductions such as:

> Stating the main point immediately, followed by outlining how the rest of the piece supports this claim.
>
> Establishing important, smaller pieces of the main idea first, and then grouping these points into a case for the main idea.
>
> Opening with a quotation, anecdote, question, seeming paradox, or other piece of interesting information, and then using it to lead to the main point.

Whatever method the writer chooses, the introduction should make their intention clear, establish their voice as a credible one, and encourage a person to continue reading.

Conclusions tend to follow a similar pattern. In them, the writer restates their main idea a final time, often after summarizing the smaller pieces of that idea. If the introduction uses a quote or anecdote to grab the reader's attention, the conclusion often makes reference to it again. Whatever way the writer chooses to arrange the conclusion, the final restatement of the main idea should be clear and simple for the reader to interpret. Finally, conclusions shouldn't introduce any new information.

Organization

Depending on what the author is attempting to accomplish, certain formats or text structures work better than others. For example, a sequence structure might work for narration but not when identifying similarities and differences between dissimilar concepts. Similarly, a comparison-contrast structure is not useful for narration. It's the author's job to put the right information in the correct format.

Readers should be familiar with the five main literary structures:

1. **Sequence** structure (sometimes referred to as the order structure) is when the order of events proceed in a predictable order. In many cases, this means the text goes through the plot elements: exposition, rising action, climax, falling action, and resolution. Readers are introduced to characters, setting, and conflict in the exposition. In the rising action, there's an increase in tension and suspense. The climax is the height of tension and the point of no return. Tension decreases during the falling action. In the resolution, any conflicts presented in the exposition are solved, and the story concludes. An informative text that is structured sequentially will often go in order from one step to the next.

2. In the **problem-solution** structure, authors identify a potential problem and suggest a solution. This form of writing is usually divided into two paragraphs and can be found in informational texts. For example, cell phone, cable and satellite providers use this structure in manuals to help customers troubleshoot or identify problems with services or products.

3. When authors want to discuss similarities and differences between separate concepts, they arrange thoughts in a **comparison-contrast** paragraph structure. Venn diagrams are an effective graphic organizer for comparison-contrast structures because they feature two overlapping circles that can be used to organize similarities and differences. A comparison-contrast essay organizes one paragraph based on similarities and another based on differences. A comparison-contrast essay can also be arranged with the similarities and differences of individual traits addressed within individual paragraphs. Words such as *however, but,* and *nevertheless* help signal a contrast in ideas.

4. **Descriptive** writing structure is designed to appeal to your senses. Much like an artist who constructs a painting, good descriptive writing builds an image in the reader's mind by appealing to the five senses: sight, hearing, taste, touch, and smell. However, overly descriptive writing can become tedious; sparse descriptions can make settings and characters seem flat. Good authors strike a balance by applying descriptions only to passages, characters, and settings that are integral to the plot.

5. Passages that use the **cause and effect** structure are simply asking *why* by demonstrating some type of connection between ideas. Words such as *if, since, because, then,* or *consequently* indicate relationship. By switching the order of a complex sentence, the writer can rearrange the emphasis on different clauses. Saying *If Sheryl is late, we'll miss the dance* is different from saying *We'll miss the dance if Sheryl is late*. One emphasizes Sheryl's tardiness while the other emphasizes missing the dance. Paragraphs can also be arranged in a cause and effect format. Since the format—before and after—is sequential, it is useful when authors wish to discuss the impact of choices. Researchers often apply this paragraph structure to the scientific method.

Point of View

Point of view is an important writing device to consider. In fiction writing, point of view refers to who tells the story or from whose perspective readers are observing as they read. In non-fiction writing, the **point of view** refers to whether authors refer to themselves, their readers, or choose not to refer to either. Whether fiction or nonfiction, the author will carefully consider the impact the perspective will have on the purpose and main point of the writing.

- **First-person point of view**: The story is told from the writer's perspective. In fiction, this would mean that the main character is also the narrator. First-person point of view is easily recognized by the use of personal pronouns such as *I, me, we, us, our, my,* and *myself.*
- **Third-person point of view**: In a more formal essay, this would be an appropriate perspective because the focus should be on the subject matter, not the writer or the reader. Third-person point of view is recognized using the pronouns *he, she, they,* and *it*. In fiction writing, third person point of view has a few variations.
- **Third-person limited point of view**: Refers to a story told by a narrator who has access to the thoughts and feelings of just one character.
- **Third-person omniscient point of view**: The narrator has access to the thoughts and feelings of all the characters.

Point of View	Pronouns Used
First person	I, me, we, us, our, my, myself
Second person	You, your, yourself
Third person	He, she, it, they

- **Third-person objective point of view**: The narrator is like a fly on the wall and can see and hear what the characters do and say but does not have access to their thoughts and feelings.
- **Second-person point of view**: This point of view isn't commonly used in fiction or non-fiction writing because it directly addresses the reader using the pronouns *you, your,* and *yourself.* Second-person perspective is more appropriate in direct communication, such as business letters or emails.

How the Position and Purpose Shape the Text

When it comes to authors' writings, readers should always identify a position or stance. No matter how objective a piece may seem, assume the author has preconceived beliefs. Reduce the likelihood of accepting an invalid argument by looking for multiple articles on the topic, including those with varying opinions. If several opinions point in the same direction, and are backed by reputable peer-reviewed sources, it's more likely the author has a valid argument. Positions that run contrary to widely held beliefs and existing data should invite scrutiny. There are exceptions to the rule, so be a careful consumer of information.

Though themes, symbols, and motifs are buried deep within the text and can sometimes be difficult to infer, an author's purpose is usually obvious from the beginning. There are four purposes of writing: to inform, to persuade, to describe, and to entertain. Informative writings present facts in an accessible way and are also known as expository writing. Persuasive writing appeals to emotions and logic to inspire the reader to adopt a specific stance. Be wary of this type of writing, as it often lacks objectivity. Descriptive writing is designed to paint a picture in the reader's mind, while writings that entertain are often narratives designed to engage and delight the reader.

The various writing styles are usually blended, with one purpose dominating the rest. For example, a persuasive piece might begin with a humorous tale to make readers more receptive to the persuasive message, or a recipe in a cookbook designed to inform might be preceded by an entertaining anecdote that makes the recipe more appealing.

Determining an Author's Point of View

A **rhetorical strategy**—also referred to as a **rhetorical mode**—is the structural way an author chooses to present his/her argument. Though the terms noted below are similar to the organizational structures noted earlier, these strategies do not imply that the entire text follows the approach. For example, a cause and effect organizational structure is solely that, nothing more. A persuasive text may use cause and effect as a strategy to convey a singular point. Thus, an argument may include several of the strategies as the author strives to convince his or her audience to take action or accept a different point of view. It's important that readers are able to identify an author's thesis and position on the topic in order to be able to identify the careful construction through which the author speaks to the reader. The following are some of the more common rhetorical strategies:

- **Cause and effect**—establishing a logical correlation or causation between two ideas
- **Classification/division**—the grouping of similar items together or division of something into parts
- **Comparison/contrast**—the distinguishing of similarities/differences to expand on an idea
- **Definition**—used to clarify abstract ideas, unfamiliar concepts, or to distinguish one idea from another
- **Description**—use of vivid imagery, active verbs, and clear adjectives to explain ideas
- **Exemplification**—the use of examples to explain an idea
- **Narration**—anecdotes or personal experience to present or expand on a concept
- **Problem/solution**—presentation of a problem or problems, followed by proposed solution(s)

Rhetorical Strategies and Devices

A **rhetorical device** is the phrasing and presentation of an idea that reinforces and emphasizes a point in an argument. A rhetorical device is often quite memorable. One of the more famous uses of a rhetorical device is in John F. Kennedy's 1961 inaugural address: "Ask not what your country can do for you, ask what you can do for your country." The contrast of ideas presented in the phrasing is an example of the rhetorical device of antimetabole.

Some other common examples are provided below, but test takers should be aware that this is not a complete list.

Device	Definition	Example
Allusion	A reference to a famous person, event, or significant literary text as a form of significant comparison	"We are apt to shut our eyes against a painful truth, and listen to the song of that siren till she transforms us into beasts." Patrick Henry
Anaphora	The repetition of the same words at the beginning of successive words, phrases, or clauses, designed to emphasize an idea	"We shall not flag or fail. We shall go on to the end. We shall fight in France, we shall fight on the seas and oceans, we shall fight with growing confidence ... we shall fight in the fields and in the streets, we shall fight in the hills. We shall never surrender." Winston Churchill
Understatement	A statement meant to portray a situation as less important than it actually is to create an ironic effect	"The war in the Pacific has not necessarily developed in Japan's favor." Emperor Hirohito, surrendering Japan in World War II
Parallelism	A syntactical similarity in a structure or series of structures used for impact of an idea, making it memorable	"A penny saved is a penny earned." Ben Franklin
Rhetorical question	A question posed that is not answered by the writer though there is a desired response, most often designed to emphasize a point	"Can anyone look at our reduced standing in the world today and say, 'Let's have four more years of this?'" Ronald Reagan

<u>Understanding Methods Used to Appeal to a Specific Audience</u>
In an argument or persuasive text, an author will strive to sway readers to an opinion or conclusion. To be effective, an author must consider his or her intended audience. Although an author may write text for a general audience, he or she will use methods of appeal or persuasion to convince that audience. Aristotle asserted that there were three methods or modes by which a person could be persuaded. These are referred to as **rhetorical appeals**.

The three main types of rhetorical appeals are shown in the following graphic.

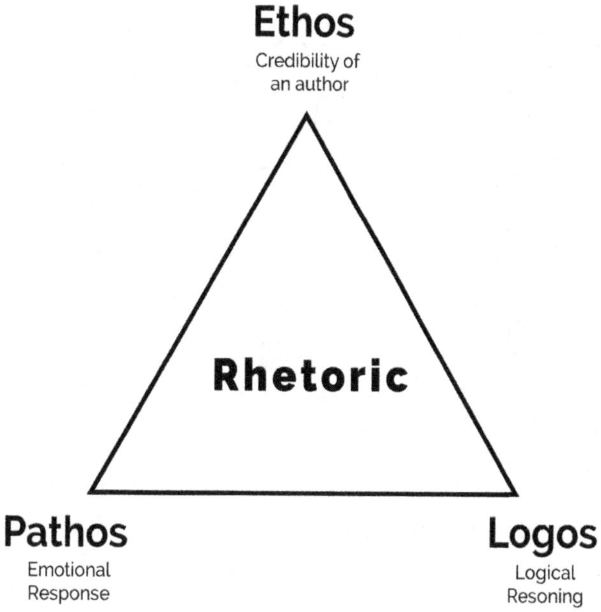

Ethos, also referred to as an **ethical appeal**, is an appeal to the audience's perception of the writer as credible (or not), based on their examination of their ethics and who the writer is, his/her experience or incorporation of relevant information, or his/her argument. For example, authors may present testimonials to bolster their arguments. The reader who critically examines the veracity of the testimonials and the credibility of those giving the testimony will be able to determine if the author's use of testimony is valid to his or her argument. In turn, this will help the reader determine if the author's thesis is valid. An author's careful and appropriate use of technical language can create an overall knowledgeable effect and, in turn, act as a convincing vehicle when it comes to credibility. Overuse of technical language, however, may create confusion in readers and obscure an author's overall intent.

Pathos, also referred to as **emotional appeal**, is an appeal to the audience's sense of identity, self-interest, or emotions. A critical reader will notice when the author is appealing to pathos through anecdotes and descriptions that elicit an emotion such as anger or pity. Readers should also beware of factual information that uses generalization to appeal to the emotions. While it's tempting to believe an author is the source of truth in his or her text, an author who presents factual information as universally true, consistent throughout time, and common to all groups is using **generalization**. Authors who exclusively use generalizations without specific facts and credible sourcing are attempting to sway readers solely through emotion.

Logos, also referred to as a **logical appeal**, is an appeal to the audience's ability to see and understand the logic in a claim offered by the writer. A critical reader has to be able to evaluate an author's arguments for validity of reasoning and for sufficiency when it comes to argument.

Applying Knowledge of Language to Aid Comprehension

<u>Affixes</u>

Individual words are constructed from building blocks of meaning. An **affix** is an element that is added to a root or stem word that can change the word's meaning.

For example, the stem word *fix* is a verb meaning *to repair*. When the ending *–able* is added, it becomes the adjective *fixable*, meaning "capable of being repaired." Adding *un–* to the beginning changes the word to *unfixable*, meaning "incapable of being repaired." In this way, affixes attach to the word stem to create a new word and a new meaning. Knowledge of affixes can assist in deciphering the meaning of unfamiliar words.

Affixes are also related to inflection. **Inflection** is the modification of a base word to express a different grammatical or syntactical function. For example, countable nouns such as *car* and *airport* become plural with the addition of *–s* at the end: *cars* and *airports*.

Verb tense is also expressed through inflection. **Regular verbs**—those that follow a standard inflection pattern—can be changed to past tense using the affixes *–ed*, *–d*, or *–ied*, as in *cooked* and *studied*. Verbs can also be modified for continuous tenses by using *–ing*, as in *working* or *exploring*. Thus, affixes are used not only to express meaning but also to reflect a word's grammatical purpose.

A **prefix** is an affix attached to the beginning of a word. The meanings of English prefixes mainly come from Greek and Latin origins. The chart below contains a few of the most commonly used English prefixes.

Prefix	**Meaning**	**Example**
a-	not	amoral, asymptomatic
anti-	against	antidote, antifreeze
auto-	self	automobile, automatic
circum-	around	circumference, circumspect
co-, com-, con-	together	coworker, companion
contra-	against	contradict, contrary
de-	negation or reversal	deflate, deodorant
extra-	outside, beyond	extraterrestrial, extracurricular
in-, im-, il-, ir-	not	impossible, irregular
inter-	between	international, intervene
intra-	within	intramural, intranet
mis-	wrongly	mistake, misunderstand
mono-	one	monolith, monopoly
non-	not	nonpartisan, nonsense
pre-	before	preview, prediction
re-	again	review, renew
semi-	half	semicircle, semicolon
sub-	under	subway, submarine
super-	above	superhuman, superintendent
trans-	across, beyond, through	trans-Siberian, transform
un-	not	unwelcome, unfriendly

While the addition of a prefix alters the meaning of the base word, the addition of a **suffix** may also affect a word's part of speech. For example, adding a suffix can change the noun *material* into the verb *materialize* and back to a noun again in *materialization*.

Suffix	Part of Speech	Meaning	Example
-able, -ible	adjective	having the ability to	honorable, flexible
-acy, -cy	noun	state or quality	intimacy, dependency
-al, -ical	adjective	having the quality of	historical, tribal
-en	verb	to cause to become	strengthen, embolden
-er, -ier	adjective	comparative	happier, longer
-est, -iest	adjective	superlative	sunniest, hottest
-ess	noun	female	waitress, actress
-ful	adjective	full of, characterized by	beautiful, thankful
-fy, -ify	verb	to cause, to come to be	liquefy, intensify
-ism	noun	doctrine, belief, action	Communism, Buddhism
-ive, -ative, -itive	adjective	having the quality of	creative, innovative
-ize	verb	to convert into, to subject to	Americanize, dramatize
-less	adjective	without, missing	emotionless, hopeless
-ly	adverb	in the manner of	quickly, energetically
-ness	noun	quality or state	goodness, darkness
-ous, -ious, -eous	adjective	having the quality of	spontaneous, pious
-ship	noun	status or condition	partnership, ownership
-tion	noun	action or state	renovation, promotion
-y	adjective	characterized by	smoky, dreamy

Through knowledge of prefixes and suffixes, a student's vocabulary can be instantly expanded with an understanding of **etymology**—the origin of words. This, in turn, can be used to add sentence structure variety to academic writing.

<u>Context Clues</u>

Familiarity with common prefixes, suffixes, and root words assists tremendously in unraveling the meaning of an unfamiliar word and making an educated guess as to its meaning. However, some words do not contain many easily-identifiable clues that point to their meaning. In this case, rather than looking at the elements within the word, it is useful to consider elements around the word—i.e., its context. **Context** refers to the other words and information within the sentence or surrounding sentences that indicate the unknown word's probable meaning. The following sentences provide context for the potentially-unfamiliar word *quixotic*:

> Rebecca had never been one to settle into a predictable, ordinary life. Her quixotic personality led her to leave behind a job with a prestigious law firm in Manhattan and move halfway around the world to pursue her dream of becoming a sushi chef in Tokyo.

A reader unfamiliar with the word *quixotic* doesn't have many clues to use in terms of affixes or root meaning. The suffix *–ic* indicates that the word is an adjective, but that is it. In this case, then, a reader would need to look at surrounding information to obtain some clues about the word. Other adjectives in the passage include *predictable* and *ordinary*, things that Rebecca was definitely not, as indicated by

"Rebecca had never been one to settle." Thus, a first clue might be that *quixotic* means the opposite of predictable.

The second sentence doesn't offer any other modifier of *personality* other than *quixotic*, but it does include a story that reveals further information about her personality. She had a stable, respectable job, but she decided to give it up to follow her dream. Combining these two ideas together, then—unpredictable and dream-seeking—gives the reader a general idea of what *quixotic* probably means. In fact, the root of the word is the character Don Quixote, a romantic dreamer who goes on an impulsive adventure.

While context clues are useful for making an approximate definition for newly-encountered words, these types of clues also come in handy when encountering common words that have multiple meanings. The word *reservation* is used differently in each the following sentences:

> A. That restaurant is booked solid for the next month; it's impossible to make a reservation unless you know somebody.
>
> B. The hospital plans to open a branch office inside the reservation to better serve Native American patients who cannot easily travel to the main hospital fifty miles away.
>
> C. Janet Clark is a dependable, knowledgeable worker, and I recommend her for the position of team leader without reservation.

All three sentences use the word to express different meanings. In fact, most words in English have more than one meaning—sometimes meanings that are completely different from one another. Thus, context can provide clues as to which meaning is appropriate in a given situation. A quick search in the dictionary reveals several possible meanings for *reservation*:

- An exception or qualification
- A tract of public land set aside, such as for the use of American Indian tribes
- An arrangement for accommodations, such as in a hotel, on a plane, or at a restaurant

Sentence A mentions a restaurant, making the third definition the correct one in this case. In sentence B, some context clues include Native Americans, as well as the implication that a reservation is a place—"inside the reservation," both of which indicate that the second definition should be used here. Finally, sentence C uses *without reservation* to mean "completely" or "without exception," so the first definition can be applied here.

Using context clues in this way can be especially useful for words that have multiple, widely varying meanings. If a word has more than one definition and two of those definitions are the opposite of each other, it is known as an **auto-antonym**—a word that can also be its own antonym. In the case of auto-antonyms, context clues are crucial to determine which definition to employ in a given sentence. For example, the word *sanction* can either mean "to approve or allow" or "a penalty." Approving and penalizing have opposite meanings, so *sanction* is an example of an auto-antonym. The following sentences reflect the distinction in meaning:

> A. In response to North Korea's latest nuclear weapons test, world leaders have called for harsher sanctions to punish the country for its actions.
>
> B. The general has sanctioned a withdrawal of troops from the area.

A context clue can be found in sentence A, which mentions "to punish." A punishment is similar to a penalty, so sentence A is using the word *sanction* according to this definition.

Other examples of auto-antonyms include *oversight*—"to supervise something" or "a missed detail"), *resign*—"to quit" or "to sign again, as a contract," and *screen*—"to show" or "to conceal." For these types of words, recognizing context clues is an important way to avoid misinterpreting the sentence's meaning.

Syntax

Syntax refers to the arrangement of words, phrases, and clauses to form a sentence. Knowledge of syntax can also give insight into a word's meaning. The section above considered several examples using the word *reservation* and applied context clues to determine the word's appropriate meaning in each sentence. Here is an example of how the placement of a word can impact its meaning and grammatical function:

> A. The development team has reserved the conference room for today.
>
> B. Her quiet and reserved nature is sometimes misinterpreted as unfriendliness when people first meet her.

In addition to using *reserved* to mean different things, each sentence also uses the word to serve a different grammatical function. In sentence A, *reserved* is part of the verb phrase *has reserved*, indicating the meaning "to set aside for a particular use." In sentence B, *reserved* acts as a modifier within the noun phrase "her quiet and reserved nature." Because the word is being used as an adjective to describe a personality characteristic, it calls up a different definition of the word—"restrained or lacking familiarity with others." As this example shows, the function of a word within the overall sentence structure can allude to its meaning. It is also useful to refer to the earlier chart about suffixes and parts of speech as another clue into what grammatical function a word is serving in a sentence.

Analyzing Nuances of Word Meaning and Figures of Speech

By now, it should be apparent that language is not as simple as one word directly correlated to one meaning. Rather, one word can express a vast array of diverse meanings, and similar meanings can be expressed through different words. However, there are very few words that express exactly the same meaning. For this reason, it is important to be able to pick up on the nuances of word meaning.

Many words contain two levels of meaning: connotation and denotation as discussed previously in the informational texts and rhetoric section. A word's **denotation** is its most literal meaning—the definition that can readily be found in the dictionary. A word's **connotation** includes all of its emotional and cultural associations.

In literary writing, authors rely heavily on connotative meaning to create mood and characterization. The following are two descriptions of a rainstorm:

> A. The rain slammed against the windowpane and the wind howled through the fireplace. A pair of hulking oaks next to the house cast eerie shadows as their branches trembled in the wind.
>
> B. The rain pattered against the windowpane and the wind whistled through the fireplace. A pair of stately oaks next to the house cast curious shadows as their branches swayed in the wind.

Description A paints a creepy picture for readers with strongly emotional words like *slammed*, connoting force and violence. *Howled* connotes pain or wildness, and *eerie* and *trembled* connote fear. Overall, the connotative language in this description serves to inspire fear and anxiety.

However, as can be seen in description B, swapping out a few key words for those with different connotations completely changes the feeling of the passage. *Slammed* is replaced with the more cheerful *pattered*, and *hulking* has been swapped out for *stately*. Both words imply something large, but *hulking* is more intimidating whereas *stately* is more respectable. *Curious* and *swayed* seem more playful than the language used in the earlier description. Although both descriptions represent roughly the same situation, the nuances of the emotional language used throughout the passages create a very different sense for readers.

Selective choice of connotative language can also be extremely impactful in other forms of writing, such as editorials or persuasive texts. Through connotative language, writers reveal their biases and opinions while trying to inspire feelings and actions in readers:

- Parents won't stop complaining about standardized tests.
- Parents continue to raise concerns about standardized tests.

Readers should be able to identify the nuance in meaning between these two sentences. The first one carries a more negative feeling, implying that parents are being bothersome or whiny. Readers of the second sentence, though, might come away with the feeling that parents are concerned and involved in their children's education. Again, the aggregate of even subtle cues can combine to give a specific emotional impression to readers, so from an early age, students should be aware of how language can be used to influence readers' opinions.

Another form of non-literal expression can be found in *figures of speech*. As with connotative language, figures of speech tend to be shared within a cultural group and may be difficult to pick up on for learners outside of that group. In some cases, a figure of speech may be based on the literal denotation of the words it contains, but in other cases, a figure of speech is far removed from its literal meaning. A case in point is **irony**, where what is said is the exact opposite of what is meant:

> The new tax plan is poorly planned, based on faulty economic data, and unable to address the financial struggles of middle class families. Yet legislators remain committed to passing this brilliant proposal.

When the writer refers to the proposal as brilliant, the opposite is implied—the plan is "faulty" and "poorly planned." By using irony, the writer means that the proposal is anything but brilliant by using the word in a non-literal sense.

Another figure of speech is **hyperbole**—extreme exaggeration or overstatement. Statements like, "I love you to the moon and back" or "Let's be friends for a million years" utilize hyperbole to convey a greater depth of emotion, without literally committing oneself to space travel or a life of immortality.

Figures of speech may sometimes use one word in place of another. **Synecdoche**, for example, uses a part of something to refer to its whole. The expression "Don't hurt a hair on her head!" implies protecting more than just an individual hair, but rather her entire body. "The art teacher is training a class of Picassos" uses Picasso, one individual notable artist, to stand in for the entire category of talented artists. Another figure of speech using word replacement is **metonymy**, where a word is replaced with something closely associated to it. For example, news reports may use the word "Washington" to refer to the American government or "the crown" to refer to the British monarch.

Discerning Fact Vs. Opinion in a Text

Teachers should educate and encourage students to view reading as an active process of discovering meaning in texts. Reading should not be passive. Readers should question what they read and apply their background knowledge to enhance their understanding and appreciation of written work. Teachers should bear in mind that the meaning derived from a given text for a student may depend on his or her background and experiences.

It's important to read any piece of writing critically. The goal is to discover the point and purpose of what the author is writing about through analysis. It's also crucial to establish the point or stance the author has taken on the topic of the piece. After determining the author's perspective, readers can then more effectively develop their own viewpoints on the subject of the piece.

It is important to distinguish between fact and opinion when reading a piece of writing. A **fact** is information that can be proven true. If information can be disproved, it is not a fact. For example, water freezes at or below thirty-two degrees Fahrenheit. An argument stating that water freezes at seventy degrees Fahrenheit cannot be supported by data and is therefore not a fact. Facts tend to be associated with science, mathematics, and statistics. **Opinions** are information open to debate. Opinions are often tied to subjective concepts like equality, morals, and rights. They can also be controversial.

Authors often use words like *think, feel, believe,* or *in my opinion* when expressing opinion, but these words won't always appear in an opinion piece, especially if it is formally written. An author's opinion may be backed up by facts, which gives it more credibility, but that opinion should not be taken as fact. A critical reader should be suspect of an author's opinion, especially if it is only supported by other opinions.

Fact	**Opinion**
There are nine innings in a game of baseball.	Baseball games run too long.
James Garfield was assassinated on July 2, 1881.	James Garfield was a good president.
McDonalds has stores in 118 countries.	McDonalds has the best hamburgers.

Critical readers examine the facts used to support an author's argument. They check the facts against other sources to be sure those facts are correct. They also check the validity of the sources used to be sure those sources are credible, academic, and/or peer- reviewed. Consider that when an author uses another person's opinion to support his or her argument, even if it is an expert's opinion, it is still only an opinion and should not be taken as fact. A strong argument uses valid, measurable facts to support ideas. Even then, the reader may disagree with the argument as it may be rooted in his or her personal beliefs.

An authoritative argument may use the facts to sway the reader. In the example of global warming, many experts differ in their opinions of what alternative fuels can be used to aid in offsetting it. Because of this, a writer may choose to only use the information and expert opinion that supports his or her viewpoint.

If the argument is that wind energy is the best solution, the author will use facts that support this idea. That same author may leave out relevant facts on solar energy. The way the author uses facts can influence the reader, so it's important to consider the facts being used, how those facts are being presented, and what information might be left out.

Critical readers should also look for errors in the argument such as logical fallacies and bias. A **logical fallacy** is a flaw in the logic used to make the argument. Logical fallacies include slippery slope, straw man, and begging the question. Authors can also reflect **bias** if they ignore an opposing viewpoint or present their side in an unbalanced way. A strong argument considers the opposition and finds a way to refute it. Critical readers should look for an unfair or one-sided presentation of the argument and be skeptical, as a bias may be present. Even if this bias is unintentional, if it exists in the writing, the reader should be wary of the validity of the argument.

Readers should also look for the use of **stereotypes**, which refer to specific groups. Stereotypes are often negative connotations about a person or place and should always be avoided. When a critical reader finds stereotypes in a piece of writing, they should immediately be critical of the argument and consider the validity of anything the author presents. Stereotypes reveal a flaw in the writer's thinking and may suggest a lack of knowledge or understanding about the subject.

Using Context Clues

A context clue is a hint that an author provides to the reader in order to help define difficult or unique words. When reading a passage, a test taker should take note of any unfamiliar words, and then examine the sentence around them to look for clues to the word meanings. Let's look at an example:

> He faced a *conundrum* in making this decision. He felt as if he had come to a crossroads. This was truly a puzzle, and what he did next would determine the course of his future.

The word **conundrum** may be unfamiliar to the reader. By looking at context clues, the reader should be able to determine its meaning. In this passage, context clues include the idea of making a decision and of being unsure. Furthermore, the author restates the definition of conundrum in using the word *puzzle* as a synonym. Therefore, the reader should be able to determine that the definition of the word *conundrum* is a difficult puzzle.

Similarly, a reader can determine difficult vocabulary by identifying antonyms. Let's look at an example:

> Her *gregarious* nature was completely opposite of her twin's, who was shy, retiring, and socially nervous.

The word *gregarious* may be unfamiliar. However, by looking at the surrounding context clues, the reader can determine that *gregarious* does not mean shy. The twins' personalities are being contrasted. Therefore, *gregarious* must mean sociable, or something similar to it.

At times, an author will provide contextual clues through a cause and effect relationship. Look at the next sentence as an example:

> The athletes were excited with *elation* when they won the tournament; unfortunately, their off-court antics caused them to forfeit the win.

The word *elation* may be unfamiliar to the reader. However, the author defines the word by presenting a cause and effect relationship. The athletes were so elated at the win that their behavior went overboard and they had to forfeit. In this instance, *elated* must mean something akin to overjoyed, happy, and overexcited.

Cause and effect is one technique authors use to demonstrate relationships. A **cause** is why something happens. The **effect** is what happens as a result. For example, a reader may encounter text such as *Because he was unable to sleep, he was often restless and irritable during the day.* The cause is insomnia due to lack of sleep. The effect is being restless and irritable. When reading for a cause and effect relationship, look for words such as "if," "then," "such," and "because." By using cause and effect, an author can describe direct relationships, and convey an overall theme, particularly when taking a stance on their topic.

An author can also provide contextual clues through comparison and contrast. Let's look at an example:

> Her torpid state caused her parents, and her physician, to worry about her seemingly sluggish well-being.

The word *torpid* is probably unfamiliar to the reader. However, the author has compared *torpid* to a state of being and, moreover, one that's worrisome. Therefore, the reader should be able to determine that *torpid* is not a positive, healthy state of being. In fact, through the use of comparison, it means sluggish. Similarly, an author may contrast an unfamiliar word with an idea. In the sentence *Her <u>torpid</u> state was completely opposite of her usual, bubbly self,* the meaning of *torpid*, or sluggish, is contrasted with the words *bubbly self*.

A test taker should be able to critically assess and determine unfamiliar word meanings through the use of an author's context clues in order to fully comprehend difficult text passages.

<u>Relating Unfamiliar Words to Familiar Words</u>

The Reading section will test a reader's ability to use context clues, and then relate unfamiliar words to more familiar ones. Using the word *torpid* as an example, the test may ask the test taker to relate the meaning of the word to a list of vocabulary options and choose the more familiar word as closest in meaning. In this case, the test may say something like the following:

> Which of the following words means the same as the word *torpid* in the above passage?

Then they will provide the test taker with a list of familiar options such as happy, disgruntled, sluggish, and animated. By using context clues, the reader has already determined the meaning of *torpid* as slow or sluggish, so the reader should be able to correctly identify the word *sluggish* as the correct answer.

One effective way to relate unfamiliar word meanings to more familiar ones is to substitute the provided word answer options with the unfamiliar word in question. Although this will not always lead to a correct answer every time, this strategy will help the test taker narrow answer options. Be careful when utilizing this strategy. Pay close attention to the meaning of sentences and answer choices because it's easy to mistake answer choices as correct when they are easily substituted, especially when they are the same part of speech. Does the sentence mean the same thing with the substituted word option in place or does it change entirely? Does the substituted word make sense? Does it possibly mean the same as the unfamiliar word in question?

Figurative Language

Literary texts also employ rhetorical devices. Figurative language like simile and metaphor is a type of rhetorical device commonly found in literature. In addition to rhetorical devices that play on the *meanings* of words, there are also rhetorical devices that use the *sounds* of words. These devices are most often found in poetry but may also be found in other types of literature and in non-fiction writing like speech texts.

Alliteration and assonance are both varieties of sound repetition. Other types of sound repetition include: **anaphora**, repetition that occurs at the beginning of the sentences; **epiphora**, repetition occurring at the end of phrases; **antimetabole**, repetition of words in reverse order; and **antiphrasis**, a form of denial of an assertion in a text.

Alliteration refers to the repetition of the first sound of each word. Recall Robert Burns' opening line:

> My love is like a red, red rose

This line includes two instances of alliteration: "love" and "like" (repeated *L* sound), as well as "red" and "rose" (repeated *R* sound). Next, assonance refers to the repetition of vowel sounds, and can occur anywhere within a word (not just the opening sound). Here is the opening of a poem by John Keats:

> When I have fears that I may cease to be
> Before my pen has glean'd my teeming brain

Assonance can be found in the words "fears," "cease," "be," "glean'd," and "teeming," all of which stress the long *E* sound. Both alliteration and assonance create a harmony that unifies the writer's language.

Another sound device is **onomatopoeia**, or words whose spelling mimics the sound they describe. Words like "crash," "bang," and "sizzle" are all examples of onomatopoeia. Use of onomatopoetic language adds auditory imagery to the text.

Readers are probably most familiar with the technique of pun. A **pun** is a play on words, taking advantage of two words that have the same or similar pronunciation. Puns can be found throughout Shakespeare's plays, for instance:

> Now is the winter of our discontent
> Made glorious summer by this son of York

These lines from *Richard III* contain a play on words. Richard III refers to his brother, the newly crowned King Edward IV, as the "son of York," referencing their family heritage from the house of York. However, while drawing a comparison between the political climate and the weather (times of political trouble were the "winter," but now the new king brings "glorious summer"), Richard's use of the word "son" also implies another word with the same pronunciation, "sun"—so Edward IV is also like the sun, bringing light, warmth, and hope to England. Puns are a clever way for writers to suggest two meanings at once.

Some examples of figurative language are included in the following table.

Term	Definition	Example
Simile	Compares two things using "like" or "as"	Her hair was like gold.
Metaphor	Compares two things as if they are the same	He was a giant teddy bear.
Idiom	Using words with predictable meanings to create a phrase with a different meaning	The world is your oyster.
Alliteration	Repeating the same beginning sound or letter in a phrase for emphasis	The busy baby babbled.
Personification	Attributing human characteristics to an object or an animal	The house glowered menacingly with a dark smile.
Foreshadowing	Giving an indication that something is going to happen later in the story	I wasn't aware at the time, but I would come to regret those words.
Symbolism	Using symbols to represent ideas and provide a different meaning	The ring represented the bond between us.
Onomatopoeia	Using words that imitate sound	The tire went off with a bang and a crunch.
Imagery	Appealing to the senses by using descriptive language	The sky was painted with red and pink and streaked with orange.
Hyperbole	Using exaggeration not meant to be taken literally	The girl weighed less than a feather.

Figurative language can be used to give additional insight into the theme or message of a text by moving beyond the usual and literal meaning of words and phrases. It can also be used to appeal to the senses of readers and create a more in-depth story.

Understanding a Range of Words and Phrases to Improve Comprehension and Read at the College Level

Vocabulary

Vocabulary consists of the bank of words that students can understand and apply fluently in order to communicate effectively. A strong vocabulary and word recognition base enables students to access prior knowledge and experiences in order to make connections in written texts. A strong vocabulary also allows students to express ideas, learn new concepts, and decode the meanings of unfamiliar words by using context clues. Conversely, if a child's vocabulary knowledge is limited and does not steadily increase, reading comprehension will be negatively affected. If students become frustrated with their lack of understanding of written texts, they will likely choose to only read texts at their comfort level or refuse to read altogether. With direct instruction, educators introduce specific words to pre-teach before reading, or examine word roots, prefixes, and suffixes. Through indirect instruction, educators ensure that students are regularly exposed to new words. This engages students in high-quality conversations and social interactions and provides access to a wide variety of challenging and enjoyable reading material.

Morphology

The study of **morphology** generally deals with the structure and formation of words. A **phoneme** is the smallest unit of sound that does not necessarily carry meaning. Essentially, phonemes are combined to form words, and words are combined to form sentences. Morphology looks at the smallest meaningful part of a word, known as a morpheme. In contrast to a phoneme, a morpheme must carry a sound and a meaning. Free morphemes are those that can stand alone, carrying both sound and meaning, as in the following words: *girl, boy, man*, and *lady*. Just as the name suggests, bound morphemes are bound to other morphemes in order to carry meaning. Examples of bound morphemes include: ish, ness, ly, and dis.

Semantics

Semantics is the branch of linguistics that addresses meanings. Morphemes, words, phrases, and sentences all carry distinct meanings. The way these individual parts are arranged can have a significant effect on meaning. In order to construct language, students must be able to use semantics to arrange and rearrange words to achieve the particular meaning they are striving for. Activities that teach semantics revolve around teaching the arrangement of word parts (morphology) and root words, and then the teaching of vocabulary. Moving from vocabulary words into studying sentences and sentence structure leads students to learn how to use context clues to determine meaning and to understand anomalies such as metaphors, idioms, and allusions. There are five types of semantic relationships that are critical to understand:

- **Hyponyms** refer to a relationship between words where general words have multiple more-specific words (hyponyms) that fall into the same category (e.g., horse: mare, stallion, foal, Appaloosa, Clydesdale).

- **Meronyms** refer to a relationship between words where a whole word has multiple parts (meronyms) that comprise it (e.g., horse: tail, mane, hooves, ears).

- **Synonyms** refer to words that have the same meaning as another word (e.g., instructor/teacher/educator, canine/dog, feline/cat, herbivore/vegetarian).

- **Antonyms** refer to words that have the opposite meaning as another word (e.g., true/false, up/down, in/out, right/wrong).

- **Homonyms** refer to words that are spelled the same (homographs) or sound the same (homophones) but mean different things (e.g., there/their/they're, two/too/to, principal/principle, plain/plane, (kitchen) sink/ sink (down as in water)).

Syntax

With its origins from the Greek word, "syntaxis," which means arrangement, **syntax** is the study of phrase and sentence formation. The study of syntax focuses on the ways in which specific words can be combined to create coherent meaning. For example: the simple rearrangement of the words, "I can run," is different from the question, "Can I run?" which is also different from the meaningless "Run I can."

The following methods can be used to teach syntax:

- **Proper Syntax Modeling**: Students don't need to be corrected for improper syntax. Instead, they should be shown ways to rephrase what they said with proper syntax. If a student says, "Run I can," then the teacher should say, "Oh, you can run how fast?" This puts syntax in place with conversational skills.

- **Open-Ended Sentences**: Students can complete open-ended sentences with proper syntax both orally and in written format, or they can correct sentences that have improper syntax so that they make sense.

- **Listening for Syntax**: Syntax is auditory. Students can often hear a syntax error before they can see it in writing. Teachers should have students use word cards or word magnets to arrange and rearrange simple sentences and read them aloud to check for syntax.

- **Repetition**: Syntax can be practiced by using songs, poems, and rhymes for repetitive automation.

Pragmatics

Pragmatics is the study of what words mean in certain situations. It helps to understand the intentions and interpretations of intentions through words used in human interaction. Different listeners and different situations call for different language and intonations of language. When people engage in a conversation, it is usually to convey a certain message, and the message (even using the same words) can change depending on the setting and the audience. The more fluent the speaker, the more success she or he will have in conveying the intended message.

The following methods can be used to teach pragmatics:

- When students state something incorrectly, a response can be given to what they intended to say in the first place. For instance, if a student says, "That's how it didn't happen." Then the teacher might say, "Of course, that's not how it happened." Instead of putting students on defense by being corrected, this method puts them at ease and helps them learn.

- Role-playing conversations with different people in different situations can help teach pragmatics. For example, pretend playing can be used where a situation remains the same but the audience changes, or the audience stays the same but the situations change. This can be followed with a discussion about how language and intonations change too.

- Different ways to convey a message can be used, such as asking vs. persuading, or giving direct vs. indirect requests and polite vs. impolite messages.

- Various non-verbal signals can be used to see how they change pragmatics. For example, students can be encouraged to use mismatched words and facial expressions, such as angry words while smiling or happy words while pretending to cry.

Strategies to Help Read New and/or Difficult Words
Students who are developing reading fluency and comprehension skills can become frustrated when presented with unfamiliar words in a given text. With direct phonics instruction, educators can teach students to decode words and then use context clues to define the words while reading. If students have a strong enough understanding of language structures, including nouns and verbs, educators can ask them to consider what part of speech the unknown word might be based on and where it might fit into the sentence. Other useful strategies involve self-monitoring, in which students are asked to think as they read and ask themselves if what they have just read makes sense. Focusing on visual clues, such as drawings and photographs, may give students valuable insight into deciphering unknown words. Looking for the word in another section of the text to see how it relates to the overall meaning could give a clue to the new vocabulary word. Spelling the word out loud or looking for word chunks, prefixes, and suffixes, as well as demonstrating how to segment the unknown word into its individual syllables, may also be effective strategies to employ.

One of the most valuable strategies, however, for helping students to read and understand new words is pre-teaching. In this strategy, educators select what they evaluate to be the unfamiliar words in the text and then introduce them to the class before reading. Educators using this method should be careful not to simply ask the students to read the text and then spell the new words correctly. They should also provide clear definitions and give the students the opportunity to read these words in various sentences to decipher word meaning. This method can dramatically reduce how often students stop reading in order to reflect on unknown words. Educators are often unsure as to whether to correct every mispronounced word a child makes when reading. If the mispronounced word still makes sense, it is sometimes better to allow the child to continue to read, since the more the child stops, the more the child's reading comprehension and fluency are negatively affected.

Integration of Knowledge and Ideas

Literature refers to a collection of written works that are the distinctive voices of peoples, time periods, and cultures. The world has gained great insight into human thought, vices, virtues, and desires through the written word. As the work pertains to the author's approach to these insights, literature can be classified as fiction or non-fiction.

Interpreting Media and Non-Print Text

This study guide has primarily focused on the printed word for Praxis test takers; however, it's important to note media and non-print text. In the 21st century, rhetoric is evident in a variety of formats. Blogs, vlogs, videos, news footage, advertisements, and live video fill informational feeds, and readers see many shortened images and snapshot texts a day. It's important to note that the majority of these formats use images to appeal to emotion over factual information. Online visuals spread more quickly and are more easily adopted by consumers as fact than printed formats.

Critical readers should be aware that media and non-print text carries some societal weight to the population. In being inundated with pictures and live footage, readers often feel compelled to skip the task of critical reading analysis and accept truth at literal face value. Authors of non-print media are aware of this fact and frequently capitalize on it.

To critically address non-print media requires that the consumer address additional sources and not exclude printed text in order to reach sound conclusions. While it's tempting for consumers to get swept away in the latest viral media, it's important to remember that creators of such have an agenda, and unless the non-print media in question is backed up with sound supporting evidence, any thesis or message cannot be considered valid or factual. Memes, gifs, and looped video cannot tell the whole, truthful story although they may appeal to opinions with which readers already agree. Sharing such non-print media online can precipitate widespread misunderstanding.

When presented with non-print media, critical readers should consider these bits of information as teasers to be investigated for accuracy and veracity. Of course, certain non-print media exists solely for entertainment, but the critical reader should be able to separate out what's generalized for entertainment's sake and what's presented for further verification, before blindly accepting the message. Increasingly, this has become more difficult for readers to do, only because of the onslaught of information to which they are exposed.

If a reader is not to fall prey to strong imagery and non-print media, he or she will need to fact-check. This, of course, requires time and attention on the reader's part, and in current culture, taking the time to fact-check seems counterproductive. However, in order to maintain credibility themselves, readers must be able to evaluate multiple sources of information across media formats and be able to identify the emotional appeal used in the smaller sound bites of non-print media. Readers must view with a discerning eye, listen with a questioning ear, and think with a critical mind.

Informational Graphics

A test taker's ability to draw conclusions from an informational graphic is a sub-skill in displaying one's command of reading evidence. Drawing conclusions requires the reader to consider all information provided in the passage, then to use logic to piece it together to form a reasonably correct resolution. In this case, a test taker must look for facts as well as opinionated statements. Both should be considered in order to arrive at a conclusion. These types of questions test one's ability to conduct logical and analytical thinking.

Identifying data-driven evidence in informational graphics is very similar to analyzing factual information. However, it often involves the use of graphics in order to do so. In these types of questions, the test taker will be presented with a graph, or organizational tool, and asked questions regarding the information it contains.

Texts may have graphical representations to help illustrate and visually support assertions made. For example, graphs can be used to express samples or segments of a population or demonstrate growth or decay. Three of the most popular graphical formats include line graphs, bar graphs, and pie charts.

Line graphs rely on a horizontal X-axis and a vertical Y-axis to establish baseline values. Dots are plotted where the horizontal and vertical axes intersect, and those dots are connected with lines. Compared to bar graphs or pie charts, line graphs are more useful for looking at the past and present and predicting future outcomes. For instance, a potential investor would look for stocks that demonstrated steady growth over many decades when examining the stock market. Note that severe spikes up and down indicate instability, while line graphs that display a slow but steady increase may indicate good returns.

Here's an example of a bar graph:

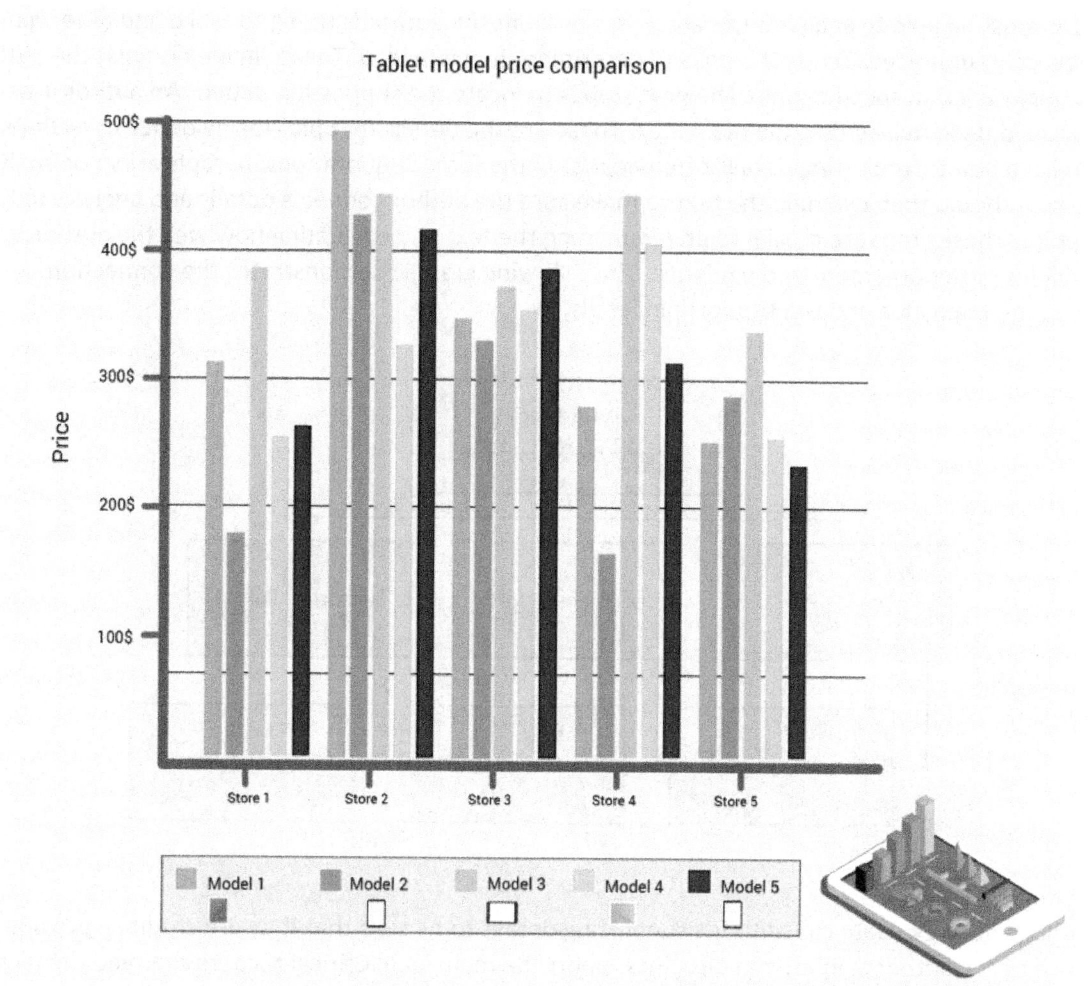

Bar graphs are usually displayed on a vertical Y-axis. The bars themselves can be two- or three-dimensional, depending on the designer's tastes. Unlike a line graph, which shows the fluctuation of only one variable, the X-axis on a bar graph is excellent for making comparisons, because it shows differences between several variables. For instance, if a consumer wanted to buy a new tablet, she could narrow the selection down to a few choices by using a bar graph to plot the prices side by side. The tallest bar would be the most expensive tablet, the shortest bar would be the cheapest.

A **pie chart** is divided into wedges that represent a numerical piece of the whole. Pie charts are useful for demonstrating how different categories add up to 100 percent. However, pie charts are not useful in comparing dissimilar items. High schools tend to use pie charts to track where students end up after graduation. Each wedge, for instance, might be labeled *vocational school, two-year college, four-year college, workforce*, or *unemployed*. By calculating the size of each wedge, schools can offer classes in the same ratios as where students will end up after high school. Pie charts are also useful for tracking finances. Items like car payments, insurance, rent, credit cards, and entertainment would each get their own wedge proportional to the amount spent in a given time period. If one wedge is inordinately bigger than the rest, or if a wedge is expendable, it might be time to create a new financial strategy.

Evaluating Arguments and Claims

A reader must be able to evaluate the argument or point the author is trying to make and determine if it is adequately supported. The first step is to determine the main idea. The main idea is what the author wants to say about a specific topic. The next step is to locate the supporting details. An author uses supporting details to illustrate the main idea. These are the details that provide evidence or examples to help make a point. Supporting details often appear in the form of quotations, paraphrasing, or analysis. Test takers should then examine the text to make sure the author connects details and analysis to the main point. These steps are crucial to understanding the text and evaluating how well the author presents his or her argument and evidence. The following graphic demonstrates the connection between the main idea and the supporting details.

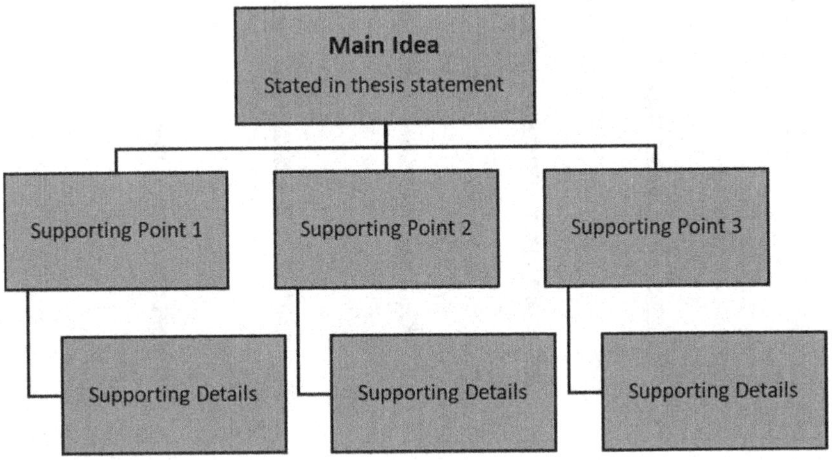

Evaluating Evidence

It is important to evaluate the author's supporting details to be sure that they are credible, provide evidence of the author's point, and directly support the main idea. Critical readers examine the facts used to support an author's argument and check those facts against other sources to make sure the facts are correct. They also check the validity of the sources used to make sure those sources are credible, academic, and/or peer-reviewed. A strong argument uses valid, measurable facts to support ideas.

Identifying False Statements

A reader must also be able to identify any *logical fallacies*—logically-flawed statements—that an author may make as those fallacies impact the validity and veracity of the author's claims.

Some of the more common fallacies are shown in the following chart.

Fallacy	Definition
Slippery Slope	A fallacy that is built on the idea that a particular action will lead to a series of events with negative results
Red Herring	The use of an observation or distraction to remove attention from the actual issue
Straw Man	An exaggeration or misrepresentation of an argument so that it is easier to refute
Post Hoc Ergo Propter Hoc	A fallacy that assumes an event to be the consequence of an earlier event merely because it came after it
Bandwagon	A fallacy that assumes because the majority of people feel or believe a certain way then it must be the right way
Ad Hominem	The use of a personal attack on the person or persons associated with a certain argument rather than focusing on the actual argument itself

Readers who are aware of the types of fallacious reasoning are able to weigh the credibility of the author's statements in terms of effective argument. Rhetorical text that contains a myriad of fallacious statements should be considered ineffectual and suspect.

Connections Between Different Texts

When analyzing two or more texts, there are several different aspects that need to be considered, particularly the styles (or the artful way in which the authors use diction to deliver a theme), points of view, and types of argument. In order to do so, one should compare and contrast the following elements between the texts:

- **Style**: narrative, persuasive, descriptive, informative, etc.
- **Tone**: sarcastic, angry, somber, humorous, etc.
- **Sentence structure**: simple (1 clause) compound (2 clauses), complex-compound (3 clauses)
- **Punctuation choice**: question marks, exclamation points, periods, dashes, etc.
- **Point of view**: first person, second person, third person
- **Paragraph structure**: long, short, both, differences between the two
- **Organizational structure**: compare/contrast, problem/solution, chronological, etc.

The following two poems and the essay concern the theme of death and are presented to demonstrate how to evaluate the above elements:

Poem 1:

How wonderful is Death,

Death, and his brother Sleep!

One, pale as yonder waning moon

With lips of lurid blue;

The other, rosy as the morn

When throned on ocean's wave

It blushes o'er the world;

Yet both so passing wonderful!

"Queen Mab," Percy Bysshe Shelley

Poem 2:

After great pain, a formal feeling comes –

The Nerves sit ceremonious, like Tombs –

The stiff Heart questions 'was it He, that bore,'

And 'Yesterday, or Centuries before'?

The Feet, mechanical, go round –

A Wooden way

Of Ground, or Air, or Ought –

Regardless grown,

A Quartz contentment, like a stone –

This is the Hour of Lead –

Remembered, if outlived,

As Freezing persons, recollect the Snow –

First – Chill – then Stupor – then the letting go –

"After Great Pain, A Formal Feeling Comes," Emily Dickinson

Essay 1

The Process of Dying

Death occurs in several stages. The first stage is the pre-active stage, which occurs a few days to weeks before death, in which the desire to eat and drink decreases, and the person may feel restless, irritable, and anxious. The second stage is the active stage, where the skin begins to cool, breathing becomes difficult as the lungs become congested (known as the "death rattle"), and the person loses control of their bodily fluids.

Once death occurs, there are also two stages. The first is clinical death, when the heart stops pumping blood and breathing ceases. This stage lasts approximately 4-6 minutes, and during this time, it is possible for a victim to be resuscitated via CPR or a defibrillator. After 6 minutes however, the oxygen stores within the brain begin to deplete, and the victim enters biological death. This is the point of no return, as the cells of the brain and vital organs begin to die, a process that is irreversible.

Now, using the outline above, the similarities and differences between the three passages are considered:

1. **Style**: The two poems are both descriptive as they focus on descriptions and sensations to convey their messages and do not follow any sort of timeline. The third selection is an expository style, presenting purely factual evidence on death, completely devoid of emotion.

2. **Tone**: Readers should notice the differences in the word choices between the two poems. Percy Shelley's word choices—"wonderful," "rosy," "blushes," "ocean"—surrounding death indicates that he views death in a welcoming manner as his words carry positive charges. The word choices by Dickinson, however, carry negative connotations—"pain," "wooden," "stone," "lead," "chill," "tombs"—which indicates an aversion to death. In contrast, the expository passage has no emotionally-charged words of any kind and seems to view death simply as a process that happens, neither welcoming nor fearing it. The tone in this passage, therefore, is neutral.

3. **Sentence structure**: Shelley's poem is composed mostly of compound sentences, which flow easily into one another. If read aloud, it sounds almost fluid, like the waves of the ocean he describes in his poem. His sentence structure mirrors the ease in which he views death. Dickinson's poem, on the other hand, is mostly simple sentences that are short and curt. They do not flow easily into one another, possibly representing her hesitancy and discomfort in her views of death. The expository passage contains many complex-compound sentences, which are used to accommodate lots of information. The structure of these sentences contributes to the overall informative nature of the selection.

4. **Punctuation choice**: Shelley uses commas, semicolons, and exclamation points in his poem, which, combined with his word choices and sentence structure, contributes to the overall positive tone of the poem. Dickinson uses lots of dashes, which make the poem feel almost cutting and jagged, which contributes to the overall negative tone of her poem. The expository text uses only commas and periods, which adds to the overall neutral tone of the selection.

5. **Point of view**: The point of view in all three selections is third person. In the two poems, there are no obvious pronouns; however, they both are presented in the third-person point of view, as Shelley speaks of Death in the third person, and Dickinson refers to "freezing persons." Generally, if there

are no first- or second-person pronouns in a selection, the view is third person. The informational selection also uses third-person point of view, as it avoids any first- or second-person pronouns.

6. **Paragraph/stanza structure**: Shelley's poem is one stanza long, making it inherently simple in nature. The simplicity of the single stanza is representative (again) of the comfort in which the author finds the topic of death. Dickinson's poem is much lengthier, and comparatively, could signify the difficulty of letting go of the death of a loved one. The paragraph structure of the essay is much longer than the two and is used to fit in a lot more information than the poems, as the poems are trying to convey emotion, and the essay is presenting facts.

7. **Organizational structure**: Shelley's poem uses a compare and contrast method to illustrate the similarities between death and sleep: that death is merely a paler, bluer brother to the warm and rosy sleep. Dickinson's structure, however, is descriptive, focusing primarily on feelings and sensations. The expository passage, on the other hand, is chronologically-organized, as it follows a timeline of events that occur in stages.

When analyzing the different structures, it may be helpful to make a table and use single words to compare and contrast the texts:

Elements	**Queen Mab**	**After Great Pain**	**Process of Dying**
Style	Descriptive	Descriptive	Expository
Tone	Warm	Cold	Neutral
Sentence Structure	Fluid	Jagged	Long
Punctuation Choice	!	–	.
Point of View	Third	Third	Third
Paragraph Structure	Short	Longer	Longest
Organizational Structure	Compare-Contrast	Descriptive	Chronological

Using this table, the differences become very clear. Although the two poems are both about death, their word tone, sentence structure, punctuation choices, and organization depict differences in how the authors perceive death, while the elements in the expository text clearly indicate an objective view of death. It should be noted that these are only a handful of the endless possible interpretations the reader could make.

Synthesis

Synthesis in reading involves the ability to fully comprehend text passages, and then going further by making new connections to see things in a new or different way. It involves a full thought process and requires readers to change the way they think about what they read.

Synthesis goes further than summary. When summarizing, a reader collects all of the information an author presents in a text passage and restates it in an effective manner. Synthesis requires that the test taker not only summarize reading material but be able to express new ideas based on the author's message. It is a full culmination of all reading comprehension strategies. It will require the test taker to order, recount, summarize, and recreate information into a whole new idea.

In utilizing synthesis, a reader must be able to form mental images about what they read, recall any background information they have about the topic, ask critical questions about the material, determine the importance of points an author makes, make inferences based on the reading, and finally be able to form new ideas based on all of the above skills. Synthesis requires the reader to make connections, visualize concepts, determine their importance, ask questions, make inferences, then fully synthesize all of this information into new thought.

Making Connections in Reading

There are three helpful thinking strategies to keep in mind when attempting to synthesize text passages:

- Think about how the content of a passage relates to life experience;
- Think about how the content of a passage relates to other text and;
- Think about how the content of a passage relates to the world in general.

When reading a given passage, the test taker should actively think about how the content relates to their life experience. While the author's message may express an opinion different from what the reader believes, or express ideas with which the reader is unfamiliar, a good reader will try to relate any of the author's details to their own familiar ground. A reader should use context clues to understand unfamiliar terminology and recognize familiar information they have encountered in prior experience. Bringing prior life experience and knowledge to the test-taking situation is helpful in making connections. The ability to relate an unfamiliar idea to something the reader already knows is critical in understanding unique and new ideas.

When trying to make connections while reading, keep the following questions in mind:

- How does this feel familiar in personal experience?
- How is this similar to or different from other reading?
- How is this familiar in the real world?
- How does this relate to the world in general?

Reader should ask themselves these questions during the act of reading in order to actively make connections to past and present experiences. Utilizing the ability to make connections is an important step in achieving synthesis.

Determining Importance in Reading

Being able to determine what is most important while reading is critical to synthesis. It is the difference between being able to tell what is necessary to full comprehension and that which is interesting but not necessary.

When determining the importance of an author's ideas, consider the following:

- Ask how critical an author's particular idea, assertion, or concept is to the overall message.

- Ask "is this an interesting fact or is this information essential to understanding the author's main idea?"

- Make a simple chart. On one side, list all of the important, essential points an author makes and on the other, list all of the interesting yet non-critical ideas.

- Highlight, circle, or underline any dates or data in non-fiction passages. Pay attention to headings, captions, and any graphs or diagrams.

- When reading a fictional passage, delineate important information such as theme, character, setting, conflict (what the problem is), and resolution (how the problem is fixed). Most often, these are the most important aspects contained in fictional text.

- If a non-fiction passage is instructional in nature, take physical note of any steps in the order of their importance as presented by the author. Look for words such as *first*, *next*, *then*, and *last*.

Determining the importance of an author's ideas is critical to synthesis in that it requires the test taker to parse out any unnecessary information and demonstrate they have the ability to make sound determination on what is important to the author, and what is merely a supporting or less critical detail.

Asking Questions While Reading

A reader must ask questions while reading. This demonstrates their ability to critically approach information and apply higher thinking skills to an author's content. Some of these questions have been addressed earlier in this section. A reader must ask what is or isn't important, what relates to their experience, and what relates to the world in general? However, it's important to ask other questions as well in order to make connections and synthesize reading material. Consider the following partial list of possibilities:

- What type of passage is this? Is it fiction? Non-fiction? Does it include data?
- Based on the type of passage, what information should be noted in order to make connections, visualize details, and determine importance?
- What is the author's message or theme? What is it they want the reader to understand?
- Is this passage trying to convince readers of something? What is it? If so, is the argument logical, convincing, and effective? How so? If not, how not?
- What do readers already know about this topic? Are there other viewpoints that support or contradict it?
- Is the information in this passage current and up to date?
- Is the author trying to teach readers a lesson? If so, what is it? Is there a moral to this story?
- How does this passage relate to experience?
- What is not as understandable in this passage? What context clues can help with understanding?
- What conclusions can be drawn? What predictions can be made?

Again, the above should be considered only a small example of the possibilities. Any question the reader asks while reading will help achieve synthesis and full reading comprehension.

Practice Questions

Questions 1–6 are based upon the following passage:

This excerpt is an adaptation of Jonathan Swift's *Gulliver's Travels into Several Remote Nations of the World.*

> My gentleness and good behaviour had gained so far on the emperor and his court, and indeed upon the army and people in general, that I began to conceive hopes of getting my liberty in a short time. I took all possible methods to cultivate this favourable disposition. The natives came, by degrees, to be less apprehensive of any danger from me. I would sometimes lie down, and let five or six of them dance on my hand; and at last the boys and girls would venture to come and play at hide-and-seek in my hair. I had now made a good progress in understanding and speaking the language. The emperor had a mind one day to entertain me with several of the country shows, wherein they exceed all nations I have known, both for dexterity and magnificence. I was diverted with none so much as that of the rope-dancers, performed upon a slender white thread, extended about two feet, and twelve inches from the ground. Upon which I shall desire liberty, with the reader's patience, to enlarge a little.
>
> This diversion is only practised by those persons who are candidates for great employments, and high favour at court. They are trained in this art from their youth, and are not always of noble birth, or liberal education. When a great office is vacant, either by death or disgrace (which often happens,) five or six of those candidates petition the emperor to entertain his majesty and the court with a dance on the rope; and whoever jumps the highest, without falling, succeeds in the office. Very often the chief ministers themselves are commanded to show their skill, and to convince the emperor that they have not lost their faculty. Flimnap, the treasurer, is allowed to cut a caper on the straight rope, at least an inch higher than any other lord in the whole empire. I have seen him do the summerset several times together, upon a trencher fixed on a rope which is no thicker than a common packthread in England. My friend Reldresal, principal secretary for private affairs, is, in my opinion, if I am not partial, the second after the treasurer; the rest of the great officers are much upon a par.

1. Which of the following statements best summarize the central purpose of this text?
    a. Gulliver details his fondness for the archaic yet interesting practices of his captors.
    b. Gulliver conjectures about the intentions of the aristocratic sector of society.
    c. Gulliver becomes acquainted with the people and practices of his new surroundings.
    d. Gulliver's differences cause him to become penitent around new acquaintances.

2. What is the word *principal* referring to in the following text?

    > My friend Reldresal, principal secretary for private affairs, is, in my opinion, if I am not partial, the second after the treasurer; the rest of the great officers are much upon a par.

    a. Primary or chief
    b. An acolyte
    c. An individual who provides nurturing
    d. One in a subordinate position

3. What can the reader infer from this passage?

> I would sometimes lie down, and let five or six of them dance on my hand; and at last the boys and girls would venture to come and play at hide-and-seek in my hair.

a. The children tortured Gulliver.
b. Gulliver traveled because he wanted to meet new people.
c. Gulliver is considerably larger than the children who are playing around him.
d. Gulliver has a genuine love and enthusiasm for people of all sizes.

4. What is the significance of the word *mind* in the following passage?

> The emperor had a mind one day to entertain me with several of the country shows, wherein they exceed all nations I have known, both for dexterity and magnificence.

a. The ability to think
b. A collective vote
c. A definitive decision
d. A mythological question

5. Which of the following assertions does not support the fact that games are a commonplace event in this culture?

a. My gentlest and good behavior . . . short time.
b. They are trained in this art from their youth . . . liberal education.
c. Very often the chief ministers themselves are commanded to show their skill . . . not lost their faculty.
d. Flimnap, the treasurer, is allowed to cut a caper on the straight rope . . . higher than any other lord in the whole empire.

6. How do the roles of Flimnap and Reldresal serve as evidence of the community's emphasis in regards to the correlation between physical strength and leadership abilities?

a. Only children used Gulliver's hands as a playground.
b. The two men who exhibited superior abilities held prominent positions in the community.
c. Only common townspeople, not leaders, walk the straight rope.
d. No one could jump higher than Gulliver.

Questions 7–12 are based upon the following passage:

This excerpt is adaptation of Robert Louis Stevenson's *The Strange Case of Dr. Jekyll and Mr. Hyde.*

> "Did you ever come across a protégé of his—one Hyde?" He asked.
>
> "Hyde?" repeated Lanyon. "No. Never heard of him. Since my time."
>
> That was the amount of information that the lawyer carried back with him to the great, dark bed on which he tossed to and fro until the small hours of the morning began to grow large. It was a night of little ease to his toiling mind, toiling in mere darkness and besieged by questions.
>
> Six o'clock struck on the bells of the church that was so conveniently near to Mr. Utterson's dwelling, and still he was digging at the problem. Hitherto it had touched him on the intellectual side alone; but; but now his imagination also was engaged, or rather enslaved; and as he lay and tossed in the gross darkness of the night in the

curtained room, Mr. Enfield's tale went by before his mind in a scroll of lighted pictures. He would be aware of the great field of lamps in a nocturnal city; then of the figure of a man walking swiftly; then of a child running from the doctor's; and then these met, and that human Juggernaut trod the child down and passed on regardless of her screams. Or else he would see a room in a rich house, where his friend lay asleep, dreaming and smiling at his dreams; and then the door of that room would be opened, the curtains of the bed plucked apart, the sleeper recalled, and, lo! There would stand by his side a figure to whom power was given, and even at that dead hour he must rise and do its bidding. The figure in these two phrases haunted the lawyer all night; and if at anytime he dozed over, it was but to see it glide more stealthily through sleeping houses, or move the more swiftly, and still the more smoothly, even to dizziness, through wider labyrinths of lamplighted city, and at every street corner crush a child and leave her screaming. And still the figure had no face by which he might know it; even in his dreams it had no face, or one that baffled him and melted before his eyes; and thus there it was that there sprung up and grew apace in the lawyer's mind a singularly strong, almost an inordinate, curiosity to behold the features of the real Mr. Hyde. If he could but once set eyes on him, he thought the mystery would lighten and perhaps roll altogether away, as was the habit of mysterious things when well examined. He might see a reason for his friend's strange preference or bondage, and even for the startling clauses of the will. And at least it would be a face worth seeing: the face of a man who was without bowels of mercy: a face which had but to show itself to raise up, in the mind of the unimpressionable Enfield, a spirit of enduring hatred.

From that time forward, Mr. Utterson began to haunt the door in the by street of shops. In the morning before office hours, at noon when business was plenty of time scarce, at night under the face of the full city moon, by all lights and at all hours of solitude or concourse, the lawyer was to be found on his chosen post.

"If he be Mr. Hyde," he had thought, "I should be Mr. Seek."

7. What is the purpose of the use of repetition in the following passage?

   It was a night of little ease to his toiling mind, toiling in mere darkness and besieged by questions.

   a. It serves as a demonstration of the mental state of Mr. Lanyon.
   b. It is reminiscent of the church bells that are mentioned in the story.
   c. It mimics Mr. Utterson's ambivalence.
   d. It emphasizes Mr. Utterson's anguish in failing to identify Hyde's whereabouts.

8. What is the setting of the story in this passage?
   a. In the city
   b. On the countryside
   c. In a jail
   d. In a mental health facility

9. What can one infer about the meaning of the word "Juggernaut" from the author's use of it in the passage?

a. It is an apparition that appears at daybreak.
b. It scares children.
c. It is associated with space travel.
d. Mr. Utterson finds it soothing.

10. What is the definition of the word *haunt* in the following passage?

From that time forward, Mr. Utterson began to haunt the door in the by street of shops. In the morning before office hours, at noon when business was plenty of time scarce, at night under the face of the full city moon, by all lights and at all hours of solitude or concourse, the lawyer was to be found on his chosen post.

a. To levitate
b. To constantly visit
c. To terrorize
d. To daunt

11. The phrase *labyrinths of lamplighted city* contains an example of what?

a. Hyperbole
b. Simile
c. Metaphor
d. Alliteration

12. What can one reasonably conclude from the final comment of this passage?

"If he be Mr. Hyde," he had thought, "I should be Mr. Seek."

a. The speaker is considering a name change.
b. The speaker is experiencing an identity crisis.
c. The speaker has mistakenly been looking for the wrong person.
d. The speaker intends to continue to look for Hyde.

Questions 13–18 are based upon the following passage:

This excerpt is adaptation from "What to the Slave is the Fourth of July?" Rochester, New York July 5, 1852

Fellow citizens—Pardon me, and allow me to ask, why am I called upon to speak here today? What have I, or those I represent, to do with your national independence? Are the great principles of political freedom and of natural justice embodied in that Declaration of Independence, Independence extended to us? And am I therefore called upon to bring our humble offering to the national altar, and to confess the benefits, and express devout gratitude for the blessings, resulting from your independence to us?

Would to God, both for your sakes and ours, ours that an affirmative answer could be truthfully returned to these questions! Then would my task be light, and my burden easy and delightful. For who is there so cold that a nation's sympathy could not warm him? Who so obdurate and dead to the claims of gratitude that would not thankfully acknowledge such priceless benefits? Who so stolid and selfish, that would not give his voice to swell the hallelujahs of a nation's jubilee, when the chains of servitude had been torn from his limbs? I am not that man. In a case like that, the dumb may eloquently speak, and the lame man leap as an hart.

But, such is not the state of the case. I say it with a sad sense of the disparity between us. I am not included within the pale of this glorious anniversary. Oh pity! Your high independence only reveals the immeasurable distance between us. The blessings in which you this day rejoice, I do not enjoy in common. The rich inheritance of justice, liberty, prosperity, and independence, bequeathed by your fathers, is shared by *you*, not by *me*. This Fourth of July is *yours,* not *mine*. You may rejoice, *I* must mourn. To drag a man in fetters into the grand illuminated temple of liberty, and call upon him to join you in joyous anthems, were inhuman mockery and sacrilegious irony. Do you mean, citizens, to mock me, by asking me to speak today? If so there is a parallel to your conduct. And let me warn you that it is dangerous to copy the example of a nation whose crimes, towering up to heaven, were thrown down by the breath of the Almighty, burying that nation and irrecoverable ruin! I can today take up the plaintive lament of a peeled and woe-smitten people.

By the rivers of Babylon, there we sat down. Yea! We wept when we remembered Zion. We hanged our harps upon the willows in the midst thereof. For there, they that carried us away captive, required of us a song; and they who wasted us required of us mirth, saying, "Sing us one of the songs of Zion." How can we sing the Lord's song in a strange land? If I forget thee, O Jerusalem, let my right hand forget her cunning. If I do not remember thee, let my tongue cleave to the roof of my mouth.

13. What is the tone of the first paragraph of this passage?
    a. Exasperated
    b. Inclusive
    c. Contemplative
    d. Nonchalant

14. Which word CANNOT be used synonymously with the term *obdurate* as it is conveyed in the text below?

    Who so obdurate and dead to the claims of gratitude, that would not thankfully acknowledge such priceless benefits?

    a. Steadfast
    b. Stubborn
    c. Contented
    d. Unwavering

15. What is the central purpose of this text?
    a. To demonstrate the author's extensive knowledge of the Bible
    b. To address the feelings of exclusion expressed by African Americans after the establishment of the Fourth of July holiday
    c. To convince wealthy landowners to adopt new holiday rituals
    d. To explain why minorities often relished the notion of segregation in government institutions

16. Which statement serves as evidence of the question above?
   a. By the rivers of Babylon . . . down.
   b. Fellow citizens . . . today.
   c. I can . . . woe-smitten people.
   d. The rich inheritance of justice . . . *not by me.*

17. The statement below features an example of which of the following literary devices?

   Oh pity! Your high independence only reveals the immeasurable distance between us.

   a. Assonance
   b. Parallelism
   c. Amplification
   d. Hyperbole

18. The speaker's use of biblical references, such as "rivers of Babylon" and the "songs of Zion," helps the reader to do all of the following EXCEPT:
   a. Identify with the speaker through the use of common text.
   b. Convince the audience that injustices have been committed by referencing another group of people who have been previously affected by slavery.
   c. Display the equivocation of the speaker and those that he represents.
   d. Appeal to the listener's sense of humanity.

19. Which organizational style is used in the following passage?

   There are several reasons why the new student café has not been as successful as expected. One factor is that prices are higher than originally advertised, so many students cannot afford to buy food and beverages there. Also, the café closes rather early; as a result, students go out in town to other late-night gathering places rather than meeting friends at the café on campus.

   a. Cause and effect order
   b. Compare and contrast order
   c. Spatial order
   d. Time order

20. What can the reader infer from this passage?

   I would sometimes lie down, and let five or six of them dance on my hand; and at last the boys and girls would venture to come and play at hide-and-seek in my hair.

   a. The children tortured Gulliver.
   b. Gulliver traveled because he wanted to meet new people.
   c. Gulliver is considerably larger than the children who are playing around him.
   d. Gulliver has a genuine love and enthusiasm for people of all sizes.

21. David Foster Wallace's *Infinite Jest* is the holy grail of modern literature. It will stand the test of time in its relevance. Every single person who starts reading *Infinite Jest* cannot physically put down the book until completing it.

Which of the following is the main point of the passage?

a. David Foster Wallace's *Infinite Jest* is the holy grail of modern literature.
b. *Infinite Jest* is a page-turner.
c. David Foster Wallace wrote *Infinite Jest*.
d. *Infinite Jest* is a modern classic for good reason and everybody should read it.

22. The assassination of Archduke Franz Ferdinand of Austria is often ascribed as the cause of World War I. However, the assassination merely lit the fuse in a combustible situation since many of the world powers were in complicated and convoluted military alliances. For example, England, France, and Russia entered into a mutual defense treaty seven years prior to World War I. Even without Franz Ferdinand's assassination ______________________.

Which of the following most logically completes the passage?

a. A war between the world powers was extremely likely.
b. World War I never would have happened.
c. England, France, and Russia would have started the war.
d. Austria would have started the war.

Questions 23–30 are based on the following passages.

Passage I

Lethal force, or deadly force, is defined as the physical means to cause death or serious harm to another individual. The law holds that lethal force is only accepted when you or another person are in immediate and unavoidable danger of death or severe bodily harm. For example, a person could be beating a weaker person in such a way that they are suffering severe enough trauma that could result in death or serious harm. This would be an instance where lethal force would be acceptable and possibly the only way to save that person from irrevocable damage.

Another example of when to use lethal force would be when someone enters your home with a deadly weapon. The intruder's presence and possession of the weapon indicate mal-intent and the ability to inflict death or severe injury to you and your loved ones. Again, lethal force can be used in this situation. Lethal force can also be applied to prevent the harm of another individual. If a woman is being brutally assaulted and is unable to fend off an attacker, lethal force can be used to defend her as a last-ditch effort. If she is in immediate jeopardy of rape, harm, and/or death, lethal force could be the only response that could effectively deter the assailant.

The key to understanding the concept of lethal force is the term *last resort*. Deadly force cannot be taken back; it should be used only to prevent severe harm or death. The law does distinguish whether the means of one's self-defense is fully warranted, or if the individual goes out of control in the process. If you continually attack the assailant after they are rendered incapacitated, this would be causing unnecessary harm, and the law can bring charges against you. Likewise, if you kill an attacker unnecessarily after defending yourself, you can be charged with murder. This would move lethal force beyond necessary defense, making it no longer a last resort but rather a use of excessive force.

Passage II

Assault is the unlawful attempt of one person to apply apprehension on another individual by an imminent threat or by initiating offensive contact. Assaults can vary, encompassing physical strikes, threatening body language, and even provocative language. In the case of the latter, even if a hand has not been laid, it is still considered an assault because of its threatening nature.

Let's look at an example: A homeowner is angered because his neighbor blows fallen leaves into his freshly mowed lawn. Irate, the homeowner gestures a fist to his fellow neighbor and threatens to bash his head in for littering on his lawn. The homeowner's physical motions and verbal threat heralds a physical threat against the other neighbor. These factors classify the homeowner's reaction as an assault. If the angry neighbor hits the threatening homeowner in retaliation, that would constitute an assault as well because he physically hit the homeowner.

Assault also centers on the involvement of weapons in a conflict. If someone fires a gun at another person, it could be interpreted as an assault unless the shooter acted in self-defense. If an individual drew a gun or a knife on someone with the intent to harm them, it would be considered assault. However, it's also considered an assault if someone simply aimed a weapon, loaded or not, at another person in a threatening manner.

23. What is the purpose of the second passage?
   a. To inform the reader about what assault is and how it is committed.
   b. To inform the reader about how assault is a minor example of lethal force.
   c. To argue that the use of assault is more common than the use of lethal force.
   d. The author is recounting an incident in which they were assaulted.

24. Which of the following situations, according to the passages, would not constitute an illegal use of lethal force?
   a. A disgruntled cashier yells obscenities at a customer.
   b. A thief is seen running away with stolen cash.
   c. A man is attacked in an alley by another man with a knife.
   d. A woman punches another woman in a bar.

25. Given the information in the passages, which of the following must be true about assault?
   a. All assault is considered expression of lethal force.
   b. There are various forms of assault.
   c. Assault is justified only as a last resort.
   d. Assault charges are more severe that unnecessary use of force charges.

26. Which of the following, if true, would most seriously undermine the explanation proposed by the author in Passage I, third paragraph?
   a. An instance of lethal force in self-defense is not absolutely absolved from blame. The law takes into account the necessary use of force at the time it is committed.
   b. An individual who uses necessary defense under lethal force is in direct compliance of the law under most circumstances.
   c. Lethal force in self-defense should be forgiven in all cases for the peace of mind of the primary victim.
   d. The use of lethal force is not evaluated on the intent of the user, but rather the severity of the primary attack that warranted self-defense.

27. Based on the passages, what can we infer about the relationship between assault and lethal force?
    a. An act of lethal force always leads to a type of assault.
    b. Assault and lethal force have no conceivable connection.
    c. An assault with deadly intent can lead to an individual using lethal force to preserve their well-being.
    d. If someone uses self-defense in a conflict, it is called deadly force; if actions or threats are intended, it is called assault.

28. Which of the following best describes the way the passages are structured?
    a. Both passages open by defining a legal concept and then continue to describe situations in order to further explain the concept.
    b. Both passages begin with situations, introduce accepted definitions, and then cite legal ramifications.
    c. Both cite specific legal doctrines, then proceed to explain the rulings.
    d. The first passage explains both concepts and then focuses on lethal force. The second passage picks up with assault and explains the concept in depth.

29. What can we infer about the role of intent in lethal force and assault?
    a. Intent is very important for determining both lethal force and assault; intent is examined in both parties and helps determine the severity of the issue.
    b. Intent is vital for determining the lawfulness of using lethal force.
    c. Intent is only taken into account for assault charges.
    d. The intent of the assailant is the main focus for determining legal ramifications; it is used to determine if the defender was justified in using force to respond.

30. The author uses the example in the second paragraph of Passage II in order to do what?
    a. To demonstrate two different types of assault by showing how each specifically relates to the other.
    b. To demonstrate a single example of two different types of assault, then adding in the third type of assault in the example's conclusion.
    c. To prove that the definition of lethal force is altered when the victim in question is a homeowner and his property is threatened.
    d. To suggest that verbal assault can be an exaggerated crime by the law and does not necessarily lead to physical violence.
    e. To demonstrate that threatening body language is only considered a type of assault if it leads to physical violence.

Questions 31–36 are based upon the following passage:

This excerpt is adapted from *Our Vanishing Wildlife,* by William T. Hornaday

> Three years ago, I think there were not many bird-lovers in the United States, who believed it possible to prevent the total extinction of both egrets from our fauna. All the known rookeries accessible to plume-hunters had been totally destroyed. Two years ago, the secret discovery of several small, hidden colonies prompted William Dutcher, President of the National Association of Audubon Societies, and Mr. T. Gilbert Pearson, Secretary, to attempt the protection of those colonies. With a fund contributed for the purpose, wardens were hired and duly commissioned. As previously stated, one of those wardens was shot dead in cold blood by a plume hunter. The task of guarding swamp

rookeries from the attacks of money-hungry desperadoes to whom the accursed plumes were worth their weight in gold, is a very chancy proceeding. There is now one warden in Florida who says that "before they get my rookery they will first have to get me."

Thus far the protective work of the Audubon Association has been successful. Now there are twenty colonies, which contain all told, about 5,000 egrets and about 120,000 herons and ibises which are guarded by the Audubon wardens. One of the most important is on Bird Island, a mile out in Orange Lake, central Florida, and it is ably defended by Oscar E. Baynard. To-day, the plume hunters who do not dare to raid the guarded rookeries are trying to study out the lines of flight of the birds, to and from their feeding-grounds, and shoot them in transit. Their motto is—"Anything to beat the law, and get the plumes." It is there that the state of Florida should take part in the war.

The success of this campaign is attested by the fact that last year a number of egrets were seen in eastern Massachusetts—for the first time in many years. And so to-day the question is, can the wardens continue to hold the plume-hunters at bay?

31. The author's use of first person pronoun in the following text does NOT have which of the following effects?

> Three years ago, I think there were not many bird-lovers in the United States, who believed it possible to prevent the total extinction of both egrets from our fauna.

a. The phrase *I think* acts as a sort of hedging, where the author's tone is less direct and/or absolute.
b. It allows the reader to more easily connect with the author.
c. It encourages the reader to empathize with the egrets.
d. It distances the reader from the text by overemphasizing the story.

32. What purpose does the quote serve at the end of the first paragraph?

a. The quote shows proof of a hunter threatening one of the wardens.
b. The quote lightens the mood by illustrating the colloquial language of the region.
c. The quote provides an example of a warden protecting one of the colonies.
d. The quote provides much needed comic relief in the form of a joke.

33. What is the meaning of the word *rookeries* in the following text?

> To-day, the plume hunters who do not dare to raid the guarded rookeries are trying to study out the lines of flight of the birds, to and from their feeding-grounds, and shoot them in transit.

a. Houses in a slum area
b. A place where hunters gather to trade tools
c. A place where wardens go to trade stories
d. A colony of breeding birds

34. What is on Bird Island?

a. Hunters selling plumes
b. An important bird colony
c. Bird Island Battle between the hunters and the wardens
d. An important egret with unique plumes

35. What is the main purpose of the passage?
  a. To persuade the audience to act in preservation of the bird colonies
  b. To show the effect hunting egrets has had on the environment
  c. To argue that the preservation of bird colonies has had a negative impact on the environment.
  d. To demonstrate the success of the protective work of the Audubon Association

36. Why are hunters trying to study the lines of flight of the birds?
  a. To study ornithology, one must know the lines of flight that birds take.
  b. To help wardens preserve the lives of the birds
  c. To have a better opportunity to hunt the birds
  d. To builds their homes under the lines of flight because they believe it brings good luck

Questions 37–42 are based upon the following passage:

This excerpt is adaptation from *The Life-Story of Insects,* by Geo H. Carpenter.

> Insects as a whole are preeminently creatures of the land and the air. This is shown not only by the possession of wings by a vast majority of the class, but by the mode of breathing to which reference has already been made, a system of branching air-tubes carrying atmospheric air with its combustion-supporting oxygen to all the insect's tissues. The air gains access to these tubes through a number of paired air-holes or spiracles, arranged segmentally in series.
>
> It is of great interest to find that, nevertheless, a number of insects spend much of their time under water. This is true of not a few in the perfect winged state, as for example aquatic beetles and water-bugs ('boatmen' and 'scorpions') which have some way of protecting their spiracles when submerged, and, possessing usually the power of flight, can pass on occasion from pond or stream to upper air. But it is advisable in connection with our present subject to dwell especially on some insects that remain continually under water till they are ready to undergo their final moult and attain the winged state, which they pass entirely in the air. The preparatory instars of such insects are aquatic; the adult instar is aerial. All may-flies, dragon-flies, and caddis-flies, many beetles and two-winged flies, and a few moths thus divide their life-story between the water and the air. For the present we confine attention to the Stone-flies, the May-flies, and the Dragon-flies, three well-known orders of insects respectively called by systematists the Plecoptera, the Ephemeroptera and the Odonata.
>
> In the case of many insects that have aquatic larvae, the latter are provided with some arrangement for enabling them to reach atmospheric air through the surface-film of the water. But the larva of a stone-fly, a dragon-fly, or a may-fly is adapted more completely than these for aquatic life; it can, by means of gills of some kind, breathe the air dissolved in water.

37. Which statement best details the central idea in this passage?
  a. It introduces certain insects that transition from water to air.
  b. It delves into entomology, especially where gills are concerned.
  c. It defines what constitutes as insects' breathing.
  d. It invites readers to have a hand in the preservation of insects.

38. Which definition most closely relates to the usage of the word *moult* in the passage?
  a. An adventure of sorts, especially underwater
  b. Mating act between two insects
  c. The act of shedding part or all of the outer shell
  d. Death of an organism that ends in a revival of life

39. What is the purpose of the first paragraph in relation to the second paragraph?
  a. The first paragraph serves as a cause and the second paragraph serves as an effect.
  b. The first paragraph serves as a contrast to the second.
  c. The first paragraph is a description for the argument in the second paragraph.
  d. The first and second paragraphs are merely presented in a sequence.

40. What does the following sentence most nearly mean?

The preparatory instars of such insects are aquatic; the adult instar is aerial.

  a. The volume of water is necessary to prep the insect for transition rather than the volume of the air.
  b. The abdomen of the insect is designed like a star in the water as well as the air.
  c. The stage of preparation in between molting is acted out in the water, while the last stage is in the air.
  d. These insects breathe first in the water through gills, yet continue to use the same organs to breathe in the air.

41. Which of the statements reflect information that one could reasonably infer based on the author's tone?
  a. The author's tone is persuasive and attempts to call the audience to action.
  b. The author's tone is passionate due to excitement over the subject and personal narrative.
  c. The author's tone is informative and exhibits interest in the subject of the study.
  d. The author's tone is somber, depicting some anger at the state of insect larvae.

42. Which statement best describes stoneflies, mayflies, and dragonflies?
  a. They are creatures of the land and the air.
  b. They have a way of protecting their spiracles when submerged.
  c. Their larvae can breathe the air dissolved in water through gills of some kind.
  d. The preparatory instars of these insects are aerial.

43. Which of the following statements least supports the argument that the American economy is healthy?
  a. The United States' Gross Domestic Product (GDP), which is the measure of all the goods and services produced in a country, increased by two percent last year.
  b. Unemployment is the lowest it's been in over a decade due to a spike in job creation.
  c. Average household income just hit a historical high point for the twentieth consecutive quarter.
  d. Last year, the output of the United States' manufacturing sector decreased despite repeated massive investments by both the private and public sectors.

44. Which of these descriptions gives the most detailed and objective support for the claim that drinking and driving is unsafe?

a. A dramatized television commercial reenacting a fatal drinking and driving accident, including heart-wrenching testimonials from loved ones
b. The Department of Transportation's press release noting the additional drinking and driving special patrol units that will be on the road during the holiday season
c. Congressional written testimony on the number of drinking and driving incidents across the country and their relationship to underage drinking statistics, according to experts
d. A highway bulletin warning drivers of penalties associated with drinking and driving

The next question is based on the following passage.

A famous children's author recently published a historical fiction novel under a pseudonym; however, it did not sell as many copies as her children's books. In her earlier years, she had majored in history and earned a graduate degree in Antebellum American History, which is the time frame of her new novel. Critics praised this newest work far more than the children's series that made her famous. In fact, her new novel was nominated for the prestigious Albert J. Beveridge Award, but still isn't selling like her children's books, which fly off the shelves because of her name alone.

45. Which one of the following statements might be accurately inferred based on the above passage?

a. The famous children's author produced an inferior book under her pseudonym.
b. The famous children's author is the foremost expert on Antebellum America.
c. The famous children's author did not receive the bump in publicity for her historical novel that it would have received if it were written under her given name.
d. People generally prefer to read children's series than historical fiction.

The next question is based on the following passage.

In 2015, 28 countries, including Estonia, Portugal, Slovenia, and Latvia, scored significantly higher than the United States on standardized high school math tests. In the 1960s, the United States consistently ranked first in the world. Today, the United States spends more than $800 billion dollars on education, which exceeds the next highest country by more than $600 billion dollars. The United States also leads the world in spending per school-aged child by an enormous margin.

46. If these statements above are factual, which of the following statements must be correct?

a. Outspending other countries on education has benefits beyond standardized math tests.
b. The United States' education system is corrupt and broken.
c. The standardized math tests are not representative of American academic prowess.
d. Spending more money does not guarantee success on standardized math tests.

The next question is based on the following conversation between a scientist and a politician.

Scientist: Last year was the warmest ever recorded in the last 134 years. During that time period, the ten warmest years have all occurred since 2000. This correlates directly with the recent increases in carbon dioxide as large countries like China, India, and Brazil continue developing and industrializing. No longer do just a handful of countries burn massive amounts of carbon-based fossil fuels; it is quickly becoming the case throughout the whole world as technology and industry spread.

Politician: Yes, but there is no causal link between increases in carbon emissions and increasing temperatures. The link is tenuous and nothing close to certain. We need to wait for all of the data before drawing hasty conclusions. For all we know, the temperature increase could be entirely natural. I believe the temperatures also rose dramatically during the dinosaurs' time, and I do not think they were burning any fossil fuels back then.

47. What is one point on which the scientist and politician agree?
    a. Burning fossil fuels causes global temperatures to rise.
    b. Global temperatures are increasing.
    c. Countries must revisit their energy policies before it's too late.
    d. Earth's climate naturally goes through warming and cooling periods.

Questions 48–54 are based on the following passage.

In the quest to understand existence, modern philosophers must question if humans can fully comprehend the world. Classical western approaches to philosophy tend to hold that one can understand something, be it an event or object, by standing outside of the phenomena and observing it. It is then by unbiased observation that one can grasp the details of the world. This seems to hold true for many things. Scientists conduct experiments and record their findings, and thus many natural phenomena become comprehendible. However, several of these observations were possible because humans used tools in order to make these discoveries.

This may seem like an extraneous matter. After all, people invented things like microscopes and telescopes in order to enhance their capacity to view cells or the movement of stars. While humans are still capable of seeing things, the question remains if human beings have the capacity to fully observe and see the world in order to understand it. It would not be an impossible stretch to argue that what humans see through a microscope is not the exact thing itself, but a human interpretation of it.

This would seem to be the case in the “Business of the Holes” experiment conducted by Richard Feynman. To study the way electrons behave, Feynman set up a barrier with two holes and a plate. The plate was there to indicate how many times the electrons would pass through the hole(s). Rather than casually observe the electrons acting under normal circumstances, Feynman discovered that electrons behave in two totally different ways depending on whether or not they are observed. The electrons that were observed had passed through either one of the holes or were caught on the plate as particles. However, electrons that weren’t observed acted as waves instead of particles and passed through both holes. This indicated that electrons have a dual nature. Electrons seen by the human eye act like particles, while unseen electrons act like waves of energy.

This dual nature of the electrons presents a conundrum. While humans now have a better understanding of electrons, the fact remains that people cannot entirely perceive how electrons behave without the use of instruments. We can only observe one of the mentioned behaviors, which only provides a partial understanding of the entire function of electrons. Therefore, we’re forced to ask ourselves whether the world we observe is objective or if it is subjectively perceived by humans. Or, an alternative question: can man understand the world only through machines that will allow them to observe natural phenomena?

Both questions humble man’s capacity to grasp the world. However, those ideas don’t take into account that many phenomena have been proven by human beings without the use of machines, such as the discovery of gravity. Like all philosophical questions, whether man's reason and observation alone can understand the universe can be approached from many angles.

48. What is the author's motivation for writing the passage?
a. Bring to light an alternative view on human perception by examining the role of technology in human understanding.
b. Educate the reader on the latest astroparticle physics discovery and offer terms that may be unfamiliar to the reader.
c. Argue that humans are totally blind to the realities of the world by presenting an experiment that proves that electrons are not what they seem on the surface.
d. Reflect on opposing views of human understanding.

49. Which of the following most closely resembles the way in which paragraph four is structured?
a. It offers one solution, questions the solution, and then ends with an alternative solution.
b. It presents an inquiry, explains the detail of that inquiry, and then offers a solution.
c. It presents a problem, explains the details of that problem, and then ends with more inquiry.
d. It gives a definition, offers an explanation, and then ends with an inquiry.

50. For the classical approach to understanding to hold true, which of the following must be required?
a. A telescope.
b. The person observing must prove their theory beyond a doubt.
c. Multiple witnesses present.
d. The person observing must be unbiased.

51. Which best describes how the electrons in the experiment behaved like waves?
a. The electrons moved up and down like actual waves.
b. The electrons passed through both holes and then onto the plate.
c. The electrons converted to photons upon touching the plate.
d. Electrons were seen passing through one hole or the other.

52. The author mentions "gravity" in the last paragraph in order to do what?
a. In order to show that different natural phenomena test man's ability to grasp the world.
b. To prove that since man has not measured it with the use of tools or machines, humans cannot know the true nature of gravity.
c. To demonstrate an example of natural phenomena humans discovered and understand without the use of tools or machines.
d. To show an alternative solution to the nature of electrons that humans have not thought of yet.

53. Which situation best parallels the revelation of the dual nature of electrons discovered in Feynman's experiment?

a. A man is born color-blind and grows up observing everything in lighter or darker shades. With the invention of special goggles he puts on, he discovers that there are other colors in addition to different shades.
b. The coelacanth was thought to be extinct, but a live specimen was just recently discovered. There are now two living species of coelacanth known to man, and both are believed to be endangered.
c. In the Middle Ages, blacksmiths added carbon to iron, thus inventing steel. The consequences of this important discovery would have its biggest effects during the industrial revolution.
d. In order to better examine and treat broken bones, the x-ray machine was invented and put to use in hospitals and medical centers.

54. Which statement about technology would the author likely disagree with?

a. Technology can help expand the field of human vision.
b. Technology renders human observation irrelevant.
c. Developing tools used in observation and research indicates growing understanding of our world in itself.
d. Studying certain phenomena necessitates the use of tools and machines.

55. The following exchange occurred after the Baseball Coach's team suffered a heartbreaking loss in the final inning.

Reporter: The team clearly did not rise to the challenge. I'm sure that getting zero hits in twenty at-bats with runners in scoring position hurt the team's chances at winning the game. What are your thoughts on this devastating loss?

Baseball Coach: Hitting with runners in scoring position was not the reason we lost this game. We made numerous errors in the field, and our pitchers gave out too many free passes. Also, we did not even need a hit with runners in scoring position. Many of those at-bats could have driven in the run by simply making contact. Our team did not deserve to win the game.

Which of the following best describes the main point of dispute between the reporter and baseball coach?

a. Whether the loss was heartbreaking.
b. Whether getting zero hits in twenty at-bats with runners in scoring position caused the loss.
c. Numerous errors in the field and pitchers giving too many free passes caused the loss.
d. Whether the team deserved to win the game.

56. Conservative Politician: Social welfare programs are destroying our country. These programs are not only adding to the annual deficit, which increases the national debt, but they also discourage hard work. Our country must continue producing leaders who bootstrap their way to the top. None of our country's citizens truly *need* assistance from the government; rather, the assistance just makes things easier.

Liberal Politician: Our great country is founded on the principle of hope. The country is built on the backs of immigrants who came here with nothing, except for the hope of a better life. Our country is too wealthy not to provide basic necessities for the less fortunate. Recent immigrants, single mothers, historically disenfranchised, disabled persons, and the elderly all require an ample safety net.

What is the main point of dispute between the politicians?

a. Spending on social welfare programs increases the national debt.
b. Certain classes of people rely on social welfare programs to meet their basic needs.
c. Certain classes of people would be irreparably harmed if the country failed to provide a social welfare program.
d. All of the country's leaders have bootstrapped their way to the top.
e. Immigrants founded the country.

Answer Explanations

1. C: Gulliver becomes acquainted with the people and practices of his new surroundings. Choice *C* is the correct answer because it most extensively summarizes the entire passage. While Choices *A* and *B* are reasonable possibilities, they reference portions of Gulliver's experiences, not the whole. Choice *D* is incorrect because Gulliver doesn't express repentance or sorrow in this particular passage.

2. A: Principal refers to *chief* or *primary* within the context of this text. Choice *A* is the answer that most closely aligns with this answer. Choices *B* and *D* make reference to a helper or followers while Choice *C* doesn't meet the description of Gulliver from the passage.

3. C: One can reasonably infer that Gulliver is considerably larger than the children who were playing around him because multiple children could fit into his hand. Choice *B* is incorrect because there is no indication of stress in Gulliver's tone. Choices *A* and *D* aren't the best answer because though Gulliver seems fond of his new acquaintances, he didn't travel there with the intentions of meeting new people or to express a definite love for them in this particular portion of the text.

4. C: The emperor made a *definitive decision* to expose Gulliver to their native customs. In this instance, the word *mind* was not related to a vote, question, or cognitive ability.

5. A: Choice *A* is correct. This assertion does *not* support the fact that games are a commonplace event in this culture because it mentions conduct, not games. Choices *B*, *C*, and *D* are incorrect because these do support the fact that games were a commonplace event.

6. B: Choice *B* is the only option that mentions the correlation between physical ability and leadership positions. Choices *A* and *D* are unrelated to physical strength and leadership abilities. Choice *C* does not make a deduction that would lead to the correct answer—it only comments upon the abilities of common townspeople.

7. D: It emphasizes Mr. Utterson's anguish in failing to identify Hyde's whereabouts. Context clues indicate that Choice *D* is correct because the passage provides great detail of Mr. Utterson's feelings about locating Hyde. Choice *A* does not fit because there is no mention of Mr. Lanyon's mental state. Choice *B* is incorrect; although the text does make mention of bells, Choice *B* is not the *best* answer overall. Choice *C* is incorrect because the passage clearly states that Mr. Utterson was determined, not unsure.

8. A: In the city. The word *city* appears in the passage several times, thus establishing the location for the reader.

9. B: It scares children. The passage states that the Juggernaut causes the children to scream. Choices *A* and *D* don't apply because the text doesn't mention either of these instances specifically. Choice *C* is incorrect because there is nothing in the text that mentions space travel.

10. B: To constantly visit. The mention of *morning*, *noon*, and *night* make it clear that the word *haunt* refers to frequent appearances at various locations. Choice *A* doesn't work because the text makes no mention of levitating. Choices *C* and *D* are not correct because the text makes mention of Mr. Utterson's anguish and disheartenment because of his failure to find Hyde but does not make mention of Mr. Utterson's feelings negatively affecting anyone else.

11. D: This is an example of alliteration. Choice *D* is the correct answer because of the repetition of the *L*-words. Hyperbole is an exaggeration, so Choice *A* doesn't work. No comparison is being made, so no simile or metaphor is being used, thus eliminating Choices *B* and *C*.

12. D: The speaker intends to continue to look for Hyde. Choices *A* and *B* are not possible answers because the text doesn't refer to any name changes or an identity crisis, despite Mr. Utterson's extreme obsession with finding Hyde. The text also makes no mention of a mistaken identity when referring to Hyde, so Choice *C* is also incorrect.

13. A: The tone is exasperated. While contemplative is an option because of the inquisitive nature of the text, Choice *A* is correct because the speaker is annoyed by the thought of being included when he felt that the fellow members of his race were being excluded. The speaker is not nonchalant, nor accepting of the circumstances which he describes.

14. C: Choice *C*, *contented*, is the only word that has different meaning. Furthermore, the speaker expresses objection and disdain throughout the entire text.

15. B: To address the feelings of exclusion expressed by African Americans after the establishment of the Fourth of July holiday. While the speaker makes biblical references, it is not the main focus of the passage, thus eliminating Choice *A* as an answer. The passage also makes no mention of wealthy landowners and doesn't speak of any positive response to the historical events, so Choices *C* and *D* are not correct.

16. D: Choice *D* is the correct answer because it clearly makes reference to justice being denied.

17. D: Hyperbole. Choices *A* and *B* are unrelated. Assonance is the repetition of sounds and commonly occurs in poetry. Parallelism refers to two statements that correlate in some manner. Choice *C* is incorrect because amplification normally refers to clarification of meaning by broadening the sentence structure, while hyperbole refers to a phrase or statement that is being exaggerated.

18. C: Display the equivocation of the speaker and those that he represents. Choice *C* is correct because the speaker is clear about his intention and stance throughout the text. Choice *A* could be true, but the words "common text" is arguable. Choice *B* is also partially true, as another group of people affected by slavery are being referenced. However, the speaker is not trying to convince the audience that injustices have been committed, as it is already understood there have been injustices committed. Choice *D* is also close to the correct answer, but it is not the *best* answer choice possible.

19. A: The passage describes a situation and then explains the causes that led to it. Also, it utilizes cause and effect signal words, such as *causes, factors, so,* and *as a result*. *B* is incorrect because a compare and contrast order considers the similarities and differences of two or more things. *C* is incorrect because spatial order describes where things are located in relation to each other. Finally, *D* is incorrect because time order describes when things occurred chronologically.

20. C: One can reasonably infer that Gulliver is considerably larger than the children who were playing around him because multiple children could fit into his hand. Choice *B* is incorrect because there is no indication of stress in Gulliver's tone. Choices *A* and *D* aren't the best answer because though Gulliver seems fond of his new acquaintances, he didn't travel there with the intentions of meeting new people or to express a definite love for them in this particular portion of the text.

21. D: Choice *D* looks like a strong answer. This answer choice references the argument's main points—*Infinite Jest* is a modern classic, the book deserves its praise, and everybody should read it. In contrast, Choice *A* restates the author's conclusion. The correct answer to main point questions will often be closely related to the conclusion. Choice *B* restates a premise. Is the author's main point that *Infinite Jest* is a page-turner? No, he uses readers' obsession with the book as a premise. Eliminate this choice. Choice *C* is definitely not the main point of the passage. It's a simple fact underlying the argument. It certainly cannot be considered the main point. Eliminate this choice.

22. A: Choice *A* is consistent with the argument's logic. The argument asserts that the world powers' military alliances amounted to a lit fuse, and the assassination merely lit it. The main point of the argument is that any event involving the military alliances would have led to a world war. Choice *B* runs counter to the argument's tone and reasoning. It can immediately be eliminated. Choice *C* is also clearly incorrect. At no point does the argument blame any single or group of countries for starting World War I. Choice *D* is incorrect for the same reason as Choice *C*. Eliminate this choice.

23. A: The purpose is to inform the reader about what assault is and how it is committed. Choice *B* is incorrect because the passage does not state that assault is a lesser form of lethal force, only that an assault can use lethal force, or alternatively, lethal force can be utilized to counter a dangerous assault. Choice *C* is incorrect because the passage is informative and does not have a set agenda. Finally, Choice *D* is incorrect because although the author uses an example in order to explain assault, it is not indicated that this is the author's personal account.

24. C: The situation of the man who is attacked in an alley by another man with a knife would most merit the use of lethal force. If the man being attached used self-defense by lethal force, it would not be considered illegal. The presence of a deadly weapon indicates mal-intent and because the individual is isolated in an alley, so lethal force in self-defense may be the only way to preserve his life. Choices *A* and *B* can be ruled out because in these situations, no one is in danger of immediate death or bodily harm by someone else. Choice *D* is an assault that does exhibit intent to harm, but this situation isn't severe enough to merit lethal force; there is no intent to kill.

25. B: As discussed in the second passage, there are several forms of assault, like assault with a deadly weapon, verbal assault, or threatening posture or language. Choice *A* is incorrect because lethal force and assault are separate as indicated by the passages. Choice *C* is incorrect because assault is never justified. Self-defense resulting in lethal force can be justified. Choice *D* is incorrect because the author does mention what the charges are on assaults; therefore, we cannot assume that they are more or less than unnecessary use of force charges.

26. D: The use of lethal force is not evaluated on the intent of the user, but rather the severity of the primary attack that warranted self-defense. This statement most undermines the last part of the passage because it directly contradicts how the law evaluates the use of lethal force. Choices *A* and *B* are stated in the paragraph, and therefore do not undermine the explanation from the author. Choice *C* does not necessarily undermine the passage, but it does not support the passage either. It is more of an opinion that does not strengthen or weaken the explanation.

27. C: An assault with deadly intent can lead to an individual using lethal force to preserve their well-being. Choice *C* is correct because it clearly establishes what both assault and lethal force are and gives the specific way in which the two concepts meet. Choice *A* is incorrect because lethal force doesn't necessarily result in assault. Choice *B* is incorrect because it contradicts the information in the passage (that assault with deadly intent can lead to an individual using lethal force). Choice *D* is compelling but ultimately too vague; the statement touches on aspects of the two ideas but fails to present the concrete way in which the two are connected to each other.

28. A: Both passages open by defining a legal concept and then describing situations in order to further explain the concept. Choice *C* is incorrect because while the passages utilize examples to help explain the concepts discussed, the author doesn't indicate that they are specific court cases. It's also clear that the passages don't open with examples, but instead, begin by defining the terms addressed in each passage. This eliminates Choice *B* and ultimately reveals Choice *A* to be the correct answer. Choice *A* accurately outlines the way both passages are structured. Because the passages follow a near identical structure; the rest of the choices can easily be ruled out.

29. A: Intent is very important for determining both lethal force and assault; intent is examined in both parties and helps determine the severity of the issue. Choices *B* and *C* are incorrect because it is clear in both passages that intent is a prevailing theme in both lethal force and assault. Choice *D* is compelling, but if a person uses lethal force to defend themselves, the intent of the defender is also examined in order to help determine if there was excessive force used. Choice *A* is correct because it states that intent is important for determining both lethal force and assault, and that intent is used to gauge the severity of the issues. Remember, just as lethal force can escalate to excessive use of force, there are different kinds of assault. Intent dictates several different forms of assault.

30. B: To demonstrate a single example of two different types of assault, then adding in a third type of assault to the example's conclusion. The example mainly serves to show an instance of "threatening body language" and "provocative language" with the homeowner gesturing threats to his neighbor. It ends the example by adding a third type of assault: physical strikes. This example is used to show the variant nature of assaults. Choice *A* is incorrect because it doesn't mention the "physical strike" assault at the end and is not specific enough. Choice *C* is incorrect because the example does not say anything about the definition of lethal force or how it might be altered. Choice *D* is incorrect, as the example mentions nothing of cause and effect.

31. D: The use of "I" could have all of the effects for the reader; it could serve to have a "hedging" effect, allow the reader to connect with the author in a more personal way, and cause the reader to empathize more with the egrets. However, it doesn't distance the reader from the text, thus eliminating Choice *D*.

32. C: The quote provides an example of a warden protecting one of the colonies. Choice *A* is incorrect because the speaker of the quote is a warden, not a hunter. Choice *B* is incorrect because the quote does not lighten the mood, but shows the danger of the situation between the wardens and the hunters. Choice *D* is incorrect because there is no humor found in the quote.

33. D: A *rookery* is a colony of breeding birds. Although *rookery* could mean Choice *A*, houses in a slum area, it does not make sense in this context. Choices *B* and *C* are both incorrect, as this is not a place for hunters to trade tools or for wardens to trade stories.

34. B: An important bird colony. The previous sentence is describing "twenty colonies" of birds, so what follows should be a bird colony. Choice *A* may be true, but we have no evidence of this in the text. Choice *C* does touch on the tension between the hunters and wardens, but there is no official "Bird Island Battle" mentioned in the text. Choice *D* does not exist in the text.

35. D: To demonstrate the success of the protective work of the Audubon Association. The text mentions several different times how and why the association has been successful and gives examples to back this fact. Choice *A* is incorrect because although the article, in some instances, calls certain people to act, it is not the purpose of the entire passage. There is no way to tell if Choices *B* and *C* are correct, as they are not mentioned in the text.

36. C: To have a better opportunity to hunt the birds. Choice *A* might be true in a general sense, but it is not relevant to the context of the text. Choice *B* is incorrect because the hunters are not studying lines of flight to help wardens, but to hunt birds. Choice *D* is incorrect because nothing in the text mentions that hunters are trying to build homes underneath lines of flight of birds for good luck.

37. A: It introduces certain insects that transition from water to air. Choice *B* is incorrect because although the passage talks about gills, it is not the central idea of the passage. Choices *C* and *D* are incorrect because the passage does not "define" or "invite," but only serves as an introduction to stoneflies, dragonflies, and mayflies and their transition from water to air.

38. C: The act of shedding part or all of the outer shell. Choices *A, B,* and *D* are incorrect.

39. B: The first paragraph serves as a contrast to the second. Notice how the first paragraph goes into detail describing how insects are able to breathe air. The second paragraph acts as a contrast to the first by stating "[i]t is of great interest to find that, nevertheless, a number of insects spend much of their time under water." Watch for transition words such as "nevertheless" to help find what type of passage you're dealing with.

40: C: The stage of preparation in between molting is acted out in the water, while the last stage is in the air. Choices *A, B,* and *D* are all incorrect. *Instars* is the phase between two periods of molting, and the text explains when these transitions occur.

41. C: The author's tone is informative and exhibits interest in the subject of the study. Overall, the author presents us with information on the subject. One moment where personal interest is depicted is when the author states, "It is of great interest to find that, nevertheless, a number of insects spend much of their time under water."

42. C: Their larva can breathe the air dissolved in water through gills of some kind. This is stated in the last paragraph. Choice *A* is incorrect because the text mentions this in a general way at the beginning of the passage concerning "insects as a whole." Choice *B* is incorrect because this is stated of beetles and water-bugs, and not the insects in question. Choice *D* is incorrect because this is the opposite of what the text says of instars.

43. D: We are looking for the claim that is least supportive of the argument that the American economy is healthy. Choice *A* says that the GDP increased by 2% last year, which supports a claim of health. Choice *B* relays that unemployment is the lowest it's been in over a decade, a sign of a strong economy. Choice *C* states that average household income is at a historical high point. In contrast, the final choice draws a negative conclusion about the economy—a decrease in output even after investments—therefore, a declining manufacturing sector is least supportive that the economy is healthy. Choice *D* is the correct answer.

44. C: The answer we seek has both the most detailed and objective information. Choice *A* describing a television commercial with a dramatized reenactment is not particularly detailed. Choice *B*, a notice to the public informing them of additional drinking and driving units on patrol, is not detailed and objective information. Choice *D*, a highway bulletin, does not present the type of information required. Choice *C* is the correct answer. The number of incidents and their relationship to a possible cause are both detailed and objective information.

45. C: We are looking for an inference—a conclusion that is reached on the basis of evidence and reasoning—from the passage that will likely explain why the famous children's author did not achieve her usual success with the new genre (despite the book's acclaim). Choice *A* is wrong because the statement is false according to the passage. Choice *B* is wrong because, although the passage says the author has a graduate degree on the subject, it would be an unrealistic leap to infer that she is the foremost expert on Antebellum America. Choice *D* is wrong because there is nothing in the passage to lead us to infer that people generally prefer a children's series to historical fiction. In contrast, Choice *C* can be logically inferred since the passage speaks of the great success of the children's series and the declaration that the fame of the author's name causes the children's books to "fly off the shelves." Thus, she did not receive any bump from her name since she published the historical novel under a pseudonym, and Choice *C* is correct.

46. D: Outspending other countries on education could have other benefits, but there is no reference to this in the passage, so Choice *A* is incorrect. Choice *B* is incorrect because the author does not mention corruption. Choice *C* is incorrect because there is nothing in the passage stating that the tests are not genuinely representative. Choice *D* is accurate because spending more money has not brought success. The United States already spends the most money, and the country is not excelling on these tests. Choice *D* is the correct answer.

47. B: The scientist and politician largely disagree, but the question asks for a point where the two are in agreement. The politician would not concur that burning fossil fuels causes global temperatures to rise; thus, Choice *A* is wrong. He would not agree with Choice *C* suggesting that countries must revisit their energy policies. By inference from the given information, the scientist would likely not concur that earth's climate naturally goes through warming and cooling cycles; so Choice *D* is incorrect. However, both the scientist and politician would agree that global temperatures are increasing. The reason for this is in dispute. The politician thinks it is part of the earth's natural cycle; the scientist thinks it is from the burning of fossil fuels. However, both acknowledge an increase, so Choice *B* is the correct answer.

48. A: Bring to light an alternative view on human perception by examining the role of technology in human understanding. This is a challenging question because the author's purpose is somewhat open-ended. The author concludes by stating that the questions regarding human perception and observation can be approached from many angles. Thus they do not seem to be attempting to prove one thing or another. Choice B is incorrect because we cannot know for certain whether the electron experiment is the latest discovery in astroparticle physics because no date is given. Choice *C* is a broad generalization that does not reflect accurately on the writer's views. While the author does appear to reflect on opposing views of human understanding (Choice *D*), the best answer is Choice *A*.

49. C: It presents a problem, explains the details of that problem, and then ends with more inquiry. The beginning of this paragraph literally "presents a conundrum," explains the problem of partial understanding, and then ends with more questions, or inquiry. There is no solution offered in this paragraph, making Choices *A* and *B* incorrect. Choice *D* is incorrect because the paragraph does not begin with a definition.

50. D: Looking back in the text, the author describes that classical philosophy holds that understanding can be reached by careful observation. This will not work if they are overly invested or biased in their pursuit. Choices *A* and *C* are in no way related and are completely unnecessary. A specific theory is not necessary to understanding, according to classical philosophy mentioned by the author. Again, the key to understanding is observing the phenomena outside of it, without biased or predisposition. Thus, Choice *B* is wrong.

51. B: The electrons passed through both holes and then onto the plate. Choices *A* and *C* are wrong because such movement is not mentioned at all in the text. In the passage the author says that electrons that were physically observed appeared to pass through one hole or another. Remember, the electrons that were observed doing this were described as acting like particles. Therefore, Choice D is wrong. Recall that the plate actually recorded electrons passing through both holes simultaneously and hitting the plate. This behavior, the electron activity that wasn't seen by humans, was characteristic of waves. Thus, Choice *B* is the right answer.

52. C: To demonstrate an example of natural phenomena humans discovered and understand without the use of tools or machines. Choice *A* mirrors the language in the beginning of the paragraph but is incorrect in its intent. Choice *B* is incorrect; the paragraph mentions nothing of "not knowing the true nature of gravity." Choice *D* is incorrect as well. There is no mention of an "alternative solution" in this paragraph.

53. A: The important thing to keep in mind is that we must choose a scenario that best parallels, or is most similar to, the discovery of the experiment mentioned in the passage. The important aspects of the experiment can be summed up like so: humans directly observed one behavior of electrons and then through analyzing a tool (the plate that recorded electron hits), discovered that there was another electron behavior that could not be physically seen by human eyes. This best parallels the scenario in Choice *A*. Like Feynman, the colorblind person is able to observe one aspect of the world but through the special goggles (a tool) he is able to see a natural phenomenon that he could not physically see on his own. While Choice *D* is compelling, the x-ray helps humans see the broken bone, not necessarily revealing that the bone is broken in the first place. The other choices do not parallel the scenario in question. Therefore, Choice *A* is the best choice.

54. B: The author would not agree that technology renders human observation irrelevant. Choice *A* is incorrect because much of the passage discusses how technology helps humans observe what cannot be seen with the naked eye, therefore the author would agree with this statement. This line of reasoning is also why the author would agree with Choice *D*, making it incorrect as well. As indicated in the second paragraph, the author seems to think that humans create inventions and tools with the goal of studying phenomena more precisely. This indicates increased understanding as people recognize limitations and develop items to help bypass the limitations and learn. Therefore, Choice *C* is incorrect as well. Again, the author doesn't attempt to disprove or dismiss classical philosophy.

55. B: Choice *A* uses similar language, but it is not the main point of disagreement. The reporter calls the loss devastating, and there's no reason to believe that the coach would disagree with this assessment. Eliminate this choice.

Choice *B* is strong since both passages mention the at-bats with runners in scoring position. The reporter asserts that the team lost due to the team failing to get such a hit. In contrast, the coach identifies several other reasons for the loss, including fielding and pitching errors. Additionally, the coach disagrees that the team even needed a hit in those situations.

Choice *C* is mentioned by the coach, but not by the reporter. It is unclear whether the reporter would agree with this assessment. Eliminate this choice.

Choice *D* is mentioned by the coach but not by the reporter. It is not stated whether the reporter believes that the team deserved to win. Eliminate this choice.

Therefore, Choice *B* is the correct answer.

56. C: Choice *A* is incorrect. The Conservative Politician definitely believes that spending on social welfare programs increases the national debt. However, the Liberal Politician does not address the cost of those programs. Choice *B* is a strong answer choice. The Liberal Politician explicitly agrees that certain classes of people rely on social welfare programs. The Conservative Politician actually agrees that people rely on the programs, but thinks this reliance is detrimental. This answer choice is slightly off base. Eliminate this choice. Choice *C* improves on Choice *B*. The Liberal Politician definitely believes that certain classes of people would be irreparably harmed. In contrast, the Conservative Politician asserts that the programs are actually harmful since people become dependent on the programs. The Conservative Politician concludes that people don't need the assistance and would be better off if left to fend for themselves. This is definitely the main point of disagreement. Choice *D* is not the main point of dispute. Neither of the politicians discusses whether *all* of the nation's leaders have bootstrapped their way to the top. Eliminate this choice.

Praxis Core Writing

Text Types, Purposes, and Production

Identifying Modes of Writing

Distinguishing Between Common Modes of Writing
To distinguish between the common modes of writing, it is important to identify the primary purpose of the work. This can be determined by considering what the author is trying to say to the reader. Although there are countless different styles of writing, all written works tend to fall under four primary categories: argumentative/persuasive, informative expository, descriptive, and narrative.

The below table highlights the purpose, distinct characteristics, and examples of each rhetorical mode.

Writing Mode	Purpose	Distinct Characteristics	Examples
Argumentative	To persuade	Opinions, loaded or subjective language, evidence, suggestions of what the reader should do, calls to action	Critical reviews Political journals Letters of recommendation Cover letters Advertising
Informative	To teach or inform	Objective language, definitions, instructions, factual information	Business and scientific reports Textbooks Instruction manuals News articles Personal letters Wills Informative essays Travel guides Study guides
Descriptive	To deliver sensory details to the reader	Heavy use of adjectives and imagery, language that appeals to any of the five senses	Poetry Journal entries Often used in narrative mode
Narrative	To tell a story, share an experience, entertain	Series of events, plot, characters, dialogue, conflict	Novels Short stories Novellas Anecdotes Biographies Epic poems Autobiographies

Identifying Common Types of Writing

The following steps help to identify examples of common types within the modes of writing:

1. Identifying the audience—to whom or for whom the author is writing
2. Determining the author's purpose—why the author is writing the piece
3. Analyzing the word choices and how they are used

To demonstrate, the following passage has been marked to illustrate *the addressee*, the **author's purpose,** and word choices:

> *To Whom It May Concern*:
>
> I am extraordinarily excited to be applying to the Master of Environmental Science program at Australian National University. I believe the richness in biological and cultural diversity, as well as Australia's close proximity to the Great Barrier Reef, would provide a deeply fulfilling educational experience. **I am writing to express why I believe I would be an excellent addition to the program.**
>
> While in college, I participated in a three-month public health internship in Ecuador, where I spent time both learning about medicine in a third world country and also about the Ecuadorian environment, including the Amazon Jungle and the Galápagos Islands. My favorite experience through the internship, besides swimming with sea lions in San Cristóbal, was helping to neutralize parasitic potable water and collect samples for analysis in Puyo.
>
> Though my undergraduate studies related primarily to the human body, I took several courses in natural science, including a year of chemistry, biology, and physics as well as a course in a calculus. I am confident that my fundamental knowledge in these fields will prepare me for the science courses integral to the Masters of Environmental Science.

Having identified the *addressee*, it is evident that this selection is a letter of some kind. Further inspection into the author's purpose, seen in **bold**, shows that the author is trying to explain why he or she should be accepted into the environmental science program, which automatically places it into the argumentative mode as the writer is trying to persuade the reader to agree and to incite the reader into action by encouraging the program to accept the writer as a candidate. In addition to revealing the purpose, the use of emotional language—extraordinarily, excellent, deeply fulfilling, favorite experience, confident—illustrates that this is a persuasive piece. It also provides evidence for why this person would be an excellent addition to the program—his/her experience in Ecuador and with scientific curriculum.

The following passage presents an opportunity to solidify this method of analysis and practice the steps above to determine the mode of writing:

> The biological effects of laughter have long been an interest of medicine and psychology. Laughing is often speculated to reduce blood pressure because it induces feelings of relaxation and elation. Participating students watched a series of videos that elicited laughter, and their blood pressure was taken before and after the viewings. An average decrease in blood pressure was observed, though resulting p-values attest that the results were not significant.

This selection contains factual and scientific information, is devoid of any adjectives or flowery descriptions, and is not trying to convince the reader of any particular stance. Though the audience is not directly addressed, the purpose of the passage is to present the results of an experiment to those who would be interested in the biological effects of laughter—most likely a scientific community. Thus, this passage is an example of informative writing.

Below is another passage to help identify examples of the common writing modes, taken from *The Endeavor Journal of Sir Joseph Banks*:

10th May 1769 – THE ENGLISH CREW GET TAHITIAN NAMES

> We have now got the Indian name of the Island, Otahite, so therefore for the future I shall call it. As for our own names the Indians find so much dificulty in pronouncing them that we are forcd to indulge them in calling us what they please, or rather what they say when they attempt to pronounce them. I give here the List: Captn Cooke *Toote*, Dr Solander *Torano*, Mr Hicks *Hete*, Mr Gore *Toárro*, Mr Molineux *Boba* from his Christian name Robert, Mr Monkhouse *Mato*, and myself *Tapáne*. In this manner they have names for almost every man in the ship.

This extract contains no elements of an informative or persuasive intent and does not seem to follow any particular line of narrative. The passage gives a list of the different names that the Indians have given the crew members, as well as the name of an island. Although there is no context for the selection, through the descriptions, it is clear that the author and his comrades are on an island trying to communicate with the native inhabitants. Hence, this passage is a journal that reflects the descriptive mode.

These are only a few of the many examples that can be found in the four primary modes of writing.

Determining the Appropriate Mode of Writing

The author's **primary purpose** is defined as the reason an author chooses to write a selection, and it is often dependent on his or her audience. A biologist writing a textbook, for example, does so to communicate scientific knowledge to an audience of people who want to study biology. An audience can be as broad as the entire global population or as specific as women fighting for equal rights in the bicycle repair industry. Whatever the audience, it is important that the author considers its demographics—age, gender, culture, language, education level, etc.

If the author's purpose is to persuade or inform, he or she will consider how much the intended audience knows about the subject. For example, if an author is writing on the importance of recycling to anyone who will listen, he or she will use the informative mode—including background information on recycling—and the argumentative mode—evidence for why it works, while also using simple diction so that it is easy for everyone to understand. If, on the other hand, the writer is proposing new methods for recycling using solar energy, the audience is probably already familiar with standard recycling processes and will require less background information, as well as more technical language inherent to the scientific community.

If the author's purpose is to entertain through a story or a poem, he or she will need to consider whom he/she is trying to entertain. If an author is writing a script for a children's cartoon, the plot, language, conflict, characters, and humor would align with the interests of the age demographic of that audience. On the other hand, if an author is trying to entertain adults, he or she may write content not suitable for children. The author's purpose and audience are generally interdependent.

Understanding the Task, Purpose, and Audience

Identifying the Task, Purpose, and Intended Audience

An author's **writing style**—the way in which words, grammar, punctuation, and sentence fluidity are used—is the most influential element in a piece of writing, and it is dependent on the purpose and the audience for whom it is intended. Together, a writing style and mode of writing form the foundation of a written work, and a good writer will choose the most effective mode and style to convey a message to readers.

Writers should first determine what they are trying to say and then choose the most effective mode of writing to communicate that message. Different writing modes and word choices will affect the tone of a piece—that is, its underlying attitude, emotion, or character. The argumentative mode may utilize words that are earnest, angry, passionate, or excited whereas an informative piece may have a sterile, germane, or enthusiastic tone. The tones found in narratives vary greatly, depending on the purpose of the writing. Tone will also be affected by the audience—teaching science to children or those who may be uninterested would be most effective with enthusiastic language and exclamation points whereas teaching science to college students may take on a more serious and professional tone, with fewer charged words and punctuation choices that are inherent to academia.

Sentence fluidity—whether sentences are long and rhythmic or short and succinct—also affects a piece of writing as it determines the way in which a piece is read. Children or audiences unfamiliar with a subject do better with short, succinct sentence structures as these break difficult concepts up into shorter points. A period, question mark, or exclamation point is literally a signal for the reader to stop and takes more time to process. Thus, longer, more complex sentences are more appropriate for adults or educated audiences as they can fit more information in between processing time.

The amount of **supporting detail** provided is also tailored to the audience. A text that introduces a new subject to its readers will focus more on broad ideas without going into greater detail whereas a text that focuses on a more specific subject is likely to provide greater detail about the ideas discussed.

Writing styles, like modes, are most effective when tailored to their audiences. Having awareness of an audience's demographic is one of the most crucial aspects of properly communicating an argument, a story, or a set of information.

Choosing the Most Appropriate Type of Writing

Before beginning any writing, it is imperative that a writer have a firm grasp on the message he or she wishes to convey and how he or she wants readers to be affected by the writing. For example, does the author want readers to be more informed about the subject? Does the writer want readers to agree with his or her opinion? Does the writer want readers to get caught up in an exciting narrative? The following steps are a guide to determining the appropriate type of writing for a task, purpose, and audience:

1. Identifying the purpose for writing the piece
2. Determining the audience
3. Adapting the writing mode, word choices, tone, and style to fit the audience and the purpose

It is important to distinguish between a work's purpose and its main idea. The essential difference between the two is that the **main idea** is what the author wants to communicate about the topic at hand whereas the **primary purpose** is why the author is writing in the first place. The primary purpose is what will determine the type of writing an author will choose to utilize, not the main idea, though the two are related. For example, if an author writes an article on the mistreatment of animals in factory farms and, at the end, suggests that people should convert to vegetarianism, the main idea is that vegetarianism would reduce the poor treatment of animals. The primary purpose is to convince the reader to stop eating animals. Since the primary purpose is to galvanize an audience into action, the author would choose the argumentative writing mode.

The next step is to consider to whom the author is appealing as this will determine the type of details to be included, the diction to be used, the tone to be employed, and the sentence structure to be used. An audience can be identified by considering the following questions:

- What is the purpose for writing the piece?
- To whom is it being written?
- What is their age range?
- Are they familiar with the material being presented, or are they just being newly introduced to it?
- Where are they from?
- Is the task at hand in a professional or casual setting?
- Is the task at hand for monetary gain?

These are just a few of the numerous considerations to keep in mind, but the main idea is to become as familiar with the audience as possible. Once the audience has been understood, the author can then adapt the writing style to align with the readers' education and interests. The audience is what determines the **rhetorical appeal** the author will use—ethos, pathos, or logos. **Ethos** is a rhetorical appeal to an audience's ethics and/or morals. Ethos is most often used in argumentative and informative writing modes. **Pathos** is an appeal to the audience's emotions and sympathies, and it is found in argumentative, descriptive, and narrative writing modes. **Logos** is an appeal to the audience's logic and reason and is used primarily in informative texts as well as in supporting details for argumentative pieces. Rhetorical appeals are discussed in depth in the informational texts and rhetoric section of the test.

If the author is trying to encourage global conversion to vegetarianism, he or she may choose to use all three rhetorical appeals to reach varying personality types. Those who are less interested in the welfare of animals but are interested in facts and science would relate more to logos. Animal lovers would relate better to an emotional appeal. In general, the most effective works utilize all three appeals.

Finally, after determining the writing mode and rhetorical appeal, the author will consider word choice, sentence structure, and tone, depending on the purpose and audience. The author may choose words that convey sadness or anger when speaking about animal welfare if writing to persuade, or he or she will stick to dispassionate and matter-of-fact tones, if informing the public on the treatment of animals in factory farms. If the author is writing to a younger or less-educated audience, he or she may choose to shorten and simplify sentence structures and word choice. If appealing to an audience with more expert knowledge on a particular subject, writers will more likely employ a style of longer sentences and more complex vocabulary.

Depending on the task, the author may choose to use a first person, second person, or third person point of view. First person and second person perspectives are inherently more casual in tone, including the author and the reader in the rhetoric, while third person perspectives are often seen in more professional settings.

Evaluating the Effectiveness of a Piece of Writing

An effective and engaging piece of writing will cause the reader to forget about the author entirely. Readers will become so engrossed in the subject, argument, or story at hand that they will almost identify with it, readily adopting beliefs proposed by the author or accepting all elements of the story as believable. On the contrary, poorly written works will cause the reader to be hyperaware of the author, doubting the writer's knowledge of a subject or questioning the validity of a narrative. Persuasive or expository works that are poorly researched will have this effect, as well as poorly planned stories with significant plot holes. An author must consider the task, purpose, and audience to sculpt a piece of writing effectively.

When evaluating the effectiveness of a piece, the most important thing to consider is how well the purpose is conveyed to the audience through the mode, use of rhetoric, and writing style.

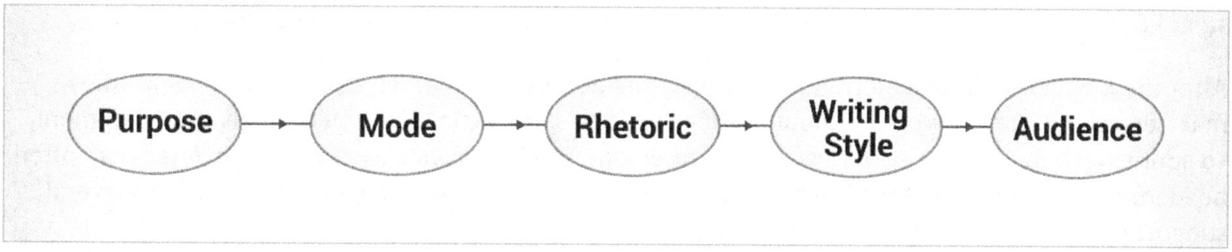

The purpose must pass through these three aspects for effective delivery to the audience. If any elements are not properly considered, the reader will be overly aware of the author, and the message will be lost. The following is a checklist for evaluating the effectiveness of a piece:

- Does the writer choose the appropriate writing mode—argumentative, narrative, descriptive, informative—for his or her purpose?
- Does the writing mode employed contain characteristics inherent to that mode?
- Does the writer consider the personalities/interests/demographics of the intended audience when choosing rhetorical appeals?
- Does the writer use appropriate vocabulary, sentence structure, voice, and tone for the audience demographic?
- Does the author properly establish himself/herself as having authority on the subject, if applicable?
- Does the piece make sense?

Another thing to consider is the medium in which the piece was written. If the medium is a blog, diary, or personal letter, the author may adopt a more casual stance towards the audience. If the piece of writing is a story in a book, a business letter or report, or a published article in a journal or if the task is to gain money or support or to get published, the author may adopt a more formal stance. Ultimately, the writer will want to be very careful in how he or she addresses the reader.

Finally, the effectiveness of a piece can be evaluated by asking how well the purpose was achieved. For example, if students are assigned to read a persuasive essay, instructors can ask whether the author influences students' opinions. Students may be assigned two differing persuasive texts with opposing perspectives and be asked which writer was more convincing. Students can then evaluate what factors contributed to this—for example, whether one author uses more credible supporting facts, appeals more effectively to readers' emotions, presents more believable personal anecdotes, or offers stronger counterargument refutation. Students can then use these evaluations to strengthen their own writing skills.

Using Clear and Coherent Writing

Identifying Details that Develop a Main Idea

The main idea of a piece is the central topic or theme. To identify the main idea, a reader should consider these questions: "What's the point? What does the author want readers to take away from this text?" Everything within the selection should relate back to the main idea because it is the center of the organizational web of any written work. Particularly in articles and reports, the main idea often appears within the opening paragraphs to orient the reader to what the author wants to say about the subject. A sentence that expresses the main idea is known as a thesis sentence or **thesis statement**.

After the main idea has been introduced, **supporting details** are what develop the main idea—they make up the bulk of the work. Without supporting details, the main idea would simply be a statement, so additional details are needed to give that statement weight and validity. Supporting details can often be identified by recognizing the key words that introduce them. The following example offers several supporting details, with key words underlined:

> Man did not evolve from apes. Though we share a common ancestor, humans and apes originated through very different evolutionary paths. There are several reasons why this is true. The first reason is that, logically, if humans evolved from apes, modern-day apes and humans would not coexist. Evolution occurs when a genetic mutation in a species ensures the survival over the rest of the species, allowing them to pass on their genes and create a new lineage of organisms. Another reason is that hominid fossils only fall into one of two categories—ape-like or human-like—and there are very strong differences between the two. Australopithecines, the hominid fossils originally believed to be ancestral to humans, are ape-like, indicated by their long arms, long and curved fingers, and funnel-shaped chests. Their hand bones suggest that they "knuckle-walked" like modern day chimpanzees and gorillas, something not found in *Homo sapien* fossils. Finally, there is no fossilized evidence to suggest a transition between the ape-like ancestor and the *Homo sapien*, indicating that a sudden mutation may have been responsible. These and many other reasons are indicative that humans and ape-like creatures are evolutionarily different.

The underlined words—*first, another,* and *finally*—are the key words that identify the supporting details. These details can be summarized as follows:

- Humans and apes could not coexist.
- Human-like and ape-like fossils are very different.
- No transition is seen between humans and ape-like ancestors.

The supporting details all relate to the central idea that "Man did not evolve from apes," which is the first sentence of the paragraph.

Even though supporting details are more specific than the main idea, they should nevertheless all be directly related to the main idea. Without sufficient supporting details, the writer's main idea will be too weak to be effective.

Organizing a Text Clearly and Coherently

There are five basic elements inherent in effective writing, and each will be discussed throughout the various subheadings of this section.

- **Main idea**: The driving message of the writing, clearly stated or implied
- **Clear organization**: The effective and purposeful arrangement of the content to support the main idea
- **Supporting details/evidence**: Content that gives appropriate depth and weight to the main idea of the story, argument, or information
- **Diction/tone**: The type of language, vocabulary, and word choice used to express the main idea, purposefully aligned to the audience and purpose
- **Adherence to conventions of English**: Correct spelling, grammar, punctuation, and sentence structure, allowing for clear communication of ideas

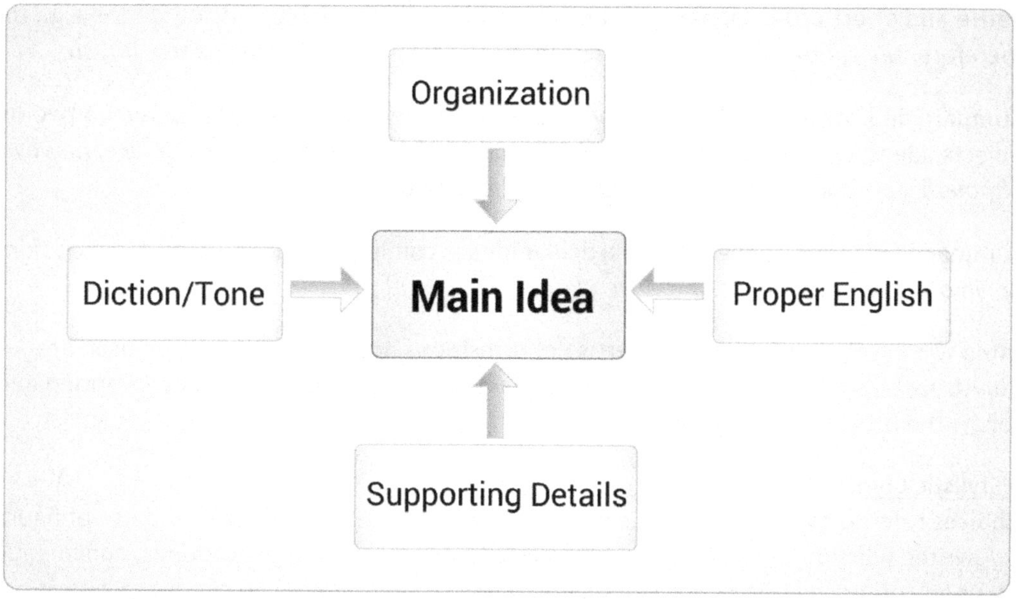

Using Varied and Effective Transitions

Transitions are the glue that holds the writing together. They function to purposefully incorporate new topics and supporting details in a smooth and coherent way. Usually, transitions are found at the beginnings of sentences, but they can also be located in the middle as a way to link clauses together. There are two types of clauses: independent and dependent as discussed in the language use and vocabulary section.

Transition words connect clauses within and between sentences for smoother writing. "I dislike apples. They taste like garbage." is choppier than "I dislike apples because they taste like garbage." Transitions demonstrate the relationship between ideas, allow for more complex sentence structures, and can alert the reader to which type of organizational format the author is using. For example, the above selection on human evolution uses the words *first, another*, and *finally* to indicate that the writer will be listing the reasons why humans and apes are evolutionarily different.

Transition words can be categorized based on the relationships they create between ideas:

- **General order**: signaling elaboration of an idea to emphasize a point—e.g., *for example, for instance, to demonstrate, including, such as, in other words, that is, in fact, also, furthermore, likewise, and, truly, so, surely, certainly, obviously, doubtless*
- **Chronological order**: referencing the time frame in which main event or idea occurs—e.g., *before, after, first, while, soon, shortly thereafter, meanwhile*
- **Numerical order/order of importance**: indicating that related ideas, supporting details, or events will be described in a sequence, possibly in order of importance—e.g., *first, second, also, finally, another, in addition, equally important, less importantly, most significantly, the main reason, last but not least*
- **Spatial order**: referring to the space and location of something or where things are located in relation to each other—e.g., *inside, outside, above, below, within, close, under, over, far, next to, adjacent to*
- **Cause and effect order**: signaling a causal relationship between events or ideas—e.g., *thus, therefore, since, resulted in, for this reason, as a result, consequently, hence, for, so*
- **Compare and contrast order**: identifying the similarities and differences between two or more objects, ideas, or lines of thought—e.g., *like, as, similarly, equally, just as, unlike, however, but, although, conversely, on the other hand, on the contrary*
- **Summary order**: indicating that a particular idea is coming to a close—e.g., *in conclusion, to sum up, in other words, ultimately, above all*

Sophisticated writing also aims to avoid overuse of transitions and ensure that those used are meaningful. Using a variety of transitions makes the writing appear more lively and informed and helps readers follow the progression of ideas.

Justifying Stylistic Choices

Stylistic choices refer to elements such as a writer's diction, sentence structure, and use of figurative language. A writer's **diction** is his or her word choice and may be elevated, academic, conversational, humorous, or any other style. The choice of diction depends on the purpose of a piece of writing. A textbook or a research paper is likely to use academic diction whereas a blog post will use more conversational expressions.

Sentence structure also affects an author's writing style. Will he or she use short, staccato sentences or longer sentences with complex structure? Effective writing tends to incorporate both styles to increase reader interest or to punctuate ideas.

Figurative language includes the use of simile, metaphor, hyperbole, or allusion, to name but a few examples. Creative or descriptive writing is likely to incorporate more non-literal expressions than academic or informative writing will. Instructors should allow students to experiment with different styles of writing and understand how style affects expression and understanding.

Introducing, Developing, and Concluding a Text Effectively

Almost all coherent written works contain three primary parts: a beginning, middle, and end. The organizational arrangements differ widely across distinct writing modes. Persuasive and expository texts utilize an introduction, body, and conclusion whereas narrative works use an orientation, series of events/conflict, and a resolution.

Every element within a written piece relates back to the main idea, and the beginning of a persuasive or expository text generally conveys the main idea or the purpose. For a narrative piece, the beginning is the section that acquaints the reader with the characters and setting, directing them to the purpose of the writing. The main idea in narrative may be implied or addressed at the end of the piece.

Depending on the primary purpose, the arrangement of the middle will adhere to one of the basic organizational structures described in the information texts and rhetoric section. They are cause and effect, problem and solution, compare and contrast, description/spatial, sequence, and order of importance.

The ending of a text is the metaphorical wrap-up of the writing. A solid ending is crucial for effective writing as it ties together loose ends, resolves the action, highlights the main points, or repeats the central idea. A conclusion ensures that readers come away from a text understanding the author's main idea. The table below highlights the important characteristics of each part of a piece of writing.

Structure	**Argumentative/Informative**	**Narrative**
Beginning	Introduction *Purpose, main idea*	Orientation *Introduces characters, setting, necessary background*
Middle	Body *Supporting details, reasons and evidence*	Events/Conflict *Story's events that revolve around a central conflict*
End	Conclusion *Highlights main points, summarizes and paraphrases ideas, reiterates the main idea*	Resolution *The solving of the central conflict*

Use of Language

<u>Making Inferences</u>

Readers should be able to make **inferences**. Making an inference requires the reader to read between the lines and look for what is *implied* rather than what is directly stated. That is, using information that is known from the text, the reader is able to make a logical assumption about information that is *not* directly stated but is probably true. Read the following passage:

> "Hey, do you wanna meet my new puppy?" Jonathan asked.
>
> "Oh, I'm sorry but please don't—" Jacinta began to protest, but before she could finish, Jonathan had already opened the passenger side door of his car and a perfect white ball of fur came bouncing towards Jacinta.
>
> "Isn't he the cutest?" beamed Jonathan.
>
> "Yes—achoo!—he's pretty—aaaachooo!!—adora—aaa—aaaachoo!" Jacinta managed to say in between sneezes. "But if you don't mind, I—I—achoo!—need to go inside."

Which of the following can be inferred from Jacinta's reaction to the puppy?

a. she hates animals
b. she is allergic to dogs
c. she prefers cats to dogs
d. she is angry at Jonathan

An inference requires the reader to consider the information presented and then form their own idea about what is probably true. Based on the details in the passage, what is the best answer to the question? Important details to pay attention to include the tone of Jacinta's dialogue, which is overall polite and apologetic, as well as her reaction itself, which is a long string of sneezes. Answer choices (a) and (d) both express strong emotions ("hates" and "angry") that are not evident in Jacinta's speech or actions. Answer choice (c) mentions cats, but there is nothing in the passage to indicate Jacinta's feelings about cats. Answer choice (b), "she is allergic to dogs," is the most logical choice—based on the fact that she began sneezing as soon as a fluffy dog approached her, it makes sense to guess that Jacinta might be allergic to dogs. So even though Jacinta never directly states, "Sorry, I'm allergic to dogs!" using the clues in the passage, it is still reasonable to guess that this is true.

Making inferences is crucial for readers of literature because literary texts often avoid presenting complete and direct information to readers about characters' thoughts or feelings, or they present this information in an unclear way, leaving it up to the reader to interpret clues given in the text. In order to make inferences while reading, readers should ask themselves:

- What details are being presented in the text?
- Is there any important information that seems to be missing?
- Based on the information that the author *does* include, what else is probably true?
- Is this inference reasonable based on what is already known?

Apply Information

A natural extension of being able to make an inference from a given set of information is also being able to apply that information to a new context. This is especially useful in non-fiction or informative writing. Considering the facts and details presented in the text, readers should consider how the same information might be relevant in a different situation. The following is an example of applying an inferential conclusion to a different context:

> Often, individuals behave differently in large groups than they do as individuals. One example of this is the psychological phenomenon known as the bystander effect. According to the bystander effect, the more people who witness an accident or crime occur, the less likely each individual bystander is to respond or offer assistance to the victim. A classic example of this is the murder of Kitty Genovese in New York City in the 1960s. Although there were over thirty witnesses to her killing by a stabber, none of them intervened to help Kitty or contact the police.

Considering the phenomenon of the bystander effect, what would probably happen if somebody tripped on the stairs in a crowded subway station?

a. Everybody would stop to help the person who tripped
b. Bystanders would point and laugh at the person who tripped
c. Someone would call the police after walking away from the station
d. Few if any bystanders would offer assistance to the person who tripped

This question asks readers to apply the information they learned from the passage, which is an informative paragraph about the bystander effect. According to the passage, this is a concept in psychology that describes the way people in groups respond to an accident—the more people are present, the less likely any one person is to intervene. While the passage illustrates this effect with the example of a woman's murder, the question asks readers to apply it to a different context—in this case, someone falling down the stairs in front of many subway passengers. Although this specific situation is not discussed in the passage, readers should be able to apply the general concepts described in the paragraph. The definition of the bystander effect includes any instance of an accident or crime in front of a large group of people. The question asks about a situation that falls within the same definition, so the general concept should still hold true: in the midst of a large crowd, few individuals are likely to actually respond to an accident. In this case, answer choice (d) is the best response.

Evaluation of Evidence

Analyzing and Evaluating Text Structure

Depending on what the author is attempting to accomplish, certain formats or text structures work better than others. For example, a sequence structure might work for narration but not when identifying similarities and differences between dissimilar concepts. Similarly, a comparison-contrast structure is not useful for narration. It's the author's job to put the right information in the correct format.

Readers should be familiar with the five main literary structures:

1. **Sequence** structure (sometimes referred to as the order structure) is when the order of events proceed in a predictable order. In many cases, this means the text goes through the plot elements: exposition, rising action, climax, falling action, and resolution. Readers are introduced to characters, setting, and conflict in the exposition. In the rising action, there's an increase in tension and suspense. The climax is the height of tension and the point of no return. Tension decreases during the falling action. In the resolution, any conflicts presented in the exposition are solved, and the story concludes. An informative text that is structured sequentially will often go in order from one step to the next.

2. In the **problem-solution** structure, authors identify a potential problem and suggest a solution. This form of writing is usually divided into two paragraphs and can be found in informational texts. For example, cell phone, cable, and satellite providers use this structure in manuals to help customers troubleshoot or identify problems with services or products.

3. When authors want to discuss similarities and differences between separate concepts, they arrange thoughts in a **comparison-contrast** paragraph structure. Venn diagrams are an effective graphic organizer for comparison-contrast structures because they feature two overlapping circles that can be used to organize similarities and differences. A comparison-contrast essay organizes one paragraph based on similarities and another based on differences. A comparison-contrast essay can also be arranged with the similarities and differences of individual traits addressed within individual paragraphs. Words such as *however*, *but*, and *nevertheless* help signal a contrast in ideas.

4. **Descriptive** writing structure is designed to appeal to your senses. Much like an artist who constructs a painting, good descriptive writing builds an image in the reader's mind by appealing to the five senses: sight, hearing, taste, touch, and smell. However, overly descriptive writing can become tedious; sparse descriptions can make settings and characters seem flat. Good

authors strike a balance by applying descriptions only to passages, characters, and settings that are integral to the plot.

5. Passages that use the **cause and effect** structure are simply asking *why* by demonstrating some type of connection between ideas. Words such as *if*, *since*, *because*, *then*, or *consequently* indicate relationship. By switching the order of a complex sentence, the writer can rearrange the emphasis on different clauses. Saying *If Sheryl is late, we'll miss the dance* is different from saying *We'll miss the dance if Sheryl is late*. One emphasizes Sheryl's tardiness while the other emphasizes missing the dance. Paragraphs can also be arranged in a cause and effect format. Since the format—before and after—is sequential, it is useful when authors wish to discuss the impact of choices. Researchers often apply this paragraph structure to the scientific method.

Text Evidence

Text evidence is the information readers find in a text or passage that supports the main idea or point(s) in a story. In turn, text evidence can help readers draw conclusions about the text or passage. The information should be taken directly from the text or passage and placed in quotation marks. Text evidence provides readers with information to support ideas about the text so that they do not rely simply on their own thoughts. Details should be precise, descriptive, and factual. Statistics are a great piece of text evidence because they provide readers with exact numbers and not just a generalization. For example, instead of saying "Asia has a larger population than Europe," authors could provide detailed information such as, "In Asia there are over 4 billion people, whereas in Europe there are a little over 750 million." More definitive information provides better evidence to readers to help support their conclusions about texts or passages.

Text Credibility

Credible sources are important when drawing conclusions because readers need to be able to trust what they are reading. Authors should always use credible sources to help gain the trust of their readers. A text is **credible** when it is believable, and the author is objective and unbiased. If readers do not trust an author's words, they may simply dismiss the text completely. For example, if an author writes a persuasive essay, he or she is outwardly trying to sway readers' opinions to align with his or her own. Readers may agree or disagree with the author, which may, in turn, lead them to believe that the author is credible or not credible. Also, readers should keep in mind the source of the text. If readers review a journal about astronomy, would a more reliable source be a NASA employee or a medical doctor? Overall, text credibility is important when drawing conclusions because readers want reliable sources that support the decisions they have made about the author's ideas.

Examining Paragraphs

While authors write, thoughts coalesce to form words on "paper" (aka a computer screen). Authors strategically place those thoughts in sentences to give them "voice" in an orderly manner, and then they manipulate them into cohesive sentences for cohesion to express ideas. Like a hunk of modeling clay (thanks to computers, people are no longer bound to erasers and whiteout), sentences can be worked and reworked until they cooperate and say what was originally intended.

Before calling a paragraph complete, identify its main point, making sure that related sentences stay on point. Pose questions such as, "Did I sufficiently develop the main point? Did I say it succinctly enough? Did I give it time to develop? *Is* it developed?"

Let's examine the following two paragraphs, each an example of a movie review. Read them and form a critique.

Example 1: *Eddie the Eagle* is a movie about a struggling athlete. Eddie was crippled at birth. He had a lot of therapy and he had a dream. Eddie trained himself for the Olympics. He went far away to learn how to ski jump. It was hard for him, but he persevered. He got a coach and kept trying. He qualified for the Olympics. He was the only one from Britain who could jump. When he succeeded, they named him, "Eddie the Eagle."

Example 2: The last movie I saw in the theater was *Eddie the Eagle,* a story of extraordinary perseverance inspired by real life events. Eddie was born in England with a birth defect that he slowly but surely overcame, but not without trial and error (not the least of which was his father's perpetual *dis*couragement). In fact, the old man did everything to get him to give up, but Eddie was dogged beyond anyone in the neighborhood; in fact, maybe beyond anyone in the whole town or even the whole world! Eddie, simply, did not know to quit. As he grew up, so did his dream; a strange one, indeed, for someone so unaccomplished: to compete in the Winter Olympics as a ski jumper (which he knew absolutely nothing about). Eddie didn't just keep on dreaming about it. He actually went to Germany and *worked* at it, facing unbelievable odds, defeats, and put-downs by Dad and the other Men in Charge, aka the Olympic decision-makers. Did that stop him? No way! Eddie got a coach and persevered. Then, when he failed, he persevered some more, again and again. You should be able to open up a dictionary, look at the word "persevere," and see a picture of Eddie the Eagle because, when everybody told him he couldn't, he did. The result? He is forever dubbed, "Eddie the Eagle."

Both reviews tell something about the movie *Eddie the Eagle*. Does one motivate the reader to want to see the movie more than the other? Does one just provide a few facts while the other paints a virtual picture of the movie? Does one give a carrot and the other a rib eye steak, mashed potatoes, and chocolate silk pie?

Paragraphs sometimes only give facts. Sometimes that's appropriate and all that is needed. Sometimes, though, writers want to use the blank documents on their computer screens to paint a picture. Writers must "see" the painting come to life. To do so, pick a familiar topic, write a simple sentence, and add to it. Pretend, for instance, there's a lovely view. What does one see? Is it a lake? Try again – picture it as though it were the sea! Visualize a big ship sailing out there. Is it sailing away or approaching? Who is on it? Is it dangerous? Is it night and are there crazy pirates on board? Uh-oh! Did one just jump ship and start swimming toward shore?

Summarizing

At the end of a text or passage, it is important to summarize what the readers read. **Summarizing** is a strategy in which readers determine what is important throughout the text or passage, shorten those ideas, and rewrite or retell it in their own words. A summary should identify the main idea of the text or passage. Important details or supportive evidence should also be accurately reported in the summary. If writers provide irrelevant details in the summary, it may cloud the greater meaning of the summary in the text. When summarizing, writers should not include their opinions, quotes, or what they thought the author should have said. A clear summary provides clarity of the text or passage to the readers. Let's review the checklist of items writers should include in their summary.

Summary Checklist

- Title of the story
- Someone: Who is or are the main character(s)?
- Wanted: What did the character(s) want?
- But: What was the problem?

- So: How did the character(s) solve the problem?
- Then: How did the story end? What was the resolution?

<u>Paraphrasing</u>

Another strategy readers can use to help them fully comprehend a text or passage is paraphrasing. **Paraphrasing** is when readers take the author's words and put them into their own words. When readers and writers paraphrase, they should avoid copying the text—that is plagiarism. It is also important to include as many details as possible when restating the facts. Not only will this help readers and writers recall information, but by putting the information into their own words, they demonstrate whether or not they fully comprehend the text or passage. Look at the example below showing an original text and how to paraphrase it.

> **Original Text**: Fenway Park is home to the beloved Boston Red Sox. The stadium opened on April 20, 1912. The stadium currently seats over 37,000 fans, many of whom travel from all over the country to experience the iconic team and nostalgia of Fenway Park.
>
> **Paraphrased**: On April 20, 1912, Fenway Park opened. Home to the Boston Red Sox, the stadium now seats over 37,000 fans. Many spectators travel to watch the Red Sox and experience the spirit of Fenway Park.

Paraphrasing, summarizing, and quoting can often cross paths with one another. Review the chart below showing the similarities and differences between the three strategies.

Paraphrasing	Summarizing	Quoting
Uses own words	Puts main ideas into own words	Uses words that are identical to text
References original source	References original source	Requires quotation marks
Uses own sentences	Shows important ideas of source	Uses author's own words and ideas

<u>Directly Stated Information Versus Implications</u>

Engaged readers should constantly self-question while reviewing texts to help them form conclusions. Self-questioning is when readers review a paragraph, page, passage, or chapter and ask themselves, "Did I understand what I read?," "What was the main event in this section?," "Where is this taking place?," and so on. Authors can provide clues or pieces of evidence throughout a text or passage to guide readers toward a conclusion. This is why active and engaged readers should read the text or passage in its entirety before forming a definitive conclusion. If readers do not gather all the pieces of evidence needed, then they may jump to an illogical conclusion.

At times, authors directly state conclusions while others simply imply them. Of course, it is easier if authors outwardly provide conclusions to readers because it does not leave any information open to interpretation. On the other hand, implications are things that authors do not directly state but can be assumed based off of information they provided. If authors only imply what may have happened, readers can form a menagerie of ideas for conclusions. For example, look at the following statement: "Once we heard the sirens, we hunkered down in the storm shelter." In this statement, the author does not directly state that there was a tornado, but clues such as "sirens" and "storm shelter" provide insight to the readers to help form that conclusion.

Language and Research Skills for Writing

Language Skills

The English language has eight parts of speech, each serving a different grammatical function.

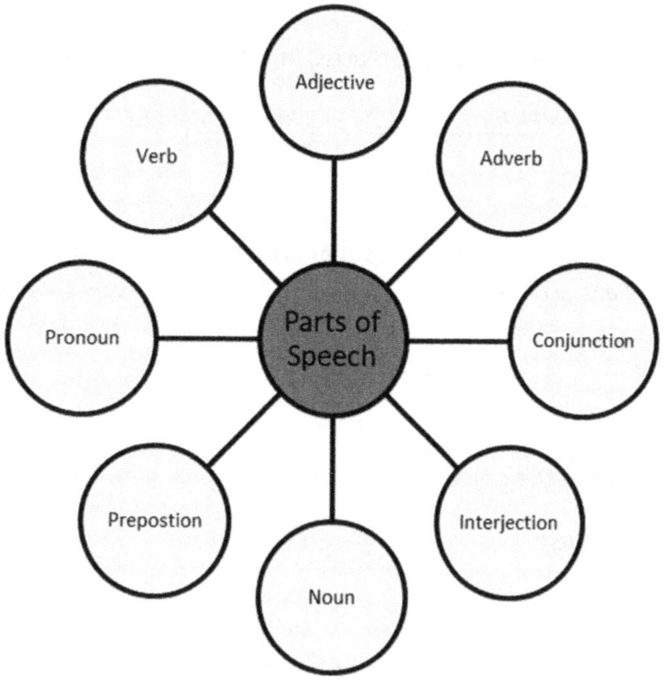

Verb
Verbs describe an action—e.g., *run, play, eat*—or a state of being—e.g., *is, are, was*. It is impossible to make a grammatically-complete sentence without a verb.

He *runs* to the store.

She *is* eight years old.

Noun
Nouns can be a person, place, or thing. They can refer to concrete objects—e.g., *chair, apple, house*—or abstract things—love, knowledge, friendliness.

Look at the *dog*!

Where are my *keys*?

Some nouns are *countable*, meaning they can be counted as separate entities—*one chair, two chairs, three chairs*. They can be either singular or plural. Other nouns, usually substances or concepts, are *uncountable*—e.g., *air, information, wealth*—and some nouns can be both countable and uncountable depending on how they are used.

I bought three *dresses*.

Respect is important to me.

I ate way too much *food* last night.

At the international festival, you can sample *foods* from around the world.

Proper nouns are the specific names of people, places, or things and are almost always capitalized.

Marie Curie studied at the Flying University in Warsaw, Poland.

Pronoun

Pronouns function as substitutes for nouns or noun phrases. Pronouns are often used to avoid constant repetition of a noun or to simplify sentences. **Personal pronouns** are used for people. Some pronouns are **subject pronouns**; they are used to replace the subject in a sentence—*I, we, he, she, they*.

Is *he* your friend?

We work together.

Object pronouns can function as the object of a sentence—*me, us, him, her, them*.

Give the documents to *her*.

Did you call *him* back yet?

Some pronouns can function as either the subject or the object—e.g., *you, it*. The subject of a sentence is the noun of the sentence that is doing or being something.

You should try it.

It tastes great.

Possessive pronouns indicate ownership. They can be used alone—*mine, yours, his, hers, theirs, ours*—or with a noun—*my, your, his, her, their, ours*. In the latter case, they function as a determiner, which is described in detail in the below section on adjectives.

This table is *ours*.

I can't find *my* phone!

Reflexive pronouns refer back to the person being spoken or written about. These pronouns end in -*self/-selves*.

I've heard that New York City is gorgeous in the autumn, but I've never seen it for *myself*.

After moving away from home, young people have to take care of *themselves*.

Indefinite pronouns are used for things that are unknown or unspecified. Some examples are *anybody, something,* and *everything*.

I'm looking for *someone* who knows how to fix computers.

I wanted to buy some shoes today, but I couldn't find *any* that I liked.

Adjective

An **adjective** modifies a noun, making it more precise or giving more information about it. Adjectives answer these questions: What kind? Which one?

I just bought a *red* car.

I don't like *cold* weather.

One special type of word that modifies a noun is a **determiner**. In fact, some grammarians classify determiners as a separate part of speech because whereas adjectives simply describe additional qualities of a noun, a determiner is often a necessary part of a noun phrase, without which the phrase is grammatically incomplete. A determiner indicates whether a noun is definite or indefinite and can identify which noun is being discussed. It also introduces context to the noun in terms of quantity and possession. The most commonly-used determiners are *articles—a, an, the*.

I ordered *a* pizza.

She lives in *the* city.

Possessive pronouns discussed above, such as *my*, *your*, and *our*, are also determiners, along with **demonstratives**—*this, that*—and **quantifiers**—*much, many, some*. These determiners can take the place of an article.

Are you using *this* chair?

I need *some* coffee!

Adverb

Adverbs modify verbs, adjectives, and other adverbs. Words that end in –ly are usually adverbs. Adverbs answer these questions: When? Where? In what manner? To what degree?

She talks *quickly*.

The mountains are *incredibly* beautiful!

The students arrived *early*.

Please take your phone call *outside*.

Preposition
Prepositions show the relationship between different elements in a phrase or sentence and connect nouns or pronouns to other words in the sentence. Some examples of prepositions are words such as *after, at, behind, by, during, from, in, on, to,* and *with*.

> Let's go *to* class.
>
> Starry Night was painted *by* Vincent van Gogh *in* 1889.

Conjunction
Conjunctions join words, phrases, clauses, or sentences together, indicating the type of connection between these elements.

> I like pizza, *and* I enjoy spaghetti.
>
> I like to play baseball, *but* I'm allergic to mitts.

Some conjunctions are **coordinating**, meaning they give equal emphasis to two main clauses. Coordinating conjunctions are short, simple words that can be remembered using the mnemonic FANBOYS: for, and, nor, but, or, yet, so. Other conjunctions are subordinating. **Subordinating conjunctions** introduce dependent clauses and include words such as *because, since, before, after, if,* and *while*.

Interjection
An **interjection** is a short word that shows greeting or emotion. Examples of interjections include *wow, ouch, hey, oops, alas,* and *hey.*

> *Wow*! Look at that sunset!
>
> Was it your birthday yesterday? *Oops*! I forgot.

<u>Errors in Standard English Grammar, Usage, Syntax, and Mechanics</u>

Sentence Fragments
A **complete sentence** requires a verb and a subject that expresses a complete thought. Sometimes, the subject is omitted in the case of the implied *you*, used in sentences that are the command or imperative form—e.g., "Look!" or "Give me that." It is understood that the subject of the command is *you*, the listener or reader, so it is possible to have a structure without an explicit subject. Without these elements, though, the sentence is incomplete—it is a **sentence fragment**. While sentence fragments often occur in conversational English or creative writing, they are generally not appropriate in academic writing. Sentence fragments often occur when dependent clauses are not joined to an independent clause:

> *Sentence fragment*: Because the airline overbooked the flight.

The sentence above is a dependent clause that does not express a complete thought. What happened as a result of this cause? With the addition of an independent clause, this now becomes a complete sentence:

> *Complete sentence*: Because the airline overbooked the flight, several passengers were unable to board.

Sentences fragments may also occur through improper use of conjunctions:

I'm going to the Bahamas for spring break. And to New York City for New Year's Eve.

While the first sentence above is a complete sentence, the second one is not because it is a prepositional phrase that lacks a subject [I] and a verb [am going]. Joining the two together with the coordinating conjunction forms one grammatically-correct sentence:

I'm going to the Bahamas for spring break and to New York City for New Year's Eve.

Run-ons

A **run-on** is a sentence with too many independent clauses that are improperly connected to each other:

This winter has been very cold some farmers have suffered damage to their crops.

The sentence above has two subject-verb combinations. The first is "this winter has been"; the second is "some farmers have suffered." However, they are simply stuck next to each other without any punctuation or conjunction. Therefore, the sentence is a run-on.

Another type of run-on occurs when writers use inappropriate punctuation:

This winter has been very cold, some farmers have suffered damage to their crops.

Though a comma has been added, this sentence is still not correct. When a comma alone is used to join two independent clauses, it is known as a **comma splice**. Without an appropriate conjunction, a comma cannot join two independent clauses by itself.

Run-on sentences can be corrected by either dividing the independent clauses into two or more separate sentences or inserting appropriate conjunctions and/or punctuation. The run-on sentence can be amended by separating each subject-verb pair into its own sentence:

This winter has been very cold. Some farmers have suffered damage to their crops.

The run-on can also be fixed by adding a comma and conjunction to join the two independent clauses with each other:

This winter has been very cold, so some farmers have suffered damage to their crops.

Parallelism

Parallel structure occurs when phrases or clauses within a sentence contain the same structure. Parallelism increases readability and comprehensibility because it is easy to tell which sentence elements are paired with each other in meaning.

Jennifer enjoys cooking, knitting, and to spend time with her cat.

This sentence is not parallel because the items in the list appear in two different forms. Some are **gerunds**, which is the verb + ing: *cooking, knitting*. The other item uses the **infinitive** form, which is to + verb: *to spend.* To create parallelism, all items in the list may reflect the same form:

Jennifer enjoys cooking, knitting, and spending time with her cat.

All of the items in the list are now in gerund forms, so this sentence exhibits parallel structure. Here's another example:

> The company is looking for employees who are responsible and with a lot of experience.

Again, the items that are listed in this sentence are not parallel. "Responsible" is an adjective, yet "with a lot of experience" is a prepositional phrase. The sentence elements do not utilize parallel parts of speech.

> The company is looking for employees who are responsible and experienced.

"Responsible" and "experienced" are both adjectives, so this sentence now has parallel structure.

Dangling and Misplaced Modifiers

Modifiers enhance meaning by clarifying or giving greater detail about another part of a sentence. However, incorrectly-placed modifiers have the opposite effect and can cause confusion. A **misplaced modifier** is a modifier that is not located appropriately in relation to the word or phrase that it modifies:

> Because he was one of the greatest thinkers of Renaissance Italy, John idolized Leonardo da Vinci.

In this sentence, the modifier is "because he was one of the greatest thinkers of Renaissance Italy," and the noun it is intended to modify is "Leonardo da Vinci." However, due to the placement of the modifier next to the subject, John, it seems as if the sentence is stating that John was a Renaissance genius, not Da Vinci.

> John idolized Leonard da Vinci because he was one of the greatest thinkers of Renaissance Italy.

The modifier is now adjacent to the appropriate noun, clarifying which of the two men in this sentence is the greatest thinker.

Dangling modifiers modify a word or phrase that is not readily apparent in the sentence. That is, they "dangle" because they are not clearly attached to anything:

> After getting accepted to college, Amir's parents were proud.

The modifier here, "after getting accepted to college," should modify who got accepted. The noun immediately following the modifier is "Amir's parents"—but they are probably not the ones who are going to college.

> After getting accepted to college, Amir made his parents proud.

The subject of the sentence has been changed to Amir himself, and now the subject and its modifier are appropriately matched.

Inconsistent Verb Tense

Verb tense reflects when an action occurred or a state existed. For example, the tense known as **simple present** expresses something that is happening right now or that happens regularly:

> She *works* in a hospital.

Present continuous tense expresses something in progress. It is formed by to be + verb + -ing.

Sorry, I can't go out right now. I *am doing* my homework.

Past tense is used to describe events that previously occurred. However, in conversational English, speakers often use present tense or a mix of past and present tense when relating past events because it gives the narrative a sense of immediacy. In formal written English, though, consistency in verb tense is necessary to avoid reader confusion.

I traveled to Europe last summer. As soon as I stepped off the plane, I feel like I'm in a movie! I'm surrounded by quaint cafes and impressive architecture.

The passage above abruptly switches from past tense—*traveled, stepped*—to present tense—*feel, am surrounded.*

I *traveled* to Europe last summer. As soon as I *stepped* off the plane, I *felt* like I was in a movie! I *was surrounded* by quaint cafes and impressive architecture.

All verbs are in past tense, so this passage now has consistent verb tense.

Split Infinitives

The **infinitive form** of a verb consists of "to + base verb"—e.g., to walk, to sleep, to approve. A **split infinitive** occurs when another word, usually an adverb, is placed between *to* and the verb:

I decided *to simply walk* to work to get more exercise every day.

The infinitive *to walk* is split by the adverb *simply.*

It was a mistake *to hastily approve* the project before conducting further preliminary research.

The infinitive *to approve* is split by *hastily.*

Although some grammarians still advise against split infinitives, this syntactic structure is common in both spoken and written English and is widely accepted in standard usage.

Subject-Verb Agreement

In English, verbs must agree with the subject. The form of a verb may change depending on whether the subject is singular or plural, or whether it is first, second, or third person. For example, the verb *to be* has various forms:

I am a student.

You are a student.

She is a student.

We are students.

They are students.

Errors occur when a verb does not agree with its subject. Sometimes, the error is readily apparent:

We is hungry.

Is is not the appropriate form of *to be* when used with the third person plural *we*.

We are hungry.

This sentence now has correct subject-verb agreement.

However, some cases are trickier, particularly when the subject consists of a lengthy noun phrase with many modifiers:

Students who are hoping to accompany the anthropology department on its annual summer trip to Ecuador needs to sign up by March 31st.

The verb in this sentence is *needs*. However, its subject is not the noun adjacent to it—Ecuador. The subject is the noun at the beginning of the sentence—students. Because *students* is plural, *needs* is the incorrect verb form.

Students who are hoping to accompany the anthropology department on its annual summer trip to Ecuador *need* to sign up by March 31st.

This sentence now uses correct agreement between *students* and *need.*

Another case to be aware of is a *collective noun*. A collective noun refers to a group of many things or people but can be singular in itself—e.g., *family, committee, army, pair team, council, jury*. Whether or not a collective noun uses a singular or plural verb depends on how the noun is being used. If the noun refers to the group performing a collective action as one unit, it should use a singular verb conjugation:

The family is moving to a new neighborhood.

The whole family is moving together in unison, so the singular verb form *is* is appropriate here.

The committee has made its decision.

The verb *has* and the possessive pronoun *its* both reflect the word *committee* as a singular noun in the sentence above; however, when a collective noun refers to the group as individuals, it can take a plural verb:

The newlywed pair spend every moment together.

This sentence emphasizes the love between two people in a pair, so it can use the plural verb *spend*.

The council are all newly elected members.

The sentence refers to the council in terms of its individual members and uses the plural verb *are*.

Overall though, American English is more likely to pair a collective noun with a singular verb, while British English is more likely to pair a collective noun with a plural verb.

Grammar, Usage, Syntax, and Mechanics Choices

Colons and Semicolons
In a sentence, **colons** are used before a list, a summary or elaboration, or an explanation related to the preceding information in the sentence:

> There are two ways to reserve tickets for the performance**:** by phone or in person.
>
> One thing is clear**:** students are spending more on tuition than ever before.

As these examples show, a colon must be preceded by an independent clause. However, the information after the colon may be in the form of an independent clause or in the form of a list.

Semicolons can be used in two different ways—to join ideas or to separate them. In some cases, semicolons can be used to connect what would otherwise be stand-alone sentences. Each part of the sentence joined by a semicolon must be an independent clause. The use of a semicolon indicates that these two independent clauses are closely related to each other:

> The rising cost of childcare is one major stressor for parents**;** healthcare expenses are another source of anxiety.
>
> Classes have been canceled due to the snowstorm**;** check the school website for updates.

Semicolons can also be used to divide elements of a sentence in a more distinct way than simply using a comma. This usage is particularly useful when the items in a list are especially long and complex and contain other internal punctuation.

> Retirees have many modes of income: some survive solely off their retirement checks**;** others supplement their income through part time jobs, like working in a supermarket or substitute teaching**;** and others are financially dependent on the support of family members, friends, and spouses.

Its and It's
These pronouns are some of the most confused in the English language as most possessives contain the suffix –'s. However, for *it*, it is the opposite. *Its* is a possessive pronoun:

> The government is reassessing *its* spending plan.

It's is a contraction of the words *it is*:

> *It's* snowing outside.

Saw and Seen
Saw and *seen* are both conjugations of the verb *to see*, but they express different verb tenses. *Saw* is used in the simple past tense. *Seen* is the past participle form of *to see* and can be used in all perfect tenses.

> I seen her yesterday.

This sentence is incorrect. Because it expresses a completed event from a specified point in time in the past, it should use simple past tense:

> I *saw* her yesterday.

This sentence uses the correct verb tense. Here's how the past participle is used correctly:

> I *have seen* her before.

The meaning in this sentence is slightly changed to indicate an event from an unspecific time in the past. In this case, present perfect is the appropriate verb tense to indicate an unspecified past experience. Present perfect conjugation is created by combining *to have* + past participle.

Then and Than
Then is generally used as an adverb indicating something that happened next in a sequence or as the result of a conditional situation:

> We parked the car and *then* walked to the restaurant.

> If enough people register for the event, *then* we can begin planning.

Than is a conjunction indicating comparison:

> This watch is more expensive *than* that one.

> The bus departed later *than* I expected.

They're, Their, and There
They're is a contraction of the words *they are*:

> *They're* moving to Ohio next week.

Their is a possessive pronoun:

> The baseball players are training for *their* upcoming season.

There can function as multiple parts of speech, but it is most commonly used as an adverb indicating a location:

> Let's go to the concert! Some great bands are playing *there*.

Insure and Ensure
These terms are both verbs. *Insure* means to guarantee something against loss, harm, or damage, usually through an insurance policy that offers monetary compensation:

> The robbers made off with her prized diamond necklace, but luckily it was *insured* for one million dollars.

Ensure means to make sure, to confirm, or to be certain:

> *Ensure* that you have your passport before entering the security checkpoint.

Accept and Except
Accept is a verb meaning to take or agree to something:

> I would like to *accept* your offer of employment.

Except is a preposition that indicates exclusion:

> I've been to every state in America *except* Hawaii.

Affect and Effect
Affect is a verb meaning to influence or to have an impact on something:

> The amount of rainfall during the growing season *affects* the flavor of wine produced from these grapes.

Effect can be used as either a noun or a verb. As a noun, *effect* is synonymous with a result:

> If we implement the changes, what will the *effect* be on our profits?

As a verb, *effect* means to bring about or to make happen:

> In just a few short months, the healthy committee has *effected* real change in school nutrition.

<u>Components of Sentences</u>

Clauses
Clauses contain a subject and a verb. An **independent clause** can function as a complete sentence on its own, but it might also be one component of a longer sentence. **Dependent clauses** cannot stand alone as complete sentences. They rely on independent clauses to complete their meaning. Dependent clauses usually begin with a subordinating conjunction. Independent and dependent clauses are sometimes also referred to as *main clauses* and *subordinate clauses*, respectively. The following structure highlights the differences:

> Apiculturists raise honeybees because they love insects.

Apiculturists raise honeybees is an independent or main clause. The subject is *apiculturists*, and the verb is *raise*. It expresses a complete thought and could be a standalone sentence.

Because they love insects is a dependent or subordinate clause. If it were not attached to the independent clause, it would be a sentence fragment. While it contains a subject and verb—*they love*—this clause is dependent because it begins with the subordinate conjunction *because*. Thus, it does not express a complete thought on its own.

Another type of clause is a **relative clause**, and it is sometimes referred to as an *adjective clause* because it gives further description about the noun. A relative clause begins with a **relative pronoun**: *that, which, who, whom, whichever, whomever,* or *whoever.* It may also begin with a *relative adverb*: *where, why,* or *when.* Here's an example of a relative clause, functioning as an adjective:

> The strawberries that I bought yesterday are already beginning to spoil.

Here, the relative clause is *that I bought yesterday*; the relative pronoun is *that*. The subject is *I*, and the verb is *bought*. The clause modifies the subject *strawberries* by answering the question, "Which strawberries?" Here's an example of a relative clause with an adverb:

> The tutoring center is a place where students can get help with homework.

The relative clause is *where students can get help with homework*, and it gives more information about a place by describing what kind of place it is. It begins with the relative adverb *where* and contains the noun *students* along with its verb phrase *can get*.

Relative clauses may be further divided into two types: essential or nonessential. **Essential clauses** contain identifying information without which the sentence would lose significant meaning or not make sense. These are also sometimes referred to as **restrictive clauses**. The sentence above contains an example of an essential relative clause. Here is what happens when the clause is removed:

> The tutoring center is a place where students can get help with homework.
>
> The tutoring center is a place.

Without the relative clause, the sentence loses the majority of its meaning; thus, the clause is essential or restrictive.

Nonessential clauses—also referred to as **non-restrictive clauses**—offer additional information about a noun in the sentence, but they do not significantly control the overall meaning of the sentence. The following example indicates a nonessential clause:

> New York City, which is located in the northeastern part of the country, is the most populated city in America.
>
> New York City is the most populated city in America.

Even without the relative clause, the sentence is still understandable and continues to communicate its central message about New York City. Thus, it is a nonessential clause.

Punctuation differs between essential and nonessential relative clauses, too. Nonessential clauses are set apart from the sentence using commas whereas essential clauses are not separated with commas. Also, the relative pronoun *that* is generally used for essential clauses, while *which* is used for nonessential clauses. The following examples clarify this distinction:

> *Romeo and Juliet* is my favorite play *that Shakespeare wrote*.

The relative clause *that Shakespeare wrote* contains essential, controlling information about the noun *play*, limiting it to those plays by Shakespeare. Without it, it would seem that *Romeo and Juliet* is the speaker's favorite play out of every play ever written, not simply from Shakespeare's repertoire.

> *Romeo and Juliet, which Shakespeare wrote*, is my favorite play.

Here, the nonessential relative clause—"which Shakespeare wrote"—modifies *Romeo and Juliet*. It doesn't provide controlling information about the play, but simply offers further background details. Thus, commas are needed.

Phrases

Phrases are groups of words that do not contain the subject-verb combination required for clauses. Phrases are classified by the part of speech that begins or controls the phrase.

A **noun phrase** consists of a noun and all its modifiers—adjectives, adverbs, and determiners. Noun phrases can serve many functions in a sentence, acting as subjects, objects, and object complements:

> *The shallow yellow bowl* sits on the top shelf.

> Nina just bought *some incredibly fresh organic produce*.

Prepositional phrases are made up of a preposition and its object. The object of a preposition might be a noun, noun phrase, pronoun, or gerund. Prepositional phrases may function as either an adjective or an adverb:

> Jack picked up the book *in front of him*.

The prepositional phrase *in front of him* acts as an adjective indicating which book Jack picked up.

> The dog ran into the back yard.

The phrase *into the backyard* describes where the dog ran, so it acts as an adverb.

Verb phrases include all of the words in a verb group, even if they are not directly adjacent to each other:

> I *should have woken up* earlier this morning.

> The company **is** now *offering* membership discounts for new enrollers.

This sentence's verb phrase is *is offering*. Even though they are separated by the word *now*, they function together as a single verb phrase.

<u>Structures of Sentences</u>

All sentences contain the same basic elements: a subject and a verb. The **subject** is who or what the sentence is about; the **verb** describes the subject's action or condition. However, these elements, subjects and verbs, can be combined in different ways. The following graphic describes the different types of sentence structures.

Sentence Structure	Independent Clauses	Dependent Clauses
Simple	1	0
Compound	2 or more	0
Complex	1	1 or more
Compound-Complex	2 or more	1 or more

A **simple sentence** expresses a complete thought and consists of one subject and verb combination:

> The children ate pizza.

The subject is *children*. The verb is *ate*.

Either the subject or the verb may be *compound*—that is, it could have more than one element:

The children and their parents ate pizza.

The children *ate pizza and watched a movie.*

All of these are still simple sentences. Despite having either compound subjects or compound verbs, each sentence still has only one subject and verb combination.

Compound sentences combine two or more simple sentences to form one sentence that has multiple subject-verb combinations:

The children ate pizza, and *their parents watched a movie.*

This structure is comprised of two independent clauses: (1) *the children ate pizza* and (2) *their parents watched a movie.* Compound sentences join different subject-verb combinations using a comma and a coordinating conjunction.

I called my mom**,** *but* she didn't answer the phone.

The weather was stormy**,** *so* we canceled our trip to the beach.

A **complex sentence** consists of an independent clause and one or more dependent clauses. Dependent clauses join a sentence using **subordinating conjunctions**. Some examples of subordinating conjunctions are *although, unless, as soon as, since, while, when, because, if,* and *before.*

I missed class yesterday *because* my mother was ill.

Before traveling to a new country, you need to exchange your money to the local currency.

The order of clauses determines their punctuation. If the dependent clause comes first, it should be separated from the independent clause with a comma. However, if the complex sentence consists of an independent clause followed by a dependent clause, then a comma is not always necessary.

A **compound-complex sentence** can be created by joining two or more independent clauses with at least one dependent clause:

After the earthquake struck, thousands of homes were destroyed, and many families were left without a place to live.

The first independent clause in the compound structure includes a dependent clause—*after the earthquake struck.* Thus, the structure is both complex and compound.

Understanding Effective and Ethical Research Practices

<u>Identifying Relevant Information During Research</u>

Relevant information is that which is pertinent to the topic at hand. Particularly when doing research online, it is easy for students to get overwhelmed with the wealth of information available to them. Before conducting research, then, students need to begin with a clear idea of the question they want to answer.

For example, a student may be interested in learning more about marriage practices in Jane Austen's England. If that student types "marriage" into a search engine, he or she will have to sift through thousands of unrelated sites before finding anything related to that topic. Narrowing down search parameters, then, can aid in locating relevant information.

When using a book, students can consult the table of contents, glossary, or index to discover whether the book contains relevant information before using it as a resource. If the student finds a hefty volume on Jane Austen, he or she can flip to the index in the back, look for the word *marriage* and find out how many page references are listed in the book. If there are few or no references to the subject, it is probably not a relevant or useful source.

In evaluating research articles, students may also consult the title, abstract, and keywords before reading the article in its entirety. Referring to the date of publication will also determine whether the research contains up-to-date discoveries, theories, and ideas about the subject or is outdated.

Evaluating the Credibility of a Print or Digital Source

There are several additional criteria that need to be examined before using a source for a research topic.

The following questions will help determine whether a source is credible:

- Author
    - Who is he or she?
    - Does he or she have the appropriate credentials—e.g., M.D, PhD?
    - Is this person authorized to write on the matter through his/her job or personal experiences?
    - Is he or she affiliated with any known credible individuals or organizations?
    - Has he or she written anything else?
- Publisher
    - Who published/produced the work? Is it a well-known journal, like National Geographic, or a tabloid, like The National Enquirer?
    - Is the publisher from a scholarly, commercial, or government association?
    - Do they publish works related to specific fields?
    - Have they published other works?
    - If a digital source, what kind of website hosts the text? Does it end in .edu, .org, or .com?
- Bias
    - Is the writing objective? Does it contain any loaded or emotional language?
    - Does the publisher/producer have a known bias, such as Fox News or CNN?
    - Does the work include diverse opinions or perspectives?
    - Does the author have any known bias—e.g., Michael Moore, Bill O'Reilly, or the Pope? Is he or she affiliated with any organizations or individuals that may have a known bias—e.g., Citizens United or the National Rifle Association?
    - Does the magazine, book, journal, or website contain any advertising?
- References
    - Are there any references?
    - Are the references credible? Do they follow the same criteria as stated above?
    - Are the references from a related field?
- Accuracy/reliability
    - Has the article, book, or digital source been peer reviewed?
    - Are all of the conclusions, supporting details, or ideas backed with published evidence?

- If a digital source, is it free of grammatical errors, poor spelling, and improper English?
  - Do other published individuals have similar findings?
- Coverage
  - Are the topic and related material both successfully addressed?
  - Does the work add new information or theories to those of their sources?
  - Is the target audience appropriate for the intended purpose?

Identifying Effective Research Practices

The purpose of all research is to provide an answer to an unknown question. Therefore, all good research papers pose the topic in the form of a question, which they will then seek to answer with clear ideas, arguments, and supporting evidence.

A **research question** is the primary focus of the research piece, and it should be formulated on a unique topic. To formulate a research question, writers begin by choosing a general topic of interest and then research the literature to determine what sort of research has already been done—the *literature review*. This helps them narrow the topic into something original and determine what still needs to be asked and researched about the topic. A solid question is very specific and avoids generalizations. The following question is offered for evaluation:

> *What is most people's favorite kind of animal?*

This research question is extremely broad without giving the paper any particular focus—it could go any direction and is not an exceptionally unique focus. To narrow it down, the question could consider a specific population:

> *What is the favorite animal of people in Ecuador?*

While this question is better, it does not address exactly why this research is being conducted or why anyone would care about the answer. Here's another possibility:

> *What does the animal considered as the most favorite of people in different regions throughout Ecuador reveal about their socioeconomic status?*

This question is extremely specific and gives a very clear direction of where the paper or project is going to go. However, sometimes the question can be too limited, where very little research has been conducted to create a solid paper, and the researcher most likely does not have the means to travel to Ecuador and travel door-to-door conducting a census on people's favorite animals. In this case, the research question would need to be broadened. Broadening a topic can mean introducing a wider range of criteria. Instead of people in Ecuador, the topic could be opened to include the population of South America or expanded to include more issues or considerations.

Identifying the Components of a Citation

Citation styles vary according to which style guide is consulted. Examples of commonly-used styles include MLA, APA, and Chicago/Turabian. Each citation style includes similar components, although the order and formatting of these components varies.

MLA Style
For an MLA style citation, components must be included or excluded depending on the source, so writers should determine which components are applicable to the source being cited. Here are the basic components:

- Author—last name, first name
- Title of source
- Title of container—e.g., a journal title or website
- Other contributors—e.g., editor or translator
- Version
- Number
- Publisher
- Publication date
- Location—e.g., the URL or DOI
- Date of Access—optional

APA Style
The following components can be found in APA style citations. Components must be included or excluded depending on the source, so writers should determine which components are applicable to the source being cited.

The basic components are as follows:

- Author—last name, first initial, middle initial
- Publication date
- Title of chapter, article, or text
- Editor— last name, first initial, middle initial
- Version/volume
- Number/issue
- Page numbers
- DOI or URL
- Database—if article is difficult to locate
- City of publication
- State of publication, abbreviated
- Publisher

Chicago/Turabian Style
Chicago/Turabian style citations are also referred to as note systems and are used most frequently in the humanities and the arts. Components must be included or excluded depending on the source, so writers should determine which components are applicable to the source being cited. They contain the following elements:

- Author—last name, first name, middle initial
- Title of chapter or article—in quotation marks
- Title of source
- Editor—first name, last name
- Page numbers
- Version/volume

- Number/issue
- Page numbers
- Date of access
- DOI
- Publication location—city and state abbreviation/country
- Publisher
- Publication Date

Citing Source Material Appropriately

The following information contains examples of the common types of sources used in research as well as the formats for each citation style. First lines of citation entries are presented flush to the left margin, and second/subsequent details are presented with a hanging indent. Some examples of bibliography entries are presented below:

Book

- MLA
- *Format*: Last name, First name, Middle initial. *Title of Source*. Publisher, Publication Date.
- *Example*: Sampson, Maximus R. *Diaries from an Alien Invasion*. Campbell Press, 1989.
- APA
  Format: Last name, First initial, Middle initial. (Year Published) *Book Title.* City, State: Publisher.
  Example: Sampson, M. R. (1989). *Diaries from an alien invasion*. Springfield, IL: Campbell Press.
- Chicago/Turabian
  Format: Last name, First name, Middle initial. *Book Title*. City, State: Publisher, Year of publication.
  Example: Sampson, Maximus R. *Diaries from an Alien Invasion*. Springfield, IL: Campbell Press, 1989.

A Chapter in an Edited Book

- MLA
  Format: Last name, First name, Middle initial. "Title of Source." *Title of Container*, Other Contributors, Publisher, Publication Date, Location.
  Example: Sampson, Maximus R. "The Spaceship." *Diaries from an Alien Invasion*, edited by Allegra M. Brewer, Campbell Press, 1989, pp. 45-62.
- APA
  Format: Last name, First Initial, Middle initial. (Year Published) Chapter title. In First initial, Middle initial, Last Name (Ed.), *Book title* (pp. page numbers). City, State: Publisher.
  Example: Sampson, M. R. (1989). The Spaceship. In A. M. Brewer (Ed.), *Diaries from an Alien Invasion* (pp. 45-62). Springfield, IL: Campbell Press.
- Chicago/Turabian
  Format: Last name, First name, Middle initial. "Chapter Title." In Book Title, edited by Editor's Name (First, Middle In. Last), Page(s). City: Publisher, Year Published.
  Example: Sampson, Maximus R. "The Spaceship," in *Diaries from an Alien Invasion*, edited by Allegra M. Brewer, 45-62. Springfield: Campbell Press, 1989.

Article in a Journal

- MLA
  Format: Last name, First name, Middle initial. "Title of Source." *Title of Container*, Number, Publication Date, Location.
  Example: Rowe, Jason R. "The Grief Monster." *Strong Living*, vol. 9, no. 9, 2016, pp 25-31.
- APA
  Format: Last name, First initial, Middle initial. (Year Published). Title of article. *Name of Journal, volume*(issue), page(s).
  Example: Rowe, J. R. (2016). The grief monster. *Strong Living, 9*(9), 25-31.
- Chicago/Turabian:
  Format: Last name, First name, Middle initial. "Title of Article." *Name of Journal* volume, issue (Year Published): Page(s).
  Example: Rowe, Jason, R. "The Grief Monster." *Strong Living* 9, no. 9 (2016): 25-31.

Page on a Website

- MLA
  Format: Last name, First name, Middle initial. "Title of Article." *Name of Website*, date published (Day Month Year), URL. Date accessed (Day Month Year).
  Example: Rowe, Jason. "The Grief Monster." *Strong Living Online*, 9 Sept. 2016. http://www.somanylosses.com/the-grief-monster/html. Accessed 13 Sept. 2016.
- APA
  Format: Last name, First initial. Middle initial. (Date Published—Year, Month Day). Page or article title. Retrieved from URL
  Example: Rowe, J. W. (2016, Sept. 9). The grief monster. Retrieved from http://www.somanylosses.com/ the-grief-monster/html
- Chicago/Turabian
  Format: Last Name, First Name, Middle initial. "Page Title." *Website Title*. Last modified Month day, year. Accessed month, day, year. URL.
  Example: Rowe, Jason. "The Grief Monster." *Strong Living Online*. Last modified September 9, 2016. Accessed September 13, 2016. http://www.somany losses.com/ the-grief-monster/html.

In-Text Citations

Most of the content found in a research paper will be supporting evidence that must be cited in-text, i.e., directly after the sentence that makes the statement. In-text citations contain details that correspond to the first detail in the bibliography entry—usually the author.

- MLA style - In-text citations will contain the author and the page number (if the source has page numbers) for direct quotations. Paraphrased source material may have just the author.
  - According to Johnson, liver cancer treatment is "just beyond our reach" (976).
  - The treatment of liver cancer is not within our reach, currently (Johnson).
  - The narrator opens the story with a paradoxical description: "It was the best of times, it was the worst of times" (Dickens 1).
- APA Style - In text citations will contain the author, the year of publication, and a page marker—if the source is paginated—for direct quotations. Paraphrased source material will include the author and year of publication.
  - According to Johnson (1986), liver cancer treatment is "just beyond our reach" (p. 976).
  - The treatment of liver cancer is not within our reach, currently (Johnson, 1986).

- Chicago Style - Chicago style has two approaches to in-text citation: notes and bibliography or author-date.
    - Notes – There are two options for notes: endnotes—provided in a sequential list at the end of the paper and separate from bibliography—or footnotes provided at the bottom of a page. In either case, the use of superscript indicates the citation number.
        - Johnson states that treatment of liver cancer is "just beyond our reach."[1]
        - 1. Robert W. Johnson, Oncology in the Twenty-first Century (Kentville, Nova Scotia: Kentville Publishing, 1986), 159.
    - Author-Date – The author-date system includes the author's name, publication year, and page number.
        - Johnson states that treatment of liver cancer is "just beyond our reach" (1986, 159).
        - Research shows that liver cancer treatment is not within our reach, currently (Johnson 1986, 159).

<u>Integrating Information from Source Material</u>

It can be daunting to integrate so many sources into a research paper while still maintaining fluency and coherency. Most source material is incorporated in the form of quotations or paraphrases, while citing the source at the end of their respective references. There are several guidelines to consider when integrating a source into writing:

- The piece should be written in the author's voice. Quotations, especially long ones, should be limited and spaced evenly throughout the paper.

- All paragraphs should begin with the author's own words and end with his or her own words; quotations should never start or end a paragraph.

- Quotations and paraphrases should be used to emphasize a point, give weight to an idea, and validate a claim.

- Supporting evidence should be introduced in a sentence or paragraph, and then explained afterwards: According to Waters (1979) [signal phrase], "All in all, we're just another brick in the wall" (p.24). The wall suggests that people are becoming more alienated, and the bricks symbolize a paradoxical connection to that alienation [Explanation].

- When introducing a source for the first time, the author's name and a smooth transition should be included: In Pink Floyd's groundbreaking album *The Wall*, Roger Waters argues that society is causing people to become more alienated.

- There should be an even balance between quotations and paraphrases.

- Quotations or paraphrases should never be taken out of context in a way that alters the original author's intent.

- Quotations should be syntactically and grammatically integrated.
- Quotations should not simply be copied and pasted in the paper. Rather, they should be introduced into a paper with natural transitions.
    - As argued in Johnson's article...
    - Evidence of this point can be found in Johnson's article, where she asserts that...
    - The central argument of John's article is...

Practice Questions

Usage

Choose the following letter choice that contains an error in the sentence.

1. After vanquishing (A) the heavily favored British forces, Washington (B) have pronounced himself as the autocratic leader (C) of the former colonies without any opposition, but (D) he famously refused and returned to his (E) Mount Vernon plantation.

2. (A) On June 14, 1775, the Second Continental Congress (B) created the (C) Continental Army, and John Adams, (D) serving in the Congress, nominated Washington to be (E) its first commander.

3. (A) Washington provided invaluable leadership, (B) training, and strategy during the Revolutionary (C) War, and he emerged from (D) the war as the embodiment of (E) liberty, and courage.

4. (A) Washington later unanimously was elected as the first (B) American president. (C) But it is (D) Washington's farewell address that cemented his legacy (E) as a visionary worthy of study.

5. (A) Washington enlisted his good (B) friend, Alexander Hamilton, in drafting his most (C) famous address, the letter expressed (D) Washington's faith in the (E) Constitution and rule of law.

6. He encouraged (A) his fellow Americans to put aside (B) partisan differences and establish a national union. (C) Washington warns Americans (D) against meddling in foreign affairs and (E) entering military alliances.

7. (A) Americans would be wise to remember (B) Washingtons farewell, especially during presidential elections when (C) politics hits a fever pitch. They might want to question the political institutions (D) that were not planned by the Founding Fathers, such as (E) the nomination process and political parties themselves.

8. Christopher Columbus (A) is often credited for discovering America. (B) This is incorrect. First, it is impossible (C) to "discover" something where people already live (D) however Christopher Columbus did explore places in the New World that were previously untouched by Europe, (E) so the term "explorer" would be more accurate.

9. Another correction (A) must be made, as well: Christopher Columbus was not the (B) first european explorer to reach the present day Americas! (C) Rather, it was Leif Erikson who first came to the (D) New World and contacted the natives, nearly five hundred years (E) before Christopher Columbus.

10. Leif Erikson, the son of (A) Erik the Red (a famous Viking outlaw and explorer in his (B) own right), was born in either 970 or (C) 980, depending on which (D) historian you seek. His own family, though, did not raise Leif, (E) being a Viking tradition.

11. (A) Leif later tried to return home (B) with the intention of taking supplies and (C) spreading Christianity to Greenland; (D) however, his ship was blown off course and he arrived in a strange new (E) land, present day Newfoundland, Canada.

12. (A) When he finally have returning to his adopted homeland, Greenland, (B) Leif consulted with a merchant (C) who had also seen the shores of this previously unknown land we now know as Canada. The son of the (D) legendary Viking explorer then gathered (E) a crew of 35 men and set sail.

13. During (A) their time in present-day Newfoundland, (B) Leif's expedition made contact with the natives (C) whom they referred to as Skraelings (which translates (D) to 'wretched ones' in Norse). There are several secondhand accounts (E) of their meetings.

Sentence Correction

Directions for questions 14–23

Select the best version of the underlined part of the sentence. The first choice is the same as the original sentence. If you think the original sentence is best, choose the first answer.

14. An important issues stemming from this meeting is that we won't have enough time to meet all of the objectives.

  a. An important issues stemming from this meeting
  b. Important issue stemming from this meeting
  c. An important issue stemming from this meeting
  d. Important issues stemming from this meeting
  e. An important issue stems from this meeting

15. The rising popularity of the clean eating movement can be attributed to the fact that experts say added sugars and chemicals in our food are to blame for the obesity epidemic.

  a. to the fact that experts say added sugars and chemicals in our food are to blame for the obesity epidemic.
  b. in the facts that experts say added sugars and chemicals in our food are to blame for the obesity epidemic.
  c. to the fact that experts saying added sugars and chemicals in our food are to blame for the obesity epidemic.
  d. with the facts that experts say added sugars and chemicals in our food are to blame for the obesity epidemic.
  e. to the fact that experts say added sugars, and chemicals, in our food are to blame for the obesity epidemic.

16. She's looking for a suitcase that can fit all of her clothes, shoes, accessory, and makeup.

  a. clothes, shoes, accessory, and makeup.
  b. clothes; shoes; accessories; and makeup.
  c. clothes, shoes, accessories, and makeups.
  d. clothes, shoe, accessory, and makeup.
  e. clothes, shoes, accessories, and makeup.

17. Shawn started taking guitar lessons while he wanted to become a better musician.

  a. while he wanted to become a better musician.
  b. because he wants to become a better musician.
  c. even though he wanted to become a better musician.
  d. because he wanted to become a better musician.
  e. however he wanted to become a better musician.

18. Considering the recent rains we have had, it's a wonder the plants haven't drowned.
   a. Considering the recent rains we have had, it's a wonder
   b. Consider the recent rains we have had, it's a wonder
   c. Considering for how much recent rain we have had, its a wonder
   d. Considering, the recent rains we have had, its a wonder
   e. Considering the recent rains we has had, it's a wonder

19. Since none of the furniture were delivered on time, we have to move in at a later date.
   a. Since none of the furniture were delivered on time,
   b. Since none of the furniture was delivered on time,
   c. Since all of the furniture were delivered on time,
   d. Since all of the furniture was delivered on time
   e. Since none of the furniture was delivering on time,

20. It is necessary for instructors to offer tutoring to any students who needs extra help in the class.
   a. to any students who needs extra help in the class.
   b. for any students that need extra help in the class.
   c. with any students who need extra help in the class.
   d. for any students needing any extra help in their class.
   e. to any students who need extra help in the class.

21. The fact the train set only includes four cars and one small track was a big disappointment to my son.
   a. the train set only includes four cars and one small track was a big disappointment
   b. that the trains set only include four cars and one small track was a big disappointment
   c. that the train set only includes four cars and one small track was a big disappointment
   d. that the train set only includes four cars and one small track were a big disappointment
   e. the train set only includes four cars and one small track that was a big disappointment

22. Because many people feel there are too many distractions to get any work done, I actually enjoy working from home.
   a. Because many people
   b. While many people
   c. Maybe many people
   d. With most people
   e. However most people

23. There were many questions about what causes the case to have gone cold, but the detective wasn't willing to discuss it with reporters.
   a. about what causes the case to have gone cold
   b. about why the case is cold
   c. about what causes the case to go cold
   d. about why the case went cold
   e. about when the causes to have the case cold

Revision in Context

Read the selection about travelling in an RV and answer Questions 24–30.

1 I have to admit that when my father bought a recreational vehicle (RV), I thought he was making a huge mistake. I didn't really know anything about RVs, but I knew that my dad was as big a "city slicker" as there was. (24) In fact, I even thought he might have gone a little bit crazy. On trips to the beach, he preferred to swim at the pool, and whenever he went hiking, he avoided touching any plants for fear that they might be poison ivy. Why would this man, with an almost irrational fear of the outdoors, want a 40-foot camping behemoth?

2 (25) The RV was a great purchase for our family and brought us all closer together. Every morning (26) we would wake up, eat breakfast, and broke camp. We laughed at our own comical attempts to back The Beast into spaces that seemed impossibly small. (27) We rejoiced as "hackers." When things inevitably went wrong and we couldn't solve the problems on our own, we discovered the incredible helpfulness and friendliness of the RV community. (28) We even made some new friends in the process.

3 (29) Above all, it allowed us to share adventures. While travelling across America, which we could not have experienced in cars and hotels. Enjoying a campfire on a chilly summer evening with the mountains of Glacier National Park in the background, or waking up early in the morning to see the sun rising over the distant spires of Arches National Park are memories that will always stay with me and our entire family. (30) Those are also memories that my siblings and me have now shared with our own children.

24. Which of the following would be the best choice for this sentence (reproduced below)?

In fact, I even thought he might have gone a little bit crazy.

a. Leave it where it is now.
b. Move the sentence so that it comes before the preceding sentence.
c. Move the sentence to the end of the first paragraph.
d. Omit the sentence.
e. Move the sentence so that it comes after the next sentence.

25. In context, which is the best version of the underlined portion of this sentence (reproduced below)?

The RV was a great purchase for our family and brought us all closer together.

a. (as it is now)
b. Not surprisingly, the RV
c. Furthermore, the RV
d. As it turns out, the RV
e. In addition, the RV

26. Which is the best version of the underlined portion of this sentence (reproduced below)?

Every morning <u>we would wake up, eat breakfast, and broke camp.</u>

a. (as it is now)
b. we would wake up, eating breakfast and breaking camp.
c. would we wake up, eat breakfast, and break camp?
d. we are waking up, eating breakfast, and breaking camp.
e. we would wake up, eat breakfast, and break camp.

27. Which is the best version of the underlined portion of this sentence (reproduced below)?

<u>We rejoiced as "hackers."</u>

a. (as it is now)
b. To a nagging problem of technology, we rejoiced as "hackers."
c. We rejoiced when we figured out how to "hack" a solution to a nagging technological problem.
d. To "hack" our way to a solution, we had to rejoice.
e. There was a nagging problem of technology that we rejoiced to as "hackers."

28. Which is the best version of the underlined portion of this sentence (reproduced below)?

<u>We even made some new friends in the process.</u>

a. (as it is now)
b. In the process was the friends we were making.
c. We are even making some new friends in the process.
d. We will make new friends in the process.
e. We even make some new friends in the process.

29. Which is the best version of the underlined portion of this sentence (reproduced below)?

<u>Above all, it allowed us to share adventures. While travelling across America,</u> which we could not have experienced in cars and hotels.

a. (as it is now)
b. Above all, it allowed us to share adventures while traveling across America,
c. Above all, it allowed us to share adventures; while traveling across America,
d. Above all, it allowed us to share adventures—while traveling across America,
e. Above all it allowed us to share adventures while travelling across America

30. Which is the best version of the underlined portion of this sentence (reproduced below)?

Those are also memories that my siblings and me have now shared with our own children.

a. (as it is now)
b. Those are also memories that me and my siblings
c. Those are also memories that my siblings and I
d. Those are also memories that I and my siblings
e. This is also memories that my siblings and I

Read the following section about Fred Hampton and answer Questions 31–36.

1 Fred Hampton desired to see lasting social change for African American people through nonviolent means and community recognition. (31) In the meantime, he became an African American activist during the American Civil Rights Movement and led the Chicago chapter of the Black Panther Party.

Hampton's Education

2 Hampton was born and raised (32) in Maywood of Chicago, Illinois in 1948. Gifted academically and a natural athlete, he became a stellar baseball player in high school. (33) Hampton graduated from Proviso East High School in 1966. He later went on to study law at Triton Junior College. While studying at Triton, Hampton joined and became a leader of the National Association for the Advancement of Colored People (NAACP). As a result of his leadership, the NAACP gained more than 500 members. Hampton worked relentlessly to acquire recreational facilities in the neighborhood and improve the educational resources provided to the impoverished black community of Maywood.

The Black Panthers

3 The Black Panther Party (BPP) (34) was another that formed around the same time as and was similar in function to the NAACP. Hampton was quickly attracted to the (35) Black Panther Party's approach to the fight for equal rights for African Americans. Hampton eventually joined the chapter and relocated to downtown Chicago to be closer to its headquarters.

4 His charismatic personality, organizational abilities, sheer determination, and rhetorical skills (36) enable him to quickly rise through the chapter's ranks. Hampton soon became the leader of the Chicago chapter of the BPP where he organized rallies, taught political education classes, and established a free medical clinic. He also took part in the community police supervision project and played an instrumental role in the BPP breakfast program for impoverished African American children.

31. In context, which is the best version of the underlined portion of this sentence (reproduced below)?

In the meantime, he became an African American activist during the American Civil Rights Movement and led the Chicago chapter of the Black Panther Party.

a. (as it is now)
b. Unfortunately,
c. Finally,
d. As a result,
e. In hindsight,

32. Which is the best version of the underlined portion of this sentence (reproduced below)?

Hampton was born and raised in Maywood of Chicago, Illinois in 1948.

a. (as it is now)
b. in Maywood, of Chicago, Illinois in 1948.
c. in Maywood of Chicago, Illinois, in 1948.
d. in Chicago, Illinois of Maywood in 1948.
e. in Chicago Illinois of Maywood in 1948.

33. Which of the following sentences, if any, should begin a new paragraph?

Hampton graduated from Proviso East High School in 1966. He later went on to study law at Triton Junior College. While studying at Triton, Hampton joined and became a leader of the National Association for the Advancement of Colored People (NAACP). As a result of his leadership, the NAACP gained more than 500 members.

a. There should be no new paragraph.
b. Hampton graduated from Proviso East High School in 1966.
c. He later went on to study law at Triton Junior College.
d. While studying at Triton, Hampton joined and became a leader of the National Association for the Advancement of Colored People (NAACP).
e. As a result of his leadership, the NAACP gained more than 500 members.

34. Which of the following facts would be the most relevant to include here?

The Black Panther Party (BPP) was another that formed around the same time as and was similar in function to the NAACP.

a. best as written
b. had lost all its members that
c. had a lot of members that
d. was another school that
e. was another activist group that

35. Which is the best version of the underlined portion of this sentence (reproduced below)?

Hampton was quickly attracted to the Black Panther Party's approach to the fight for equal rights for African Americans.

a. (as it is now)
b. Black Panther Parties approach
c. Black Panther Partys' approach
d. Black Panther Parties' approach
e. Black Panther Partys approach

36. Which is the best version of the underlined portion of this sentence (reproduced below)?

His charismatic personality, organizational abilities, sheer determination, and rhetorical skills enable him to quickly rise through the chapter's ranks.

a. (as it is now)
b. are enabling him to quickly rise
c. enabled him to quickly rise
d. will enable him to quickly rise
e. enables him to quickly rise

Research Skills

37. A student is starting a research assignment on Japanese-American internment camps during World War II, but she is unsure of how to gather relevant resources. Which of the following would be the most helpful advice for the student?
a. Conduct a broad internet search to get a wide view of the subject.
b. Consult an American history textbook.
c. Find websites about Japanese culture such as fashion and politics.
d. Locate texts in the library related to World War II in America and look for references to internment camps in the index.
e. Find a historical fiction novel about Japanese-American internment camps.

38. Which of the following should be evaluated to ensure the credibility of a source?
a. The publisher, the author, and the references
b. The subject, the title, and the audience
c. The organization, stylistic choices, and transition words
d. The length, the tone, and the contributions of multiple authors
e. The author's purpose, the audience, and the syntax

39. Which of the following is true of using citations in a research paper?
a. If a source is cited in the bibliography, it is not necessary to cite it in the paper as well.
b. In-text citations differ in format from bibliographic citations.
c. Students should learn one standard method of citing sources.
d. Books and articles need to be cited, but not websites or multimedia sources.
e. Websites and multimedia sources need to be cited, but not books or articles.

40. Which of the following is true regarding the integration of source material to maintain the flow of ideas in a research project or paper?

a. There should be at least one quotation in every paragraph.

b. If a source is paraphrased instead of being directly quoted, it is not necessary to include a citation.

c. An author's full name must be used in every signal phrase.

d. In-text citations should be used to support the paper's argument without overwhelming the student's writing.

e. There should be at least one paraphrase in every paragraph.

Answer Explanations

Usage

1. B: Choice *B* has a sentence error. "Washington have pronounced" should be "Washington could have pronounced." "Have pronounced" is incorrect usage for the subject "Washington," as it should go with a plural subject, and Washington is singular.

2. E: Choice *E* has the sentence error because it's unclear what the pronoun "its" is referring to; it could be the "Continental Army or the "Congress." Overall, there's a better way to write the sentence so that the pronoun clearly refers to its antecedent.

3. E: Choice *E* has the sentence error because it has an extra comma. Usually we want to place commas right before a conjunction when either side of the comma is a complete sentence or independent clause. Or, like the list at Choice *B*, we can use commas to list. But the comma in Choice *E* is unnecessary.

4. A: Choice *A* has a sentence error because it is awkwardly worded. The phrasing should say "Washington was later unanimously elected," rather than "Washington later unanimously was elected." It helps to have "unanimously" and "elected" beside each other, since the word "unanimously" is the adverb describing "elected."

5. C: Choice *C* has a comma splice. There should be a period after the word "address." The comma splice creates a run-on sentence.

6. C: Choice *C* is correct because it creates inconsistent verb tense. Since the passage is talking about history, we should stay in past tense. The verb "warns" is in present tense.

7. B: Choice *B* is lacking an apostrophe for possession. Choice *C* is tricky; we have "politics hits," which at first may be considered incorrect subject/verb agreement. However, the word "politics" can be placed with either a singular or plural verb, so this is not grammatically incorrect. We can substitute "politics" with "it" and we would have "it hits," making the phrase correct.

8. D: Choice *D* has a sentence error because it lacks proper punctuation around the word "however." Since "however" acts as a transition word here, it needs to have a period or semicolon in front of it and a comma behind it, like this: "where people already live. However, Christopher Columbus . . ." It currently acts as a run-on sentence.

9. B: Choice *B* has a sentence error in it; the term "european" should be capitalized because it is used to denote a person from a specific region.

10. E: The phrase "being a Viking tradition" is not grammatically correct. Replacing "being" with "which was" makes the dependent clause clearer.

11. E: Choice *E* has a sentence error. A colon should appear after the word "land," not a comma. It should look like the following: "in a strange new land: present day Newfoundland, Canada. This colon is used to provide an explanation for the sentence before it.

12. A: Choice *A* has a sentence error because "have returning" should be "returned." The helping verb "have" would go with "returned," but not the word "returning." This is incorrect verb usage.

13. D: Choice *D* has a grammatical error. The single quotes should be double quotes. Single quotes are used for quotes within a quote.

Sentence Correction

14. C: In this answer, the article and subject agree, and the subject and predicate agree. Choice *A* is incorrect because the article (*an*) and the noun (*issues*) do not agree in number. Choice *B* is incorrect because an article is needed before *important issue*. Choice *D* is incorrect because the plural subject *issues* does not agree with the singular verb *is*. Choice *E* is incorrect because the clause at the beginning of the sentence calls for the –ing *stemming*; with "stems," we've added a verb when there is already the main verb "is."

15. A: Choices *B* and *D* both use the expression *attributed to the fact* incorrectly. It can only be attributed *to* the fact, not *with* or *in* the fact. Choice *C* incorrectly uses a gerund, *saying*, when it should use the present tense of the verb *say*. Choice *E* is incorrect because it adds commas around "and chemicals," which is incorrect.

16. E: Choice *E* is correct because it uses correct parallel structure of plural nouns. *A* is incorrect because the word *accessory* is in singular form. Choice *B* is incorrect; semicolons are used in lists only if there is a list within a list. Choice *C* is incorrect because it pluralizes *makeup*, which is already in plural form. Choice *D* is incorrect because it again uses the singular *accessory*, and it uses the singular *shoe*.

17. D: In a cause/effect relationship, it is correct to use word *because* in the clausal part of the sentence. This can eliminate both Choices *A, C,* and *E*, which don't clearly show the cause/effect relationship. Choice *B* is incorrect because it uses the present tense, when the first part of the sentence is in the past tense. It makes grammatical sense for both parts of the sentence to be in present tense.

18. A: In Choice *B*, the present tense form of the verb *consider* creates an independent clause joined to another independent clause with only a comma, which is a comma splice and grammatically incorrect. Both *C* and *D* use the possessive form of *its*, when it should be the contraction *it's* for *it is*. Choice *D* also includes incorrect comma placement. Choice *E* is also incorrect; the helping verb here should be "have," not "has."

19. B: Choice *A* uses the plural form of the verb, when the subject is the pronoun *none*, which needs a singular verb. Choice *C* also uses the wrong verb form and uses the word *all* in place of *none*, which doesn't make sense in the context of the sentence. Choice *D* uses *all* again, and is missing the comma, which is necessary to set the dependent clause off from the independent clause. Choice *E* is incorrect, as it uses the progressive form of the verb "deliver" instead of the past tense.

20. E: Answer Choice *E* uses the best, most concise word choice. Choice *A* is incorrect because "needs" should be "need" in order to agree with the subject. Choice *B* uses the pronoun *that* to refer to people instead of *who*. *C* incorrectly uses the preposition *with*. Choice *D* uses the preposition *for* and the additional word *any*, making the sentence wordy and less clear.

21. C: Choice *A* is missing the word *that*, which is necessary for the sentence to make sense. Choice *B* pluralizes *trains* and uses the singular form of the word *include*, so it does not agree with the word *set*. Choice *D* changes the verb to *were*, which is in plural form and does not agree with the singular subject. Choice *E* is incorrect because the "that" is placed after "track," which makes the sentence awkwardly worded and thus incorrect.

22. B: Choice *B* uses the best choice of words to create a subordinate and independent clause. In Choice *A*, *because* makes it seem like this is the reason I enjoy working from home, which is incorrect. In *C*, the word *maybe* creates two independent clauses, which are not joined properly with a comma. Choice *D* uses *with*, which does not make grammatical sense. "However" in Choice *E* is also an awkward addition, so mark this as incorrect.

23. D: Choices *A*, *C*, and *E* use additional words and phrases that are not necessary. Choice *B* is more concise, but uses the present tense of *is*. This does not agree with the rest of the sentence, which uses past tense. The best choice is Choice *D*, which uses the most concise sentence structure and is grammatically correct.

Revision in Context

24. B: Move the sentence so that it comes before the preceding sentence. For this question, place the underlined sentence in each prospective choice's position. To keep as-is is incorrect because the father "going crazy" doesn't logically follow the fact that he was a "city slicker." Choice C is incorrect because the sentence in question is not a concluding sentence and does not transition smoothly into the second paragraph. Choice *D* is incorrect because the sentence doesn't necessarily need to be omitted since it logically follows the very first sentence in the passage. Choice *E* is incorrect because the "In fact" transition does not logically follow the sentence that begins with "On trips to the beach."

25. D: Choice *D* is correct because "As it turns out" indicates a contrast from the previous sentiment, that the RV was a great purchase. Choice *A* is incorrect because the sentence needs an effective transition from the paragraph before. Choice *B* is incorrect because the text indicates it *is* surprising that the RV was a great purchase because the author was skeptical beforehand. Choices *C* and *E* are incorrect because the transitions "Furthermore" and "In addition" do not indicate a contrast.

26. E: This sentence calls for parallel structure. Choice *E* is correct because the verbs "wake," "eat," and "break" are consistent in tense and parts of speech. Choice *A* is incorrect because the words "wake" and "eat" are present tense while the word "broke" is in past tense. Choice *C* is incorrect because this turns the sentence into a question, which doesn't make sense within the context. Choice *D* is incorrect because it breaks tense with the rest of the passage. "Waking," "eating," and "breaking" are all present participles, and the context around the sentence is in past tense. Choice *E* is incorrect because it does not display parallel structure in verb form.

27. C: Choice *C* is correct because it is clear, concise, and fits within the context of the passage. Choice *A* is incorrect because "We rejoiced as 'hackers'" does not give reason *why* hacking was rejoiced. Choices *B* and *E* are incorrect because they do not mention a solution being found and is therefore not specific enough. Choice *D* is incorrect because the meaning is eschewed by the helping verb "had to rejoice," and the sentence does not give enough detail as to what the problem entails.

28. A: The original sentence is correct because the verb tense as well as the order of the sentence makes sense in the given context. Choice *B* is incorrect because the order of the words makes the sentence more confusing than it otherwise would be. Choices *C* and *E* are incorrect because "We are even making" and "We even make" are in present tense. Choice *D* is incorrect because "We will make" is future tense. The surrounding text of the sentence is in past tense.

29. B: Choice *B* is correct because there is no punctuation needed if a dependent clause ("while traveling across America") is located behind the independent clause ("it allowed us to share adventures"). Choice *A* is incorrect because there are two dependent clauses connected and no independent clause, and a complete sentence requires at least one independent clause. Choice *C* is incorrect because of the same reason as Choice *A*. Semicolons have the same function as periods: there must be an independent clause on either side of the semicolon. Choice *D* is incorrect because the dash simply interrupts the complete sentence. Choice *E* is incorrect because it omits all commas; there is a comma needed after the introductory phrase "above all" as well as after the independent clause after "across America."

30. C: The rules for "me" and "I" is that one should use "I" when it is the subject pronoun of a sentence, and "me" when it is the object pronoun of the sentence. Break the sentence up to see if "I" or "me" should be used. To say "Those are memories that I have now shared" makes more sense than to say "Those are memories that me have now shared." Choice *D* is incorrect because "my siblings" should come before "I." Choice *E* is incorrect because the pronoun "this" doesn't agree with the noun, "memories."

31. D: Choice *D* is correct because Fred Hampton becoming an activist was a direct result of him wanting to see lasting social change for African American people. Choice *A* doesn't make sense because "In the meantime" denotes something happening at the same time as another thing. Choice *B* is incorrect because the text's tone does not indicate that becoming a civil rights activist is an unfortunate path. Choice *C* is incorrect because "Finally" indicates something that comes last in a series of events, and the word in question is at the beginning of the introductory paragraph. "In hindsight" means the ability to understand something after it has happened, so this is not the correct context.

32. A: Choice *A* is correct because there should be a comma between the city and state. Choice *B* is incorrect because the comma after "Maywood" interrupts the phrase "Maywood of Chicago." Choice *C* is incorrect because a comma after "Illinois" is unnecessary. Finally, Choice *D* is incorrect because the order of the sentence designates that Chicago, Illinois is in Maywood, which is incorrect. Choice *E* is incorrect for the same reason, and for the fact that there is no comma between "Chicago" and "Illinois."

33. C: This is a difficult question. The paragraph is incorrect as-is because it is too long and thus loses the reader halfway through. Choice *C* is correct because if the new paragraph began with "While studying at Triton," we would see a smooth transition from one paragraph to the next. We can also see how the two paragraphs are logically split in two. The first half of the paragraph talks about where he studied. The second half of the paragraph talks about the NAACP and the result of his leadership in the association. If we look at the passage as a whole, we can see that there are two main topics that should be broken in two.

34. E: The BPP was another activist group. We can figure out this answer by looking at context clues. We know that the BPP is "similar in function" to the NAACP. To find out what the NAACP's function is, we must look at the previous sentences. We know from above that the NAACP is an activist group, so we can assume that the BPP is also an activist group.

35. A: Choice *A* is correct because the Black Panther Party is one entity, therefore the possession should show the "Party's approach" with the apostrophe between the "y" and the "s." Choice *B* is incorrect because the word "Parties" should not be plural. Choice *C* is incorrect because the apostrophe indicates that the word "Partys" is plural. The plural of "party" is "parties." Choice *D* is incorrect because, again, the word "parties" should not be plural; instead, it is one unified party. Choice *E* is incorrect because it is missing the apostrophe before the "s."

36. C: Choice *C* is correct because the passage is told in past tense, and "enabled" is a past tense verb. Choices *A* and *E,* "enable" and "enables," are present tense. Choice *B*, "are enabling," is a present participle, which suggests a continuing action. Choice *D*, "will enable," is future tense.

Research Skills

37. D: Relevant information refers to information that is closely related to the subject being researched. Students might get overwhelmed by information when they first begin researching, so they should learn how to narrow down search terms for their field of study. Choices *A* and *B* are incorrect because they start with a range that is far too wide; the student will spend too much time sifting through unrelated information to gather only a few related facts. Choice *C* introduces a more limited range, but it is not closely related to the topic that is being researched. Choice *E* would not be a credible enough source, since it is in part fiction. Finally, Choice *D* is correct because the student is choosing books that are more closely related to the topic and is using the index or table of contents to evaluate whether the source contains the necessary information.

38. A: The publisher, author, and references are elements of a resource that determine credibility. If the publisher has published more than one work, the author has written more than one piece on the subject, or the work references other recognized research, the credibility of a source will be stronger. Choice *B* is incorrect because the subject and title may be used to determine relevancy, not credibility, and the audience does not have much to do with the credibility of a source. Choice *C* is incorrect because the organization, stylistic choices, and transition words are all components of an effectively-written piece, but they have less to do with credibility, other than to ensure that the author knows how to write. The length and tone of a piece are a matter of author's preference, and a work does not have to be written by multiple people to be considered a credible source. Choice *E* is incorrect; although the syntax helps with the credibility of a source, this is not the best answer.

39. B: In-text citations are much shorter and usually only include the author's last name, page numbers being referenced, and for some styles, the publication year. Bibliographic citations contain much more detailed reference information. *B* is incorrect because citations are necessary both in the text and in a bibliography. *C* is incorrect because there are several different citation styles depending on the type of paper or article being written. Rather, students should learn when it is appropriate to apply each different style. *D* and *E* are incorrect because all sources need to be cited regardless of medium.

40. D: The purpose of integrating research is to add support and credibility to the student's ideas, not to replace the student's own ideas altogether. Choices *A* and *E* are incorrect as the bulk of the paper or project should be comprised of the author's own words, and quotations and paraphrases should be used to support them. Outside sources should be included when they enhance the writer's argument, but they are not required in every single paragraph. Choice *B* is also incorrect because regardless of whether ideas are directly quoted or paraphrased, it is essential to always credit authors for their ideas. The use of the author's full name in every signal phrase is unnecessary, so Choice *C* is also incorrect.

Essay Prompt

Directions: Please read the prompts below and answer in an essay format.

Essay 1

Some people feel that sharing their lives on social media sites such as Facebook, Instagram, and Snapchat is fine. They share every aspect of their lives, including pictures of themselves and their families, what they ate for lunch, who they are dating, and when they are going on vacation. They even say that if it's not on social media, it didn't happen. Other people believe that sharing so much personal information is an invasion of privacy and could prove dangerous. They think sharing personal pictures and details invites predators, cyberbullying, and identity theft.

Write an essay to someone who is considering whether to participate in social media. Take a side on the issue and argue whether or not he/she should join a social media network. Use specific examples to support your argument.

Essay 2

Read the two articles below. Then, write a 500-word essay in which you synthesize the two articles with your own opinion of the topic. That is, you must develop a position of the topic then use both sources to draw upon your knowledge of the topic and appeal to your audience. Refer to each source by the author's last name or title.

Excerpt from *Preface to Lyrical Ballads* by William Wordsworth (1800)

From such verses the Poems in these volumes will be found distinguished at least by one mark of difference, that each of them has a worthy *purpose.* Not that I always began to write with a distinct purpose formerly conceived; but habits of meditation have, I trust, so prompted and regulated my feelings, that my descriptions of such objects as strongly excite those feelings, will be found to carry along with them a *purpose.* If this opinion be erroneous, I can have little right to the name of a Poet. For all good poetry is the spontaneous overflow of powerful feelings: and though this be true, Poems to which any value can be attached were never produced on any variety of subjects but by a man who, being possessed of more than usual organic sensibility, had also thought long and deeply. For our continued influxes of feeling are modified and directed by our thoughts, which are indeed the representatives of all our past feelings; and, as by contemplating the relation of these general representatives to each other, we discover what is really important to men, so, by the repetition and continuance of this act, our feelings will be connected with important subjects, till at length, if we be originally possessed of much sensibility, such habits of mind will be produced, that, by obeying blindly and mechanically the impulses of those habits, we shall describe objects, and utter sentiments, of such a nature, and in such connexion with each other, that the understanding of the Reader must necessarily be in some degree enlightened, and his affections strengthened and purified.

Excerpt from *Tradition and the Individual Talent* by T.S. Eliot (1921)

If you compare several representative passages of the greatest poetry you see how great is the variety of types of combination, and also how completely any semi-ethical criterion of "sublimity" misses the mark. For it is not the "greatness," the intensity, of the emotions, the components, but the intensity of the artistic process, the pressure, so to speak, under which the fusion takes place, that counts. The episode of Paolo and Francesca employs a definite emotion, but the intensity of the poetry is something quite different from whatever intensity in the supposed experience it may give the impression of. It is no more intense, furthermore, than Canto XXVI, the voyage of Ulysses, which has not the direct dependence upon an emotion. Great variety is possible in the process of transmution of emotion: the murder of Agamemnon, or the agony of Othello, gives an artistic effect apparently closer to a possible original than the scenes from Dante. In the *Agamemnon,* the artistic emotion approximates to the emotion of an actual spectator; in *Othello* to the emotion of the protagonist himself. But the difference between art and the event is always absolute; the combination which is the murder of Agamemnon is probably as complex as that which is the voyage of Ulysses. In either case there has been a fusion of elements. The ode of Keats contains a number of feelings which have nothing particular to do with the nightingale, but which the nightingale, partly, perhaps, because of its attractive name, and partly because of its reputation, served to bring together.

Number and Quantity

Ratios and Proportional Relationships

Ratios are used to show the relationship between two quantities. The ratio of oranges to apples in the grocery store may be 3 to 2. That means that for every 3 oranges, there are 2 apples. This comparison can be expanded to represent the actual number of oranges and apples. Another example may be the number of boys to girls in a math class. If the ratio of boys to girls is given as 2 to 5, that means there are 2 boys to every 5 girls in the class. Ratios can also be compared if the units in each ratio are the same. The ratio of boys to girls in the math class can be compared to the ratio of boys to girls in a science class by stating which ratio is higher and which is lower.

Rates are used to compare two quantities with different units. **Unit rates** are the simplest form of rate. With unit rates, the denominator in the comparison of two units is one. For example, if someone can type at a rate of 1000 words in 5 minutes, then his or her unit rate for typing is $\frac{1000}{5} = 200$ words in one minute or 200 words per minute. Any rate can be converted into a unit rate by dividing to make the denominator one. 1000 words in 5 minutes has been converted into the unit rate of 200 words per minute.

Ratios and rates can be used together to convert rates into different units. For example, if someone is driving 50 kilometers per hour, that rate can be converted into miles per hour by using a ratio known as the **conversion factor**. Since the given value contains kilometers and the final answer needs to be in miles, the ratio relating miles to kilometers needs to be used. There are 0.62 miles in 1 kilometer. This, written as a ratio and in fraction form, is $\frac{0.62\ miles}{1\ km}$. To convert 50km/hour into miles per hour, the following conversion needs to be set up: $\frac{50\ km}{hour} \times \frac{0.62\ miles}{1\ km} = 31\ miles\ per\ hour.$

The ratio between two similar geometric figures is called the **scale factor**. For example, a problem may depict two similar triangles, A and B. The scale factor from the smaller triangle A to the larger triangle B is given as 2 because the length of the corresponding side of the larger triangle, 16, is twice the corresponding side on the smaller triangle, 8. This scale factor can also be used to find the value of a missing side, x, in triangle A. Since the scale factor from the smaller triangle (A) to larger one (B) is 2, the larger corresponding side in triangle B (given as 25), can be divided by 2 to find the missing side in A (x = 12.5). The scale factor can also be represented in the equation $2A = B$ because two times the lengths of A gives the corresponding lengths of B. This is the idea behind similar triangles.

<u>Unit Rate</u>

Unit rate word problems will ask to calculate the rate or quantity of something in a different value. For example, a problem might say that a car drove a certain number of miles in a certain number of minutes and then ask how many miles per hour the car was traveling. These questions involve solving proportions. Consider the following examples:

1) Alexandra made $96 during the first 3 hours of her shift as a temporary worker at a law office. She will continue to earn money at this rate until she finishes in 5 more hours. How much does Alexandra make per hour? How much will Alexandra have made at the end of the day?

This problem can be solved in two ways. The first is to set up a proportion, as the rate of pay is constant. The second is to determine her hourly rate, multiply the 5 hours by that rate, and then add the $96.

To set up a proportion, put the money already earned over the hours already worked on one side of an equation. The other side has x over 8 hours (the total hours worked in the day). It looks like this: $\frac{96}{3} = \frac{x}{8}$. Now, cross-multiply to get $768 = 3x$. To get x, divide by 3, which leaves $x = 256$. Alternatively, as x is the numerator of one of the proportions, multiplying by its denominator will reduce the solution by one step. Thus, Alexandra will make $256 at the end of the day. To calculate her hourly rate, divide the total by 8, giving $32 per hour.

Alternatively, it is possible to figure out the hourly rate by dividing $96 by 3 hours to get $32 per hour. Now her total pay can be figured by multiplying $32 per hour by 8 hours, which comes out to $256.

2) Jonathan is reading a novel. So far, he has read 215 of the 335 total pages. It takes Jonathan 25 minutes to read 10 pages, and the rate is constant. How long does it take Jonathan to read one page? How much longer will it take him to finish the novel? Express the answer in time.

To calculate how long it takes Jonathan to read one page, divide the 25 minutes by 10 pages to determine the page per minute rate. Thus, it takes 2.5 minutes to read one page.

Jonathan must read 120 more pages to complete the novel. (This is calculated by subtracting the pages already read from the total.) Now, multiply his rate per page by the number of pages. Thus, $120 \div 2.5 = 300$. Expressed in time, 300 minutes is equal to 5 hours.

3) At a hotel, $\frac{4}{5}$ of the 120 rooms are booked for Saturday. On Sunday, $\frac{3}{4}$ of the rooms are booked. On which day are more of the rooms booked, and by how many more?

The first step is to calculate the number of rooms booked for each day. Do this by multiplying the fraction of the rooms booked by the total number of rooms.

Saturday: $\frac{4}{5} \times 120 = \frac{4}{5} \times \frac{120}{1} = \frac{480}{5} = 96$ rooms

Sunday: $\frac{3}{4} \times 120 = \frac{3}{4} \times \frac{120}{1} = \frac{360}{4} = 90$ rooms

Thus, more rooms were booked on Saturday by 6 rooms.

4) In a veterinary hospital, the veterinarian-to-pet ratio is 1:9. The ratio is always constant. If there are 45 pets in the hospital, how many veterinarians are currently in the veterinary hospital?

Set up a proportion to solve for the number of veterinarians: $\frac{1}{9} = \frac{x}{45}$

Cross-multiplying results in $9x = 45$, which works out to 5 veterinarians.

Alternatively, as there are always 9 times as many pets as veterinarians, is it possible to divide the number of pets (45) by 9. This also arrives at the correct answer of 5 veterinarians.

5) At a general practice law firm, 30% of the lawyers work solely on tort cases. If 9 lawyers work solely on tort cases, how many lawyers work at the firm?

First, solve for the total number of lawyers working at the firm, which will be represented here with x. The problem states that 9 lawyers work solely on torts cases, and they make up 30% of the total lawyers at the firm. Thus, 30% multiplied by the total, x, will equal 9. Written as equation, this is: $30\% \times x = 9$.

It's easier to deal with the equation after converting the percentage to a decimal, leaving $0.3x = 9$. Thus, $x = \frac{9}{0.3} = 30$ lawyers working at the firm.

6) Xavier was hospitalized with pneumonia. He was originally given 35mg of antibiotics. Later, after his condition continued to worsen, Xavier's dosage was increased to 60mg. What was the percent increase of the antibiotics? Round the percentage to the nearest tenth.

An increase or decrease in percentage can be calculated by dividing the difference in amounts by the original amount and multiplying by 100. Written as an equation, the formula is:

$$\frac{new\ quantity\ -\ old\ quantity}{old\ quantity} \times 100$$

Here, the question states that the dosage was increased from 35mg to 60mg, so these are plugged into the formula to find the percentage increase.

$$\frac{60\ -\ 35}{35} \times\ 100\ =\ \frac{25}{35}\ \times 100 =\ .7142\ \times 100\ = 71.4\%$$

Analyzing Proportional Relationships and Using Them to Solve Real-World Problems

Much like a scale factor can be written using an equation like $2A = B$, a **relationship** is represented by the equation $Y = kX$. X and Y are proportional because as values of X increase, the values of Y also increase. A relationship that is inversely proportional can be represented by the equation $Y = \frac{k}{X}$, where the value of Y decreases as the value of x increases and vice versa.

Proportional reasoning can be used to solve problems involving ratios, percentages, and averages. Ratios can be used in setting up proportions and solving them to find unknowns. For example, if a student completes an average of 10 pages of math homework in 3 nights, how long would it take the student to complete 22 pages? Both ratios can be written as fractions. The second ratio would contain the unknown.

The following proportion represents this problem, where x is the unknown number of nights:

$$\frac{10\,pages}{3\,nights} = \frac{22\,pages}{x\,nights}$$

Solving this proportion entails cross-multiplying and results in the following equation: $10x = 22 \times 3$. Simplifying and solving for x results in the exact solution: $x = 6.6\,nights$. The result would be rounded up to 7 because the homework would actually be completed on the 7th night.

The following problem uses ratios involving percentages:

If 20% of the class is girls and 30 students are in the class, how many girls are in the class?

To set up this problem, it is helpful to use the common proportion: $\frac{\%}{100} = \frac{is}{of}$. Within the proportion, % is the percentage of girls, 100 is the total percentage of the class, *is* is the number of girls, and *of* is the total number of students in the class. Most percentage problems can be written using this language. To solve this problem, the proportion should be set up as $\frac{20}{100} = \frac{x}{30}$, and then solved for x. Cross-multiplying results in the equation $20 \times 30 = 100x$, which results in the solution $x = 6$. There are 6 girls in the class.

Problems involving volume, length, and other units can also be solved using ratios. For example, a problem may ask for the volume of a cone to be found that has a radius, $r = 7m$ and a height, $h = 16m$. Referring to the formulas provided on the test, the volume of a cone is given as: $V = \pi r^2 \frac{h}{3}$, where r is the radius, and h is the height. Plugging $r = 7$ and $h = 16$ into the formula, the following is obtained: $V = \pi(7^2)\frac{16}{3}$. Therefore, volume of the cone is found to be approximately 821m^3. Sometimes, answers in different units are sought. If this problem wanted the answer in liters, 821m^3 would need to be converted. Using the equivalence statement 1m^3 = 1000L, the following ratio would be used to solve for liters: $821\text{m}^3 \times \frac{1000L}{1m^3}$. Cubic meters in the numerator and denominator cancel each other out, and the answer is converted to 821,000 liters, or 8.21×10^5 L.

Other conversions can also be made between different given and final units. If the temperature in a pool is 30°C, what is the temperature of the pool in degrees Fahrenheit? To convert these units, an equation is used relating Celsius to Fahrenheit. The following equation is used: $T_{°F} = 1.8T_{°C} + 32$. Plugging in the given temperature and solving the equation for T yields the result: $T_{°F} = 1.8(30) + 32 = 86°F$. Both units in the metric system and U.S. customary system are widely used.

Here are some more examples of how to solve for proportions:

1) $\frac{75\%}{90\%} = \frac{25\%}{x}$

To solve for x, the fractions must be cross multiplied: $(75\%x = 90\% \times 25\%)$. To make things easier, let's convert the percentages to decimals: $(0.9 \times 0.25 = 0.225 = 0.75x)$. To get rid of x's co-efficient, each side must be divided by that same coefficient to get the answer $x = 0.3$. The question could ask for the answer as a percentage or fraction in lowest terms, which are 30% and $\frac{3}{10}$, respectively.

2) $\frac{x}{12} = \frac{30}{96}$

Cross-multiply: $96x = 30 \times 12$

Multiply: $96x = 360$

Divide: $x = 360 \div 96$

Answer: $x = 3.75$

3) $\frac{0.5}{3} = \frac{x}{6}$

Cross-multiply: $3x = 0.5 \times 6$

Multiply: $3x = 3$

Divide: $x = 3 \div 3$

Answer: $x = 1$

You may have noticed there's a faster way to arrive at the answer. If there is an obvious operation being performed on the proportion, the same operation can be used on the other side of the proportion to solve for x. For example, in the first practice problem, 75% became 25% when divided by 3, and upon doing the same to 90%, the correct answer of 30% would have been found with much less legwork. However, these questions aren't always so intuitive, so it's a good idea to work through the steps, even if the answer seems apparent from the outset.

Operations with Fractions

A **fraction** is an equation that represents a part of a whole but can also be used to present ratios or division problems. An example of a fraction is $\frac{x}{y}$. In this example, x is called the numerator, while y is the denominator. The numerator represents the number of parts, and the denominator is the total number of parts. They are separated by a line or slash, known as a fraction bar.. In simple fractions, the numerator and denominator can be nearly any integer. However, the denominator of a fraction can never be zero, because dividing by zero is a function which is undefined.

Imagine that an apple pie has been baked for a holiday party, and the full pie has eight slices. After the party, there are five slices left. How could the amount of the pie that remains be expressed as a fraction? The numerator is 5 since there are five parts left, and the denominator is 8 since there were eight total slices in the whole pie. Thus, expressed as a fraction, the leftover pie totals $\frac{5}{8}$ of the original amount.

Fractions come in three different varieties: proper fractions, improper fractions, and mixed numbers. Proper fractions have a numerator less than the denominator, such as $\frac{3}{8}$, but improper fractions have a numerator greater than the denominator, such as $\frac{15}{8}$. Mixed numbers combine a whole number with a proper fraction, such as $3\frac{1}{2}$. Any mixed number can be written as an improper fraction by multiplying the integer by the denominator, adding the product to the value of the numerator, and dividing the sum by the original denominator. For example, $3\frac{1}{2} = \frac{3\times2+1}{2} = \frac{7}{2}$. Whole numbers can also be converted into fractions by placing the whole number as the numerator and making the denominator 1. For example, $3 = \frac{3}{1}$.

One of the most fundamental concepts of fractions is their ability to be manipulated by multiplication or division. This is possible since $\frac{n}{n} = 1$ for any non-zero integer. As a result, multiplying or dividing by $\frac{n}{n}$ will not alter the original fraction since any number multiplied or divided by 1 doesn't change the value of that number. Fractions of the same value are known as equivalent fractions. For example, $\frac{2}{4}, \frac{4}{8}, \frac{50}{100}$, and $\frac{75}{150}$ are equivalent, as they all equal $\frac{1}{2}$.

Although many equivalent fractions exist, they are easier to compare and interpret when reduced or simplified. The numerator and denominator of a simple fraction will have no factors in common other than 1. When reducing or simplifying fractions, divide the numerator and denominator by the greatest common factor. A simple strategy is to divide the numerator and denominator by low numbers, like 2, 3, or 5 until arriving at a simple fraction, but the same thing could be achieved by determining the greatest common factor for both the numerator and denominator and dividing each by it. Using the first method is preferable when both the numerator and denominator are even, end in 5, or are obviously a multiple of another number. However, if no numbers seem to work, it will be necessary to factor the numerator and denominator to find the GCF. Let's look at examples:

1) Simplify the fraction $\frac{6}{8}$:

Dividing the numerator and denominator by 2 results in $\frac{3}{4}$, which is a simple fraction.

2) Simplify the fraction $\frac{12}{36}$:

Dividing the numerator and denominator by 2 leaves $\frac{6}{18}$. This isn't a simple fraction, as both the numerator and denominator have factors in common. Diving each by 3 results in $\frac{2}{6}$, but this can be further simplified by dividing by 2 to get $\frac{1}{3}$. This is the simplest fraction, as the numerator is 1. In cases like this, multiple division operations can be avoided by determining the greatest common factor between the numerator and denominator.

3) Simplify the fraction $\frac{18}{54}$ by dividing by the greatest common factor:

First, determine the factors for the numerator and denominator. The factors of 18 are 1, 2, 3, 6, 9, and 18. The factors of 54 are 1, 2, 3, 6, 9, 18, 27, and 54. Thus, the greatest common factor is 18. Dividing $\frac{18}{54}$ by 18 leaves $\frac{1}{3}$, which is the simplest fraction. This method takes slightly more work, but it definitively arrives at the simplest fraction.

Of the four basic operations that can be performed on fractions, the one which involves the least amount of work is multiplication. To multiply two fractions, simply multiply the numerators, multiply the denominators, and place the products as a fraction. Whole numbers and mixed numbers can also be expressed as a fraction, as described above, to multiply with a fraction. Let's work through a couple of examples.

1) $\frac{2}{5} \times \frac{3}{4} = \frac{6}{20} = \frac{3}{10}$

2) $\frac{4}{9} \times \frac{7}{11} = \frac{28}{99}$

Dividing fractions is similar to multiplication with one key difference. To divide fractions, flip the numerator and denominator of the second fraction, and then proceed as if it were a multiplication problem:

1) $\frac{7}{8} \div \frac{4}{5} = \frac{7}{8} \times \frac{5}{4} = \frac{35}{32}$

2) $\frac{5}{9} \div \frac{1}{3} = \frac{5}{9} \times \frac{3}{1} = \frac{15}{9} = \frac{5}{3}$

Addition and subtraction require more steps than multiplication and division, as these operations require the fractions to have the same denominator, also called a common denominator. It is always possible to find a common denominator by multiplying the denominators. However, when the denominators are large numbers, this method is unwieldy, especially if the answer must be provided in its simplest form. Thus, it's beneficial to find the least common denominator of the fractions—the least common denominator is incidentally also the least common multiple.

Once equivalent fractions have been found with common denominators, simply add or subtract the numerators to arrive at the answer:

1) $\frac{1}{2} + \frac{3}{4} = \frac{2}{4} + \frac{3}{4} = \frac{5}{4}$

2) $\frac{3}{12} + \frac{11}{20} = \frac{15}{60} + \frac{33}{60} = \frac{48}{60} = \frac{4}{5}$

3) $\frac{7}{9} - \frac{4}{15} = \frac{35}{45} - \frac{12}{45} = \frac{23}{45}$

4) $\frac{5}{6} - \frac{7}{18} = \frac{15}{18} - \frac{7}{18} = \frac{8}{18} = \frac{4}{9}$

Solving Multi-Digit Problems, Common Factors, and Multiples

<u>Problem Situations for Operations</u>
Addition and subtraction are **inverse operations**. Adding a number and then subtracting the same number will cancel each other out, resulting in the original number, and vice versa. For example, $8 + 7 - 7 = 8$ and $137 - 100 + 100 = 137$. Similarly, multiplication and division are inverse operations. Therefore, multiplying by a number and then dividing by the same number results in the original number, and vice versa. For example, $8 \times 2 \div 2 = 8$ and $12 \div 4 \times 4 = 12$. Inverse operations are used to work backwards to solve problems. In the case that 7 and a number add to 18, the inverse operation of subtraction is used to find the unknown value ($18 - 7 = 11$). If a school's entire 4th grade was divided evenly into 3 classes each with 22 students, the inverse operation of multiplication is used to determine the total students in the grade ($22 \times 3 = 66$). Additional scenarios involving inverse operations are included in the tables below.

There are a variety of real-world situations in which one or more of the operators is used to solve a problem. The tables below display the most common scenarios.

Addition & Subtraction

	Unknown Result	**Unknown Change**	**Unknown Start**
Adding to	5 students were in class. 4 more students arrived. How many students are in class? $5+4=?$	8 students were in class. More students arrived late. There are now 18 students in class. How many students arrived late? $8+?=18$ Solved by inverse operations $18-8=?$	Some students were in class early. 11 more students arrived. There are now 17 students in class. How many students were in class early? $?+11=17$ Solved by inverse operations $17-11=?$
Taking from	15 students were in class. 5 students left class. How many students are in class now? $15-5=?$	12 students were in class. Some students left class. There are now 8 students in class. How many students left class? $12-?=8$ Solved by inverse operations $8+?=12 \rightarrow 12-8=?$	Some students were in class. 3 students left class. Then there were 13 students in class. How many students were in class before? $?-3=13$ Solved by inverse operations $13+3=?$

	Unknown Total	**Unknown Addends (Both)**	**Unknown Addends (One)**
Putting together/ taking apart	The homework assignment is 10 addition problems and 8 subtraction problems. How many problems are in the homework assignment? $10+8=?$	Bobby has $9. How much can Bobby spend on candy and how much can Bobby spend on toys? $9=?+?$	Bobby has 12 pairs of pants. 5 pairs of pants are shorts, and the rest are long. How many pairs of long pants does he have? $12=5+?$ Solved by inverse operations $12-5=?$

	Unknown Difference	**Unknown Larger Value**	**Unknown Smaller Value**
Comparing	Bobby has 5 toys. Tommy has 8 toys. How many more toys does Tommy have than Bobby? $5 + ? = 8$ Solved by inverse operations $8 - 5 = ?$ Bobby has \$6. Tommy has \$10. How many fewer dollars does Bobby have than Tommy? $10 - 6 = ?$	Tommy has 2 more toys than Bobby. Bobby has 4 toys. How many toys does Tommy have? $2 + 4 = ?$ Bobby has 3 fewer dollars than Tommy. Bobby has \$8. How many dollars does Tommy have? $? - 3 = 8$ Solved by inverse operations $8 + 3 = ?$	Tommy has 6 more toys than Bobby. Tommy has 10 toys. How many toys does Bobby have? $? + 6 = 10$ Solved by inverse operations $10 - 6 = ?$ Bobby has \$5 less than Tommy. Tommy has \$9. How many dollars does Bobby have? $9 - 5 = ?$

Multiplication and Division

	Unknown Product	**Unknown Group Size**	**Unknown Number of Groups**
Equal groups	There are 5 students, and each student has 4 pieces of candy. How many pieces of candy are there in all? $5 \times 4 = ?$	14 pieces of candy are shared equally by 7 students. How many pieces of candy does each student have? $7 \times ? = 14$ Solved by inverse operations $14 \div 7 = ?$	If 18 pieces of candy are to be given out 3 to each student, how many students will get candy? $? \times 3 = 18$ Solved by inverse operations $18 \div 3 = ?$

	Unknown Product	Unknown Factor	Unknown Factor
Arrays	There are 5 rows of students with 3 students in each row. How many students are there? $5 \times 3 = ?$	If 16 students are arranged into 4 equal rows, how many students will be in each row? $4 \times ? = 16$ Solved by inverse operations $16 \div 4 = ?$	If 24 students are arranged into an array with 6 columns, how many rows are there? $? \times 6 = 24$ Solved by inverse operations $24 \div 6 = ?$

	Larger Unknown	Smaller Unknown	Multiplier Unknown
Comparing	A small popcorn costs \$1.50. A large popcorn costs 3 times as much as a small popcorn. How much does a large popcorn cost? $1.50 \times 3 = ?$	A large soda costs \$6 and that is 2 times as much as a small soda costs. How much does a small soda cost? $2 \times ? = 6$ Solved by inverse operations $6 \div 2 = ?$	A large pretzel costs \$3 and a small pretzel costs \$2. How many times as much does the large pretzel cost as the small pretzel? $? \times 2 = 3$ Solved by inverse operations $3 \div 2 = ?$

Factorization

Factors are the numbers multiplied to achieve a product. Thus, every product in a multiplication equation has, at minimum, two factors. Of course, some products will have more than two factors. For the sake of most discussions, assume that factors are positive integers.

To find a number's factors, start with 1 and the number itself. Then divide the number by 2, 3, 4, and so on, seeing if any divisors can divide the number without a remainder, keeping a list of those that do. Stop upon reaching either the number itself or another factor.

Let's find the factors of 45. Start with 1 and 45. Then try to divide 45 by 2, which fails. Now divide 45 by 3. The answer is 15, so 3 and 15 are now factors. Dividing by 4 doesn't work and dividing by 5 leaves 9. Lastly, dividing 45 by 6, 7, and 8 all don't work. The next integer to try is 9, but this is already known to be a factor, so the factorization is complete. The factors of 45 are 1, 3, 5, 9, 15 and 45.

Prime Factorization

Prime factorization involves an additional step after breaking a number down to its factors: breaking down the factors until they are all prime numbers. A prime number is any number that can only be divided by 1 and itself. The prime numbers between 1 and 20 are 2, 3, 5, 7, 11, 13, 17, and 19. As a simple test, numbers that are even or end in 5 are not prime.

Let's break 129 down into its prime factors. First, the factors are 3 and 43. Both 3 and 43 are prime numbers, so we're done. But if 43 was not a prime number, then it would also need to be factorized until all of the factors are expressed as prime numbers.

Common Factor

A **common factor** is a factor shared by two numbers. Let's take 45 and 30 and find the common factors:

The factors of 45 are: 1, 3, 5, 9, 15, and 45.
The factors of 30 are: 1, 2, 3, 5, 6, 10, 15, and 30.
The common factors are 1, 3, 5, and 15.

Greatest Common Factor

The **greatest common factor** is the largest number among the shared, common factors. From the factors of 45 and 30, the common factors are 3, 5, and 15. Thus, 15 is the greatest common factor, as it's the largest number.

Least Common Multiple

The **least common multiple** is the smallest number that's a multiple of two numbers. Let's try to find the least common multiple of 4 and 9. The multiples of 4 are 4, 8, 12, 16, 20, 24, 28, 32, 36, and so on. For 9, the multiples are 9, 18, 27, 36, 45, 54, etc. Thus, the least common multiple of 4 and 9 is 36, the lowest number where 4 and 9 share multiples.

If two numbers share no factors besides 1 in common, then their least common multiple will be simply their product. If two numbers have common factors, then their least common multiple will be their product divided by their greatest common factor. This can be visualized by the formula $LCM = \frac{x \times y}{GCF}$, where *x* and *y* are some integers and *LCM* and *GCF* are their least common multiple and greatest common factor, respectively.

Performing Operations on Rational Numbers

A **rational number** is any number that can be written in the form of a ratio or fraction. Integers can be written as fractions with a denominator of 1 ($5 = \frac{5}{1}$; $-342 = \frac{-342}{1}$; etc.). Decimals that terminate and/or repeat can also be written as fractions ($47 = \frac{47}{100}$; $.\overline{33} = \frac{1}{3}$).

When adding or subtracting fractions, the numbers must have the same denominators. In these cases, numerators are added or subtracted, and denominators are kept the same. For example, $\frac{2}{7} + \frac{3}{7} = \frac{5}{7}$ and $\frac{4}{5} - \frac{3}{5} = \frac{1}{5}$. If the fractions to be added or subtracted do not have the same denominator, a common denominator must be found. This is accomplished by changing one or both fractions to a different but equivalent fraction. Consider the example $\frac{1}{6} + \frac{4}{9}$. First, a common denominator must be found. One method is to find the least common multiple (LCM) of the denominators 6 and 9. This is the lowest number that both 6 and 9 will divide into evenly. In this case the LCM is 18. Both fractions should be changed to equivalent fractions with a denominator of 18. To obtain the numerator of the new fraction, the old numerator is multiplied by the same number by which the old denominator is multiplied. For the fraction $\frac{1}{6}$, 6 multiplied by 3 will produce a denominator of 18. Therefore, the numerator is multiplied by 3 to produce the new numerator $\left(\frac{1 \times 3}{6 \times 3} = \frac{3}{18}\right)$. For the fraction $\frac{4}{9}$, multiplying both the numerator and denominator by 2 produces $\frac{8}{18}$. Since the two new fractions have common denominators, they can be added $\left(\frac{3}{18} + \frac{8}{18} = \frac{11}{18}\right)$.

When multiplying or dividing rational numbers, these numbers may be converted to fractions and multiplied or divided accordingly. When multiplying fractions, all numerators are multiplied by each other and all denominators are multiplied by each other. For example, $\frac{1}{3}\times\frac{6}{5}=\frac{1\times6}{3\times5}=\frac{6}{15}$ and $\frac{-1}{2}\times\frac{3}{1}\times\frac{11}{100}=\frac{-1\times3\times11}{2\times1\times100}=\frac{-33}{200}$. When dividing fractions, the problem is converted by multiplying by the reciprocal of the divisor. This is done by changing division to multiplication and "flipping" the second fraction, or divisor. For example, $\frac{1}{2}\div\frac{3}{5}\rightarrow\frac{1}{2}\times\frac{5}{3}$ and $\frac{5}{1}\div\frac{1}{3}\rightarrow\frac{5}{1}\times\frac{3}{1}$. To complete the problem, the rules for multiplying fractions should be followed.

Note that when adding, subtracting, multiplying, and dividing mixed numbers (ex. $4\frac{1}{2}$), it is easiest to convert these to improper fractions (larger numerator than denominator). To do so, the denominator is kept the same. To obtain the numerator, the whole number is multiplied by the denominator and added to the numerator. For example, $4\frac{1}{2}=\frac{9}{2}$ and $7\frac{2}{3}=\frac{23}{3}$. Also, note that answers involving fractions should be converted to the simplest form.

Rational and Irrational Numbers

All real numbers can be separated into two groups: rational and irrational numbers. **Rational numbers** are any numbers that can be written as a fraction, such as $\frac{1}{3}, \frac{7}{4}$, and -25. Alternatively, **irrational numbers** are those that cannot be written as a fraction, such as numbers with never-ending, non-repeating decimal values. Many irrational numbers result from taking roots, such as $\sqrt{2}$ or $\sqrt{3}$. An irrational number may be written as:

34.5684952...

The ellipsis (...) represents the line of numbers after the decimal that does not repeat and is never-ending.

When rational and irrational numbers interact, there are different types of number outcomes. For example, when adding or multiplying two rational numbers, the result is a rational number. No matter what two fractions are added or multiplied together, the result can always be written as a fraction. The following expression shows two rational numbers multiplied together:

$$\frac{3}{8}\times\frac{4}{7}=\frac{12}{56}$$

The product of these two fractions is another fraction that can be simplified to $\frac{3}{14}$.

As another interaction, rational numbers added to irrational numbers will always result in irrational numbers. No part of any fraction can be added to a never-ending, non-repeating decimal to make a rational number. The same result is true when multiplying a rational and irrational number. Taking a fractional part of a never-ending, non-repeating decimal will always result in another never-ending, non-repeating decimal. An example of the product of rational and irrational numbers is shown in the following expression: $2\times\sqrt{7}$.

The last type of interaction concerns two irrational numbers, where the sum or product may be rational or irrational depending on the numbers being used. The following expression shows a rational sum from two irrational numbers:

$$\sqrt{3}+\left(6-\sqrt{3}\right)=6$$

The product of two irrational numbers can be rational or irrational. A rational result can be seen in the following expression:

$$\sqrt{2} \times \sqrt{8} = \sqrt{2 \times 8} = \sqrt{16} = 4$$

An irrational result can be seen in the following:

$$\sqrt{3} \times \sqrt{2} = \sqrt{6}$$

<u>Structure of the Number System</u>
The mathematical number system is made up of two general types of numbers: real and complex. **Real numbers** are those that are used in normal settings, while **complex numbers** are those composed of both a real number and an imaginary one. Imaginary numbers are the result of taking the square root of -1, and $\sqrt{-1} = i$.

The real number system is often explained using a Venn diagram similar to the one below. After a number has been labeled as a real number, further classification occurs when considering the other groups in this diagram. If a number is a never-ending, non-repeating decimal, it falls in the irrational category. Otherwise, it is rational. More information on these types of numbers is provided in the previous section. Furthermore, if a number does not have a fractional part, it is classified as an integer, such as -2, 75, or zero. Whole numbers are an even smaller group that only includes positive integers and zero. The last group of natural numbers is made up of only positive integers, such as 2, 56, or 12.

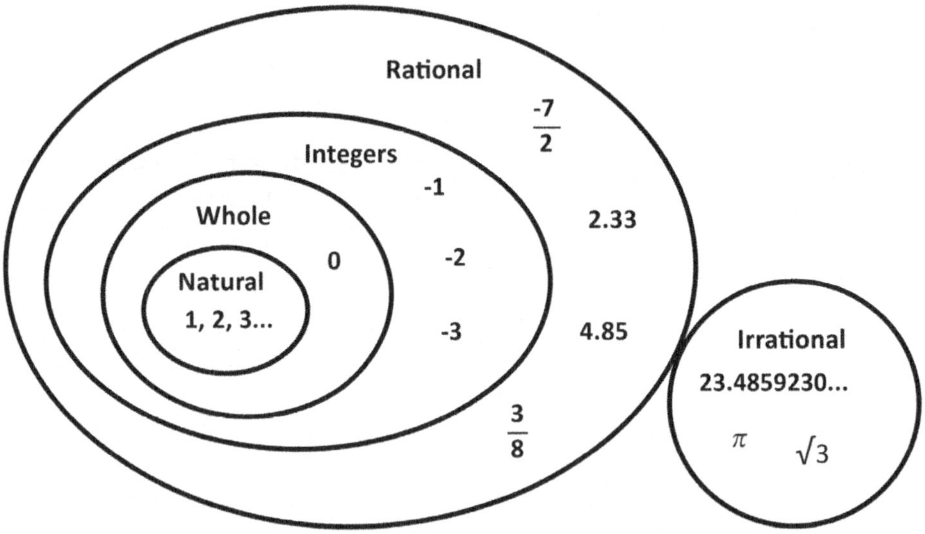

Real numbers can be compared and ordered using the number line. If a number falls to the left on the real number line, it is less than a number on the right. For example, $-2 < 5$ because -2 falls to the left of zero, and 5 falls to the right. Numbers to the left of zero are negative while those to the right are positive.

Complex numbers are made up of the sum of a real number and an imaginary number. Some examples of complex numbers include $6 + 2i$, $5 - 7i$, and $-3 + 12i$. Adding and subtracting complex numbers is similar to collecting like terms. The real numbers are added together, and the imaginary numbers are added together. For example, if the problem asks to simplify the expression $6 + 2i - 3 + 7i$, the 6 and (-3) are combined to make 3, and the $2i$ and $7i$ combine to make $9i$. Multiplying and dividing complex numbers is similar to working with exponents. One rule to remember when multiplying is that $i \times i = -1$. For example, if a problem asks to simplify the expression $4i(3 + 7i)$, the $4i$ should be distributed throughout the 3 and the $7i$. This leaves the final expression $12i - 28$. The 28 is negative because $i \times i$ results in a negative number. The last type of operation to consider with complex numbers is the conjugate. The **conjugate** of a complex number is a technique used to change the complex number into a real number. For example, the conjugate of $4 - 3i$ is $4 + 3i$. Multiplying $(4 - 3i)(4 + 3i)$ results in $16 + 12i - 12i + 9$, which has a final answer of $16 + 9 = 25$.

The order of operations—PEMDAS—simplifies longer expressions with real or imaginary numbers. Each operation is listed in the order of how they should be completed in a problem containing more than one operation. Parenthesis can also mean grouping symbols, such as brackets and absolute value. Then, exponents are calculated. Multiplication and division should be completed from left to right, and addition and subtraction should be completed from left to right.

Simplification of another type of expression occurs when radicals are involved. Root is another word for radical. For example, the following expression is a radical that can be simplified: $\sqrt{24x^2}$. First, the number must be factored out to the highest perfect square. Any perfect square can be taken out of a radical. Twenty-four can be factored into 4 and 6, and 4 can be taken out of the radical. $\sqrt{4} = 2$ can be taken out, and 6 stays underneath. If $x > 0$, x can be taken out of the radical because it is a perfect square. The simplified radical is $2x\sqrt{6}$. An approximation can be found using a calculator.

There are also properties of numbers that are true for certain operations. The **commutative** property allows the order of the terms in an expression to change while keeping the same final answer. Both addition and multiplication can be completed in any order and still obtain the same result. However, order does matter in subtraction and division. The **associative** property allows any terms to be "associated" by parenthesis and retain the same final answer. For example, $(4 + 3) + 5 = 4 + (3 + 5)$. Both addition and multiplication are associative; however, subtraction and division do not hold this property. The **distributive** property states that $a(b + c) = ab + ac$. It is a property that involves both addition and multiplication, and the *a* is distributed onto each term inside the parentheses.

Radicals and Exponents

Exponents are used in mathematics to express a number or variable multiplied by itself a certain number of times. For example, x^3 means x is multiplied by itself three times. In this expression, x is called the **base**, and 3 is the **exponent**. Exponents can be used in more complex problems when they contain fractions and negative numbers.

Fractional exponents can be explained by looking first at the inverse of exponents, which are **roots**. Given the expression x^2, the square root can be taken, $\sqrt{x^2}$, cancelling out the 2 and leaving *x* by itself, if *x* is positive. Cancellation occurs because $\sqrt{x}$ can be written with exponents, instead of roots, as $x^{\frac{1}{2}}$. The numerator of 1 is the exponent, and the denominator of 2 is called the root (which is why it's referred to as **square root**). Taking the square root of x^2 is the same as raising it to the $\frac{1}{2}$ power. Written out in mathematical form, it takes the following progression:

$$\sqrt{x^2} = (x^2)^{\frac{1}{2}} = x$$

From properties of exponents, $2 \times \frac{1}{2} = 1$ is the actual exponent of *x*. Another example can be seen with $x^{\frac{4}{7}}$. The variable *x*, raised to four-sevenths, is equal to the seventh root of *x* to the fourth power: $\sqrt[7]{x^4}$. In general,

$$x^{\frac{1}{n}} = \sqrt[n]{x}$$

and

$$x^{\frac{m}{n}} = \sqrt[n]{x^m}$$

Negative exponents also involve fractions. Whereas y^3 can also be rewritten as $\frac{y^3}{1}$, y^{-3} can be rewritten as $\frac{1}{y^3}$. A negative exponent means the exponential expression must be moved to the opposite spot in a fraction to make the exponent positive. If the negative appears in the numerator, it moves to the denominator. If the negative appears in the denominator, it is moved to the numerator. In general, $a^{-n} = \frac{1}{a^n}$, and a^{-n} and a^n are reciprocals.

Take, for example, the following expression:

$$\frac{a^{-4}b^2}{c^{-5}}$$

Since *a* is raised to the negative fourth power, it can be moved to the denominator. Since *c* is raised to the negative fifth power, it can be moved to the numerator. The *b* variable is raised to the positive second power, so it does not move.

The simplified expression is as follows:

$$\frac{b^2c^5}{a^4}$$

In mathematical expressions containing exponents and other operations, the order of operations must be followed. PEMDAS states that exponents are calculated after any parenthesis and grouping symbols, but before any multiplication, division, addition, and subtraction.

There are a few rules for working with exponents. For any numbers a, b, m, n, the following hold true:

$$a^1 = a$$

$$1^a = 1$$

$$a^0 = 1$$

$$a^m \times a^n = a^{m+n}$$

$$a^m \div a^n = a^{m-n}$$

$$(a^m)^n = a^{m \times n}$$

$$(a \times b)^m = a^m \times b^m$$

$$(a \div b)^m = a^m \div b^m$$

Any number, including a fraction, can be an exponent. The same rules apply.

Manipulating Roots and Exponents

A **root** is a different way to write an exponent when the exponent is the reciprocal of a whole number. We use the **radical** symbol to write this in the following way: $\sqrt[n]{a} = a^{\frac{1}{n}}$. This quantity is called the *n-th root* of *a*. The *n* is called the **index** of the radical.

Note that if the *n*-th root of *a* is multiplied by itself *n* times, the result will just be *a*. If no number *n* is written by the radical, it is assumed that *n* is 2: $\sqrt{5} = 5^{\frac{1}{2}}$. The special case of the 2nd root is called the **square root**, and the third root is called the **cube root**.

A **perfect square** is a whole number that is the square of another whole number. For example, sixteen and 64 are perfect squares because 16 is the square of 4, and 64 is the square of 8.

Solving Problems by Quantitative Reasoning

Dimensional analysis is the process of converting between different units using equivalent measurement statements. For instance, running 5 kilometers is approximately the same as running 3.1 miles. This conversion can be found by knowing that 1 kilometer is equal to approximately 0.62 miles.

When setting up the dimensional analysis calculations, the original units need to be opposite one another in each of the two fractions: one in the original amount (essentially in the numerator) and one in the denominator of the conversion factor. This enables them to cancel after multiplying, leaving the converted result.

Calculations involving formulas, such as determining volume and area, are a common situation in which units need to be interpreted and used. However, graphs can also carry meaning through units. The graph below is an example. It represents a graph of the position of an object over time. The y-axis represents the position or the number of meters the object is from the starting point at time *s*, in seconds. Interpreting this graph, the origin shows that at time zero seconds, the object is zero meters away from the starting point. As the time increases to one second, the position increases to five meters away.

This trend continues until 6 seconds, where the object is 30 meters away from the starting position. After this point in time—since the graph remains horizontal from 6 to 10 seconds—the object must have stopped moving.

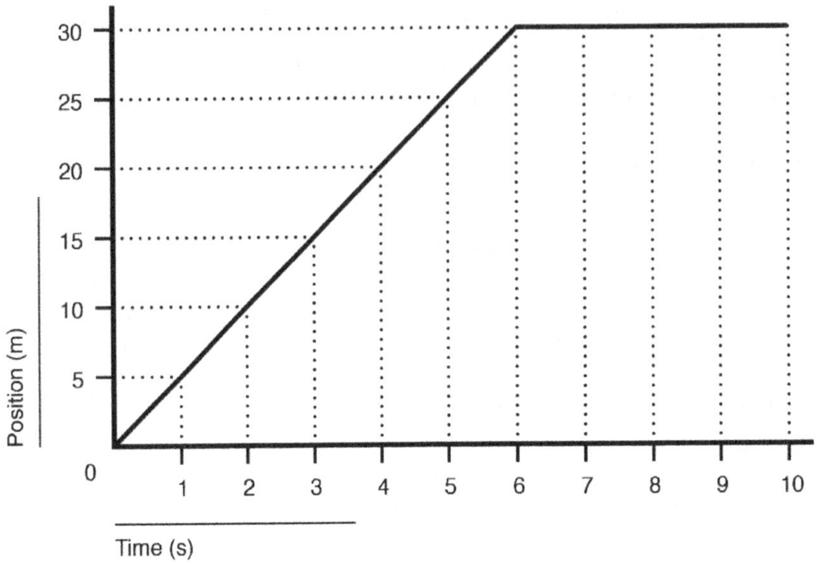

When solving problems with units, it's important to consider the reasonableness of the answer. If conversions are used, it's helpful to have an estimated value to compare the final answer to. This way, if the final answer is too distant from the estimate, it will be obvious that a mistake was made.

Algebra and Functions

Applying Understanding of Arithmetic to Algebraic Expressions

A fraction, or ratio, wherein each part is a polynomial, defines **rational expressions**. Some examples include $\frac{2x+6}{x}$, $\frac{1}{x^2-4x+8}$, and $\frac{z^2}{x+5}$. Exponents on the variables are restricted to whole numbers, which means roots and negative exponents are not included in rational expressions.

Rational expressions can be transformed by factoring. For example, the expression $\frac{x^2-5x+6}{(x-3)}$ can be rewritten by factoring the numerator to obtain $\frac{(x-3)(x-2)}{(x-3)}$. Therefore, the common binomial $(x-3)$ can cancel so that the simplified expression is $\frac{(x-2)}{1} = (x-2)$.

Additionally, other rational expressions can be rewritten to take on different forms. Some may be factorable in themselves, while others can be transformed through arithmetic operations. Rational expressions are closed under addition, subtraction, multiplication, and division by a nonzero expression. **Closed** means that if any one of these operations is performed on a rational expression, the result will still be a rational expression. The set of all real numbers is another example of a set closed under all four operations.

Adding and subtracting rational expressions is based on the same concepts as adding and subtracting simple fractions. For both concepts, the denominators must be the same for the operation to take place. For example, here are two rational expressions:

$$\frac{x^3 - 4}{(x-3)} + \frac{x+8}{(x-3)}$$

Since the denominators are both $(x - 3)$, the numerators can be combined by collecting like terms to form:

$$\frac{x^3 + x + 4}{(x-3)}$$

If the denominators are different, they need to be made common (the same) by using the Least Common Denominator (LCD). Each denominator needs to be factored, and the LCD contains each factor that appears in any one denominator the greatest number of times it appears in any denominator. The original expressions need to be multiplied times a form of 1, which will turn each denominator into the LCD. This process is like adding fractions with unlike denominators. It is also important when working with rational expressions to define what value of the variable makes the denominator zero. For this particular value, the expression is undefined.

Multiplication of rational expressions is performed like multiplication of fractions. The numerators are multiplied; then, the denominators are multiplied. The final fraction is then simplified. The expressions are simplified by factoring and cancelling out common terms. In the following example, the numerator of the second expression can be factored first to simplify the expression before multiplying:

$$\frac{x^2}{(x-4)} \times \frac{x^2 - x - 12}{2}$$

$$\frac{x^2}{(x-4)} \times \frac{(x-4)(x+3)}{2}$$

The $(x - 4)$ on the top and bottom cancel out:

$$\frac{x^2}{1} \times \frac{(x+3)}{2}$$

Then multiplication is performed, resulting in:

$$\frac{x^3 + 3x^2}{2}$$

Dividing rational expressions is similar to the division of fractions, where division turns into multiplying by a reciprocal. So the following expression can be rewritten as a multiplication problem:

$$\frac{x^2 - 3x + 7}{x - 4} \div \frac{x^2 - 5x + 3}{x - 4}$$

$$\frac{x^2 - 3x + 7}{x - 4} \times \frac{x - 4}{x^2 - 5x + 3}$$

The $x - 4$ cancels out, leaving:

$$\frac{x^2 - 3x + 7}{x^2 - 5x + 3}$$

The final answers should always be completely simplified. If a function is composed of a rational expression, the zeros of the graph can be found from setting the polynomial in the numerator as equal to zero and solving. The values that make the denominator equal to zero will either exist on the graph as a hole or a vertical asymptote.

Solving Problems Using Numerical and Algebraic Expressions

Linear expressions and equations are concise mathematical statements that can be written to model a variety of scenarios. Questions found pertaining to this topic will contain one variable only. A variable is an unknown quantity, usually denoted by a letter (*x, n, p,* etc.). In the case of linear expressions and equations, the power of the variable (its exponent) is 1. A variable without a visible exponent is raised to the first power.

Writing Linear Expressions

A linear expression is a statement about an unknown quantity expressed in mathematical symbols. The statement "five times a number added to forty" can be expressed as $5x + 40$. A linear equation is a statement in which two expressions (at least one containing a variable) are equal to each other. The statement "five times a number added to forty is equal to ten" can be expressed as $5x + 40 = 10$. Real-world scenarios can also be expressed mathematically. Consider the following:

> Bob had \$20 and Tom had \$4. After selling 4 ice cream cones to Bob, Tom has as much money as Bob.

The cost of an ice cream cone is an unknown quantity and can be represented by a variable. The amount of money Bob has after his purchase is four times the cost of an ice cream cone subtracted from his original \$20. The amount of money Tom has after his sale is four times the cost of an ice cream cone added to his original \$4. This can be expressed as: $20 - 4x = 4x + 4$, where *x* represents the cost of an ice cream cone.

When expressing a verbal or written statement mathematically, it is key to understand words or phrases that can be represented with symbols. The following are examples:

Symbol	Phrase
$+$	added to, increased by, sum of, more than
$-$	decreased by, difference between, less than, take away
x	multiplied by, 3 (4, 5 . . .) times as large, product of
$\div$	divided by, quotient of, half (third, etc.) of
$=$	is, the same as, results in, as much as
$x, t, n, etc.$	a number, unknown quantity, value of

Evaluating and Simplifying Algebraic Expressions

Given an algebraic expression, students may be asked to evaluate for given values of variable(s). In doing so, students will arrive at a numerical value as an answer. For example:

Evaluate $a - 2b + ab \ for \ a = 3 \text{ and } b = -1$

To evaluate an expression, the given values should be substituted for the variables and simplified using the order of operations. In this case: $(3) - 2(-1) + (3)(-1)$. Parentheses are used when substituting.

Given an algebraic expression, students may be asked to simplify the expression. For example:

Simplify $5x^2 - 10x + 2 - 8x^2 + x - 1$.

Simplifying algebraic expressions requires combining like terms. A term is a number, variable, or product of a number and variables separated by addition and subtraction. The terms in the above expressions are: $5x^2, -10x, 2, -8x^2, x$, and -1. Like terms have the same variables raised to the same powers (exponents). To combine like terms, the coefficients (numerical factor of the term including sign) are added, while the variables and their powers are kept the same. The example above simplifies to $-3x^2 - 9x + 1$.

Generating Equivalent Expressions

Algebraic expressions are made up of numbers, variables, and combinations of the two, using mathematical operations. Expressions can be rewritten based on their factors. For example, the expression $6x + 4$ can be rewritten as $2(3x + 2)$ because 2 is a factor of both $6x$ and 4. More complex expressions can also be rewritten based on their factors. The expression $x^4 - 16$ can be rewritten as $(x^2 - 4)(x^2 + 4)$. This is a different type of factoring, where a difference of squares is factored into a sum and difference of the same two terms. With some expressions, the factoring process is simple and only leads to a different way to represent the expression. With others, factoring and rewriting the expression leads to more information about the given problem.

In the following quadratic equation, factoring the binomial leads to finding the zeros of the function:

$$x^2 - 5x + 6 = y$$

This equation factors into $(x - 3)(x - 2) = y$, where 2 and 3 are found to be the zeros of the function when y is set equal to zero. The zeros of any function are the x-values where the graph of the function on the coordinate plane crosses the x-axis.

Factoring an equation is a simple way to rewrite the equation and find the zeros, but factoring is not possible for every quadratic. Completing the square is one way to find zeros when factoring is not an option. The following equation cannot be factored: $x^2 + 10x - 9 = 0$. The first step in this method is to move the constant to the right side of the equation, making it $x^2 + 10x = 9$. Then, the coefficient of x is divided by 2 and squared. This number is then added to both sides of the equation, to make the equation still true. For this example, $\left(\frac{10}{2}\right)^2 = 25$ is added to both sides of the equation to obtain:

$$x^2 + 10x + 25 = 9 + 25$$

This expression simplifies to $x^2 + 10x + 25 = 34$, which can then be factored into $(x + 5)^2 = 34$. Solving for x then involves taking the square root of both sides and subtracting 5. This leads to two zeros of the function:

$$x = \pm\sqrt{34} - 5$$

Depending on the type of answer the question seeks, a calculator may be used to find exact numbers.

Given a quadratic equation in standard form— $ax^2 + bx + c = 0$—the sign of a tells whether the function has a minimum value or a maximum value. If $a > 0$, the graph opens up and has a minimum value. If $a < 0$, the graph opens down and has a maximum value. Depending on the way the quadratic equation is written, multiplication may need to occur before a max/min value is determined.

Exponential expressions can also be rewritten, just as quadratic equations. Properties of exponents must be understood.

The Connection Between Proportional Relationships and Linear Equations

Linear relationships describe the way two quantities change with respect to each other. The relationship is defined as linear because a line is produced if all the sets of corresponding values are graphed on a coordinate grid. When expressing the linear relationship as an equation, the equation is often written in the form $y = mx + b$ (slope-intercept form) where *m* and *b* are numerical values and *x* and *y* are variables (for example, $y = 5x + 10$). Given a linear equation and the value of either variable (*x* or *y*), the value of the other variable can be determined.

Suppose a teacher is grading a test containing 20 questions with 5 points given for each correct answer, adding a curve of 10 points to each test. This linear relationship can be expressed as the equation $y = 5x + 10$ where *x* represents the number of correct answers and *y* represents the test score. To determine the score of a test with a given number of correct answers, the number of correct answers is substituted into the equation for *x* and evaluated. For example, for 10 correct answers, 10 is substituted for *x*: $y = 5(10) + 10 \rightarrow y = 60$. Therefore, 10 correct answers will result in a score of 60. The number of correct answers needed to obtain a certain score can also be determined. To determine the number of correct answers needed to score a 90, 90 is substituted for *y* in the equation (*y* represents the test score) and solved: $90 = 5x + 10 \rightarrow 80 = 5x \rightarrow 16 = x$. Therefore, 16 correct answers are needed to score a 90.

Linear relationships may be represented by a table of 2 corresponding values. Certain tables may determine the relationship between the values and predict other corresponding sets. Consider the table below, which displays the money in a checking account that charges a monthly fee:

Month	0	1	2	3	4
Balance	$210	$195	$180	$165	$150

An examination of the values reveals that the account loses $15 every month (the month increases by one and the balance decreases by 15). This information can be used to predict future values. To determine what the value will be in month 6, the pattern can be continued, and it can be concluded that the balance will be $120. To determine which month the balance will be $0, $210 is divided by $15 (since the balance decreases $15 every month), resulting in month 14.

Similar to a table, a graph can display corresponding values of a linear relationship.

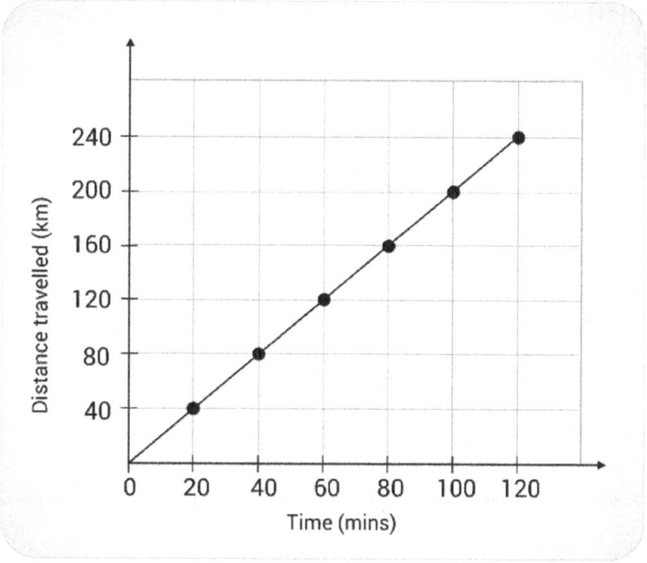

The graph above represents the relationship between distance traveled and time. To find the distance traveled in 80 minutes, the mark for 80 minutes is located at the bottom of the graph. By following this mark directly up on the graph, the corresponding point for 80 minutes is directly across from the 160-kilometer mark. This information indicates that the distance travelled in 80 minutes is 160 kilometers. To predict information not displayed on the graph, the way in which the variables change with respect to one another is determined. In this case, distance increases by 40 kilometers as time increases by 20 minutes. This information can be used to continue the data in the graph or convert the values to a table.

Identifying Variables for Linear Models

The first step to writing a linear model is to identify what the variables represent. A **variable** represents an unknown quantity, and in the case of a linear equation, a specific relationship exists between the two variables (usually x and y). Within a given scenario, the variables are the two quantities that are changing. The variable x is considered the independent variable and represents the inputs of a function. The variable y is considered the dependent variable and represents the outputs of a function. For example, if a scenario describes distance traveled and time traveled, distance would be represented by y and time represented by x. The distance traveled depends on the time spent traveling (time is independent). If a scenario describes the cost of a cab ride and the distance traveled, the cost would be represented by y and the distance represented by x. The cost of a cab ride depends on the distance traveled.

Identifying the Slope and Y-Intercept for Linear Models

The **slope of the graph of a line** represents the rate of change between the variables of an equation. In the context of a real-world scenario, the slope will tell the way in which the unknown quantities (variables) change with respect to each other. A scenario involving distance and time might state that someone is traveling at a rate of 45 miles per hour. The slope of the linear model would be 45. A scenario involving the cost of a cab ride and distance traveled might state that the person is charged $3 for each mile. The slope of the linear model would be 3.

The **y-intercept of a linear function** is the value of *y* when $x = 0$ (the point where the line intercepts the *y*-axis on the graph of the equation). It is sometimes helpful to think of this as a "starting point" for a linear function. Suppose for the scenario about the cab ride that the person is told that the cab company charges a flat fee of $5 plus $3 for each mile. Before traveling any distance ($x = 0$), the cost is $5. The *y*-intercept for the linear model would be 5.

<u>Identifying Ordered Pairs for Linear Models</u>

A linear equation with two variables can be written given a point (ordered pair) and the slope or given two points on a line. An ordered pair gives a set of corresponding values for the two variables (*x* and *y*). As an example, for a scenario involving distance and time, it is given that the person traveled 112.5 miles in 2 ½ hours. Knowing that *x* represents time and *y* represents distance, this information can be written as the ordered pair (2.5, 112.5).

<u>Linear Functions Model a Linear Relationship Between Two Quantities</u>

Linear relationships between two quantities can be expressed in two ways: function notation or as a linear equation with two variables. The relationship is referred to as linear because its graph is represented by a line. For a relationship to be linear, both variables must be raised to the first power only.

Function/Linear Equation Notation

A **relation** is a set of input and output values that can be written as ordered pairs. A function is a relation in which each input is paired with exactly one output. The domain of a function consists of all inputs, and the range consists of all outputs. Graphing the ordered pairs of a linear function produces a straight line. An example of a function would be $f(x) = 4x + 4$, read "*f* of *x* is equal to four times *x* plus four." In this example, the input would be *x* and the output would be f(*x*). Ordered pairs would be represented as (*x*, f(*x*)). To find the output for an input value of 3, 3 would be substituted for *x* into the function as follows: $f(3) = 4(3) + 4$, resulting in $f(3) = 16$. Therefore, the ordered pair $(3, f(3)) = (3, 16)$. Note f(*x*) is a function of *x* denoted by *f*. Functions of *x* could be named *g*(*x*), read "*g* of *x*"; *p*(*x*), read "*p* of *x*"; etc.

A linear function could also be written in the form of an equation with two variables. Typically, the variable *x* represents the inputs and the variable *y* represents the outputs. The variable *x* is considered the independent variable and *y* the dependent variable. The above function would be written as $y = 4x + 4$. Ordered pairs are written in the form (*x*, *y*).

Writing Linear Equations in Two Variables

When writing linear equations in two variables, the process depends on the information given. Questions will typically provide the slope of the line and its *y*-intercept, an ordered pair and the slope, or two ordered pairs.

Linear equations are commonly written in slope-intercept form, $y = mx + b$, where *m* represents the slope of the line and *b* represents the *y*-intercept. The slope is the rate of change between the variables, usually expressed as a whole number or fraction. The *y*-intercept is the value of *y* when *x* = 0 (the point where the line intercepts the *y*-axis on a graph). Given the slope and *y*-intercept of a line, the values are substituted for *m* and *b* into the equation. A line with a slope of $\frac{1}{2}$ and *y*-intercept of -2 would have an equation $y = \frac{1}{2}x - 2$.

The point-slope form of a line, $y - y_1 = m(x - x_1)$, is used to write an equation when given an ordered pair (point on the equation's graph) for the function and its rate of change (slope of the line). The values for the slope, m, and the point (x_1, y_1) are substituted into the point-slope form to obtain the equation of the line. A line with a slope of 3 and an ordered pair (4, -2) would have an equation $y - (-2) = 3(x - 4)$. If a question specifies that the equation be written in slope-intercept form, the equation should be manipulated to isolate *y*:

Solve: $y - (-2) = 3(x - 4)$

Distribute: $y + 2 = 3x - 12$

Subtract 2 from both sides: $y = 3x - 14$

Given two ordered pairs for a function, (x_1, y_1) and (x_2, y_2), it is possible to determine the rate of change between the variables (slope of the line). To calculate the slope of the line, m, the values for the ordered pairs should be substituted into the formula: $m = \frac{y_2 - y_1}{x_2 - x_1}$. The expression is substituted to obtain a whole number or fraction for the slope. Once the slope is calculated, the slope and either of the ordered pairs should be substituted into the point-slope form to obtain the equation of the line.

Solving Equations Using Reasoning

Solving equations in one variable is the process of isolating that variable on one side of the equation. The letters in an equation and any numbers attached to them are the variables as they stand for unknown quantities that you are trying to solve for. *X* is commonly used as a variable, though any letter can be used. For example, in $3x - 7 = 20$, the variable is $3x$, and it needs to be isolated. The numbers (also called constants) are -7 and 20. That means $3x$ needs to be on one side of the equals sign (either side is fine), and all the numbers need to be on the other side of the equals sign.

To accomplish this, the equation must be manipulated by performing opposite operations of what already exists. Remember that addition and subtraction are opposites and that multiplication and division are opposites. Any action taken to one side of the equation must be taken on the other side to maintain equality.

So, since the 7 is being subtracted, it can be moved to the right side of the equation by adding seven to both sides:

$$3x - 7 = 20$$

$$3x - 7 + 7 = 20 + 7$$

$$3x = 27$$

Now that the variable $3x$ is on one side and the constants (now combined into one constant) are on the other side, the 3 needs to be moved to the right side. 3 and x are being multiplied together, so 3 then needs to be divided from each side.

$$\frac{3x}{3} = \frac{27}{3}$$

$$x = 9$$

Now x has been completely isolated, and thus we know its value.

The solution is found to be $x = 9$. This solution can be checked for accuracy by plugging $x = 9$ in the original equation. After simplifying the equation, $20 = 20$ is found, which is a true statement:

$$3 \times 9 - 7 = 20$$

$$27 - 7 = 20$$

$$20 = 20$$

Equations that require solving for a variable (**algebraic equations**) come in many forms. Here are some more examples:

No number attached to the variable:

$$x + 8 = 20$$

$$x + 8 - 8 = 20 - 8$$

$$x = 12$$

Fraction in the variable:

$$\frac{1}{2}z + 24 = 36$$

$$\frac{1}{2}z + 24 - 24 = 36 - 24$$

$$\frac{1}{2}z = 12$$

Now we multiply the fraction by its inverse:

$$\frac{2}{1} \times \frac{1}{2}z = 12 \times \frac{2}{1}$$

$$z = 24$$

Multiple instances of x:

$$14x + x - 4 = 3x + 2$$

All instances of x can be combined.

$$15x - 4 = 3x + 2$$

$$15x - 4 + 4 = 3x + 2 + 4$$

$$15x = 3x + 6$$

$$15x - 3x = 3x + 6 - 3x$$

$$12x = 6$$

$$\frac{12x}{12} = \frac{6}{12}$$

$$x = \frac{1}{2}$$

<u>Methods for Solving Equations</u>

Equations with one variable can be solved using the addition principle and multiplication principle. If $a = b$, then $a + c = b + c$, and $ac = bc$. Given the equation $2x - 3 = 5x + 7$, the first step is to combine the variable terms and the constant terms. Using the principles, expressions can be added and subtracted onto and off both sides of the equals sign, so the equation turns into $-10 = 3x$. Dividing by 3 on both sides through the multiplication principle with $c = \frac{1}{3}$ results in the final answer of $x = \frac{-10}{3}$.

Some equations have a higher degree and are not solved by simply using opposite operations. When an equation has a degree of 2, completing the square is an option. For example, the quadratic equation $x^2 - 6x + 2 = 0$ can be rewritten by completing the square. The goal of completing the square is to get the equation into the form $(x - p)^2 = q$. Using the example, the constant term 2 first needs to be moved over to the opposite side by subtracting. Then, the square can be completed by adding 9 to both sides, which is the square of half of the coefficient of the middle term $-6x$. The current equation is $x^2 - 6x + 9 = 7$. The left side can be factored into a square of a binomial, resulting in $(x - 3)^2 = 7$. To solve for x, the square root of both sides should be taken, resulting in:

$$(x - 3) = \pm\sqrt{7}$$

$$x = 3 \pm \sqrt{7}$$

Other ways of solving quadratic equations include graphing, factoring, and using the quadratic formula. The equation $y = x^2 - 4x + 3$ can be graphed on the coordinate plane, and the solutions can be observed where it crosses the x-axis. The graph will be a parabola that opens up with two solutions at 1 and 3.

The equation can also be factored to find the solutions. The original equation, $y = x^2 - 4x + 3$ can be factored into $y = (x - 1)(x - 3)$. Setting this equal to zero, the x-values are found to be 1 and 3, just as on the graph. Solving by factoring and graphing are not always possible. The quadratic formula is a method of solving quadratic equations that always results in exact solutions.

The formula is:

$$x = \frac{-b \pm \sqrt{b^2 - 4ac}}{2a}$$

where a, b, and c are the coefficients in the original equation in standard form $y = ax^2 + bx + c$. For this example,

$$x = \frac{4 \pm \sqrt{(-4)^2 - 4(1)(3)}}{2(1)} = \frac{4 \pm \sqrt{16 - 12}}{2} = \frac{4 \pm 2}{2} = 1, 3$$

The expression underneath the radical is called the **discriminant**. Without working out the entire formula, the value of the discriminant can reveal the nature of the solutions. If the value of the discriminant $b^2 - 4ac$ is positive, then there will be two real solutions. If the value is zero, there will be one real solution. If the value is negative, the two solutions will be imaginary or complex. If the solutions are complex, it means that the parabola never touches the x-axis. An example of a complex solution can be found by solving the following quadratic: $y = x^2 - 4x + 8$. By using the quadratic formula, the solutions are found to be:

$$x = \frac{4 \pm \sqrt{(-4)^2 - 4(1)(8)}}{2(1)} = \frac{4 \pm \sqrt{16 - 32}}{2} = \frac{4 \pm \sqrt{-16}}{2} = 2 \pm 2i$$

The solutions both have a real part, 2, and an imaginary part, $2i$.

One-Variable Linear Equations and Inequalities

Linear equations and linear inequalities are both comparisons of two algebraic expressions. However, unlike equations in which the expressions are equal, linear inequalities compare expressions that may be unequal. Linear equations typically have one value for the variable that makes the statement true. Linear inequalities generally have an infinite number of values that make the statement true.

When solving a linear equation, the desired result requires determining a numerical value for the unknown variable. If given a linear equation involving addition, subtraction, multiplication, or division, working backwards isolates the variable. Addition and subtraction are inverse operations, as are multiplication and division. Therefore, they can be used to cancel each other out.

For example, solve $4(t - 2) + 2t - 4 = 2(9 - 2t)$

Distributing: $4t - 8 + 2t - 4 = 18 - 4t$

Combining like terms: $6t - 12 = 18 - 4t$

Adding $4t$ to each side to move the variable: $10t - 12 = 18$

Adding 12 to each side to isolate the variable: $10t = 30$

Dividing each side by 10 to isolate the variable: $t = 3$

The answer can be checked by substituting the value for the variable into the original equation, ensuring that both sides calculate to be equal.

Linear inequalities express the relationship between unequal values. More specifically, they describe in what way the values are unequal. A value can be greater than (>), less than (<), greater than or equal to (≥), or less than or equal to (≤) another value. $5x + 40 > 65$ is read as *five times a number added to forty is greater than sixty-five.*

When solving a linear inequality, the solution is the set of all numbers that make the statement true. The inequality $x + 2 \geq 6$ has a solution set of 4 and every number greater than 4 (4.01; 5; 12; 107; etc.). Adding 2 to 4 or any number greater than 4 results in a value that is greater than or equal to 6. Therefore, $x \geq 4$ is the solution set.

To algebraically solve a linear inequality, follow the same steps as those for solving a linear equation. The inequality symbol stays the same for all operations *except* when multiplying or dividing by a negative number. If multiplying or dividing by a negative number while solving an inequality, the relationship reverses (the sign flips). In other words, > switches to < and vice versa. Multiplying or dividing by a positive number does not change the relationship, so the sign stays the same. An example is shown below.

Solve $-2x - 8 \leq 22$

Add 8 to both sides: $-2x \leq 30$

Divide both sides by -2: $x \geq -15$

Solutions of a linear equation or a linear inequality are the values of the variable that make a statement true. In the case of a linear equation, the solution set (list of all possible solutions) typically consists of a single numerical value. To find the solution, the equation is solved by isolating the variable. For example, solving the equation $3x - 7 = -13$ produces the solution $x = -2$. The only value for *x* which produces a true statement is -2. This can be checked by substituting -2 into the original equation to check that both sides are equal. In this case, $3(-2) - 7 = -13 \rightarrow -13 = -13$; therefore, -2 is a solution.

Although linear equations generally have one solution, this is not always the case. If there is no value for the variable that makes the statement true, there is no solution to the equation. Consider the equation $x + 3 = x - 1$. There is no value for *x* in which adding 3 to the value produces the same result as subtracting one from the value. Conversely, if any value for the variable makes a true statement, the equation has an infinite number of solutions. Consider the equation $3x + 6 = 3(x + 2)$. Any number substituted for *x* will result in a true statement (both sides of the equation are equal).

By manipulating equations like the two above, the variable of the equation will cancel out completely. If the remaining constants express a true statement (ex. $6 = 6$), then all real numbers are solutions to the equation. If the constants left express a false statement (ex. $3 = -1$), then no solution exists for the equation.

Solving a linear inequality requires all values that make the statement true to be determined. For example, solving $3x - 7 \geq -13$ produces the solution $x \geq -2$. This means that -2 and any number greater than -2 produces a true statement. Solution sets for linear inequalities will often be displayed using a number line. If a value is included in the set (≥ or ≤), a shaded dot is placed on that value and an arrow extending in the direction of the solutions. For a variable > or ≥ a number, the arrow will point right on a number line, the direction where the numbers increase. If a variable is < or ≤ a number, the arrow will point left on a number line, which is the direction where the numbers decrease. If the value is not included in the set (> or <), an open (unshaded) circle on that value is used with an arrow in the appropriate direction.

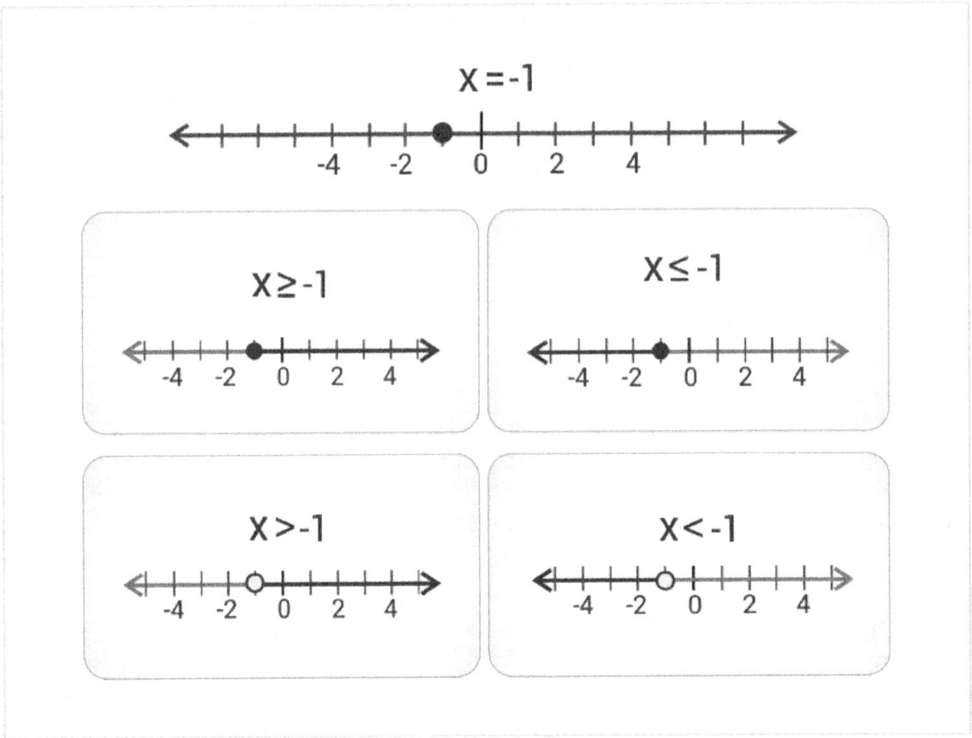

Similar to linear equations, a linear inequality may have a solution set consisting of all real numbers or can contain no solution. When solved algebraically, a linear inequality in which the variable cancels out and results in a true statement (ex. $7 \geq 2$) has a solution set of all real numbers. A linear inequality in which the variable cancels out and results in a false statement (ex. $7 \leq 2$) has no solution.

Linear Inequalities in One Variable

Linear inequalities and linear equations are both comparisons of two algebraic expressions. However, unlike equations in which the expressions are equal to each other, linear inequalities compare expressions that are unequal. Linear equations typically have one value for the variable that makes the statement true. Linear inequalities generally have an infinite number of values that make the statement true. Exceptions to these last two statements are covered in Section 6.

Writing Linear Inequalities

Linear inequalities are a concise mathematical way to express the relationship between unequal values. More specifically, they describe in what way the values are unequal. A value could be greater than ($>$); less than ($<$); greater than or equal to ($\geq$); or less than or equal to ($\leq$) another value. The statement "five times a number added to forty is more than sixty-five" can be expressed as $5x + 40 > 65$. Common words and phrases that express inequalities are:

Symbol	**Phrase**
$<$	is under, is below, smaller than, beneath
$>$	is above, is over, bigger than, exceeds
$\leq$	no more than, at most, maximum
$\geq$	no less than, at least, minimum

Systems of Equations and Inequalities

A **system of equations** is a group of equations that have the same variables or unknowns. These equations can be linear, but they are not always so. Finding a solution to a system of equations means finding the values of the variables that satisfy each equation. For a linear system of two equations and two variables, there could be a single solution, no solution, or infinitely many solutions.

A single solution occurs when there is one value for x and y that satisfies the system. This would be shown on the graph where the lines cross at exactly one point. When there is no solution, the lines are parallel and do not ever cross. With infinitely many solutions, the equations may look different, but they are the same line. One equation will be a multiple of the other, and on the graph, they lie on top of each other.

The process of elimination can be used to solve a system of equations. For example, the following equations make up a system:

$$x + 3y = 10 \text{ and } 2x - 5y = 9$$

Immediately adding these equations does not eliminate a variable, but it is possible to change the first equation by multiplying the whole equation by -2. This changes the first equation to

$$-2x - 6y = -20$$

The equations can be then added to obtain $-11y = -11$. Solving for y yields $y = 1$. To find the rest of the solution, 1 can be substituted in for y in either original equation to find the value of $x = 7$. The solution to the system is (7, 1) because it makes both equations true, and it is the point in which the lines intersect. If the system is **dependent**—having infinitely many solutions—then both variables will cancel out when the elimination method is used, resulting in an equation that is true for many values of *x* and *y*. Since the system is dependent, both equations can be simplified to the same equation or line.

A system can also be solved using **substitution**. This involves solving one equation for a variable and then plugging that solved equation into the other equation in the system. This equation can be solved for one variable, which can then be plugged in to either original equation and solved for the other variable. For example, $x - y = -2$ and $3x + 2y = 9$ can be solved using substitution. The first equation can be solved for x, where $x = -2 + y$.

Then it can be plugged into the other equation:

$$3(-2 + y) + 2y = 9$$

Solving for y yields:

$$-6 + 3y + 2y = 9$$

That shows that $y = 3$. If $y = 3$, then $x = 1$.

This solution can be checked by plugging in these values for the variables in each equation to see if it makes a true statement.

Finally, a solution to a system of equations can be found graphically. The solution to a linear system is the point or points where the lines cross. The values of x and y represent the coordinates (x, y) where the lines intersect. Using the same system of equation as above, they can be solved for y to put them in slope-intercept form, $y = mx + b$. These equations become $y = x + 2$ and $y = -\frac{3}{2}x + 4.5$. The slope is the coefficient of x, and the y-intercept is the constant value.

This system with the solution is shown below:

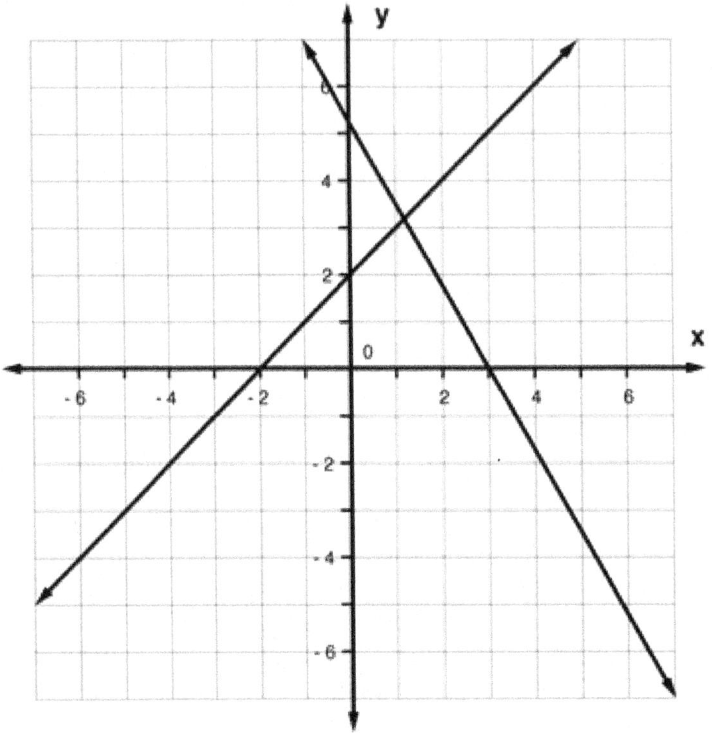

A system of equations may also be made up of a linear and a quadratic equation. These systems may have one solution, two solutions, or no solutions. The graph of these systems involves one straight line and one parabola. Algebraically, these systems can be solved by solving the linear equation for one variable and plugging that answer in to the quadratic equation. If possible, the equation can then be solved to find part of the answer. The graphing method is commonly used for these types of systems. On a graph, these two lines can be found to intersect at one point, at two points across the parabola, or at no points.

Matrices can also be used to solve systems of linear equations. Specifically, for systems, the coefficients of the linear equations in standard form are the entries in the matrix. Using the same system of linear equations as above, $x - y = -2$ and $3x + 2y = 9$, the matrix to represent the system is:

$$\begin{bmatrix} 1 & -1 \\ 3 & 2 \end{bmatrix} \begin{bmatrix} x \\ y \end{bmatrix} = \begin{bmatrix} -2 \\ 9 \end{bmatrix}$$

To solve this system using matrices, the inverse matrix must be found. For a general 2x2 matrix:

$$\begin{bmatrix} a & b \\ c & d \end{bmatrix}$$

The inverse matrix is found by the expression:

$$\frac{1}{ad-bc}\begin{bmatrix} d & -b \\ -c & a \end{bmatrix}$$

The inverse matrix for the system given above is:

$$\frac{1}{2--3}\begin{bmatrix} 2 & 1 \\ -3 & 1 \end{bmatrix} = \frac{1}{5}\begin{bmatrix} 2 & 1 \\ -3 & 1 \end{bmatrix}$$

The next step in solving is to multiply this identity matrix by the system matrix above. This is given by the following equation:

$$\frac{1}{5}\begin{bmatrix} 2 & 1 \\ -3 & 1 \end{bmatrix}\begin{bmatrix} 1 & -1 \\ 3 & 2 \end{bmatrix}\begin{bmatrix} x \\ y \end{bmatrix} = \begin{bmatrix} -2 \\ 9 \end{bmatrix}\begin{bmatrix} 2 & 1 \\ -3 & 1 \end{bmatrix}\frac{1}{5}$$

which simplifies to

$$\frac{1}{5}\begin{bmatrix} 5 & 0 \\ 0 & 5 \end{bmatrix}\begin{bmatrix} x \\ y \end{bmatrix} = \frac{1}{5}\begin{bmatrix} 5 \\ 15 \end{bmatrix}$$

Solving for the solution matrix, the answer is:

$$\begin{bmatrix} 1 & 0 \\ 0 & 1 \end{bmatrix}\begin{bmatrix} x \\ y \end{bmatrix} = \begin{bmatrix} 1 \\ 3 \end{bmatrix}$$

Since the first matrix is the identity matrix, the solution is $x = 1$ and $y = 3$.

Finding solutions to systems of equations is essentially finding what values of the variables make both equations true. It is finding the input value that yields the same output value in both equations. For functions $g(x)$ and $f(x)$, the equation $g(x) = f(x)$ means the output values are being set equal to each other. Solving for the value of x means finding the x-coordinate that gives the same output in both functions. For example, $f(x) = x + 2$ and $g(x) = -3x + 10$ is a system of equations. Setting $f(x) = g(x)$ yields the equation $x + 2 = -3x + 10$. Solving for x, gives the x-coordinate $x = 2$ where the two lines cross. This value can also be found by using a table or a graph. On a table, both equations can be given the same inputs, and the outputs can be recorded to find the point(s) where the lines cross. Any method of solving finds the same solution, but some methods are more appropriate for some systems of equations than others.

Systems of Linear Inequalities

Systems of **linear inequalities** are like systems of equations, but the solutions are different. Since inequalities have infinitely many solutions, their systems also have infinitely many solutions. Finding the solutions of inequalities involves graphs. A system of two equations and two inequalities is linear; thus, the lines can be graphed using slope-intercept form. If the inequality has an equals sign, the line is solid. If the inequality only has a greater than or less than symbol, the line on the graph is dotted. Dashed lines indicate that points lying on the line are not included in the solution. After the lines are graphed, a region is shaded on one side of the line. This side is found by determining if a point—known as a **test point**—lying on one side of the line produces a true inequality. If it does, that side of the graph is shaded. If the point produces a false inequality, the line is shaded on the opposite side from the point. The graph of a system of inequalities involves shading the intersection of the two shaded regions.

Representing and Solving Equations and Inequalities Graphically

The difference of a number and 5 is equal to 10 times the number. To find this unknown number, a simple equation can be written to represent the problem. Key words such as *difference, equal*, and *times* are used to form the following equation with one variable: $n - 5 = 10n$. When solving for n, opposite operations are used. First, n is subtracted from $10n$ across the equals sign, resulting in $-5 = 9n$. Then, 9 is divided on both sides, leaving $n = -\frac{5}{9}$. This solution can be graphed on the number line with a dot as shown below:

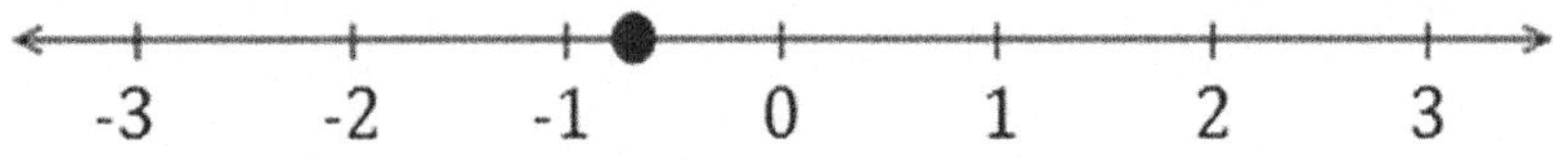

If the problem were changed to say, "The difference of a number and 5 is greater than 10 times the number," then an inequality would be used instead of an equation. Using key words again, *greater than* is represented by the symbol >. The inequality $n - 5 > 10n$ can be solved using the same techniques, resulting in $n > -\frac{5}{9}$. The only time solving an inequality differs from solving an equation is when a negative number is either multiplied times or divided by each side of the inequality.

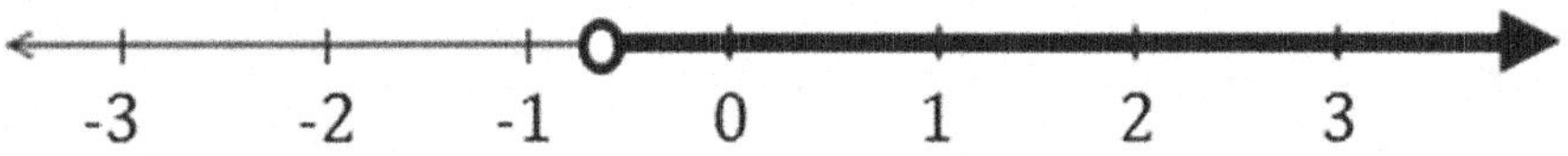

Equations and inequalities in two variables represent a relationship. Jim owns a car wash and charges \$40 per car. The rent for the facility is \$350 per month. An equation can be written to relate the number of cars Jim cleans to the money he makes per month. Let x represent the number of cars and y represent the profit Jim makes each month from the car wash. The equation $y = 40x - 350$ can be used to show Jim's profit or loss. Since this equation has two variables, the coordinate plane can be used to show the relationship and predict profit or loss for Jim. The following graph shows that Jim must wash at least nine cars to pay the rent, where $x = 9$. Anything nine cars and above yield a profit shown in the value on the y-axis.

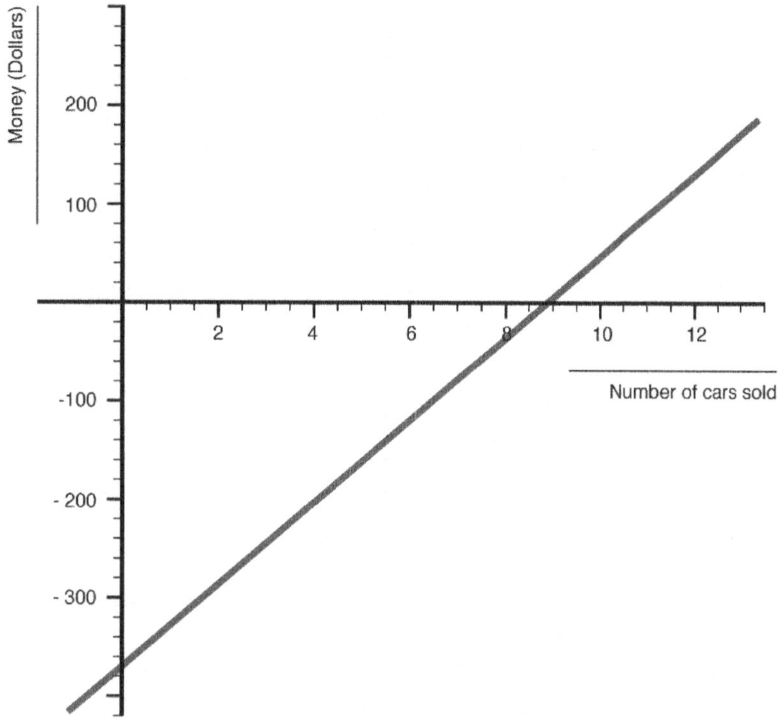

With a single equation in two variables, the solutions are limited only by the situation the equation represents. When two equations or inequalities are used, more constraints are added. For example, in a system of linear equations, there is often—although not always—only one answer. The point of intersection of two lines is the solution. For a system of inequalities, there are infinitely many answers.

The intersection of two solution sets gives the solution set of the system of inequalities. In the following graph, the darker shaded region is where two inequalities overlap. Any set of x and y found in that region satisfies both inequalities. The line with the positive slope is solid, meaning the values on that line are included in the solution.

The line with the negative slope is dotted, so the coordinates on that line are not included.

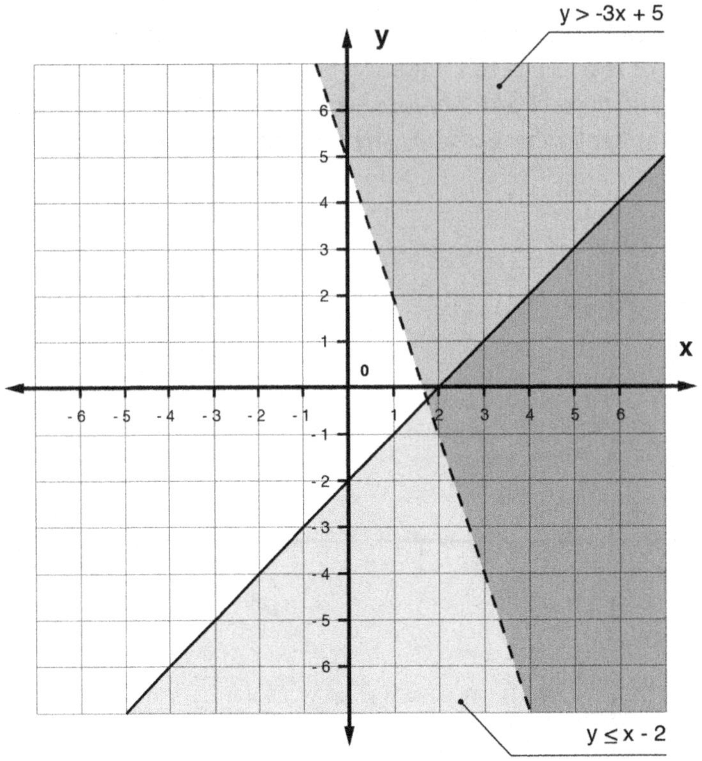

Formulas with two variables are equations used to represent a specific relationship. For example, the formula $d = rt$ represents the relationship between distance, rate, and time. If Bob travels at a rate of 35 miles per hour on his road trip from Westminster to Seneca, the formula $d = 35t$ can be used to represent his distance traveled in a specific length of time. Formulas can also be used to show different roles of the variables, transformed without any given numbers. Solving for r, the formula becomes $\frac{d}{t} = r$. The t is moved over by division so that *rate* is a function of distance and time.

Understanding Connections Between Algebraic and Graphical Representations

The solution set to a linear equation in two variables can be represented visually by a line graphed on the coordinate plane. Every point on this line represents an ordered pair (*x*, *y*), which makes the equation true. The process for graphing a line depends on the form in which its equation is written: slope-intercept form or standard form.

Graphing a Line in Slope-Intercept Form

When an equation is written in slope-intercept form, $y = mx + b$, *m* represents the slope of the line and *b* represents the *y*-intercept. The *y*-intercept is the value of *y* when $x = 0$ and the point at which the graph of the line crosses the *y*-axis. The slope is the rate of change between the variables, expressed as a fraction. The fraction expresses the change in *y* compared to the change in *x*. If the slope is an integer, it should be written as a fraction with a denominator of 1. For example, 5 would be written as 5/1.

To graph a line given an equation in slope-intercept form, the *y*-intercept should first be plotted. For example, to graph $y = -\frac{2}{3}x + 7$, the *y*-intercept of 7 would be plotted on the *y*-axis (vertical axis) at the point (0, 7). Next, the slope would be used to determine a second point for the line. Note that all that is necessary to graph a line is two points on that line. The slope will indicate how to get from one point on the line to another. The slope expresses vertical change (*y*) compared to horizontal change (*x*) and therefore is sometimes referred to as $\frac{rise}{run}$. The numerator indicates the change in the *y* value (move up for positive integers and move down for negative integers), and the denominator indicates the change in the *x* value. For the previous example, using the slope of $-\frac{2}{3}$, from the first point at the *y*-intercept, the second point should be found by counting down 2 and to the right 3. This point would be located at (3, 5).

Graphing a Line in Standard Form

When an equation is written in standard form, $Ax + By = C$, it is easy to identify the *x*- and *y*-intercepts for the graph of the line. Just as the *y*-intercept is the point at which the line intercepts the *y*-axis, the *x*-intercept is the point at which the line intercepts the *x*-axis. At the *y*-intercept, $x = 0$; and at the *x*-intercept, $y = 0$. Given an equation in standard form, $x = 0$ should be used to find the *y*-intercept. Likewise, $y = 0$ should be used to find the *x*-intercept. For example, to graph $3x + 2y = 6$, 0 for *y* results in $3x + 2(0) = 6$. Solving for *y* yields $x = 2$; therefore, an ordered pair for the line is (2, 0). Substituting 0 for *x* results in $3(0) + 2y = 6$. Solving for *y* yields $y = 3$; therefore, an ordered pair for the line is (0, 3). The two ordered pairs (the *x*- and *y*-intercepts) can be plotted and a straight line through them can be constructed.

T - chart

x	y
0	3
2	0

Intercepts

x - intercept : (2,0)

y - intercept : (0,3)

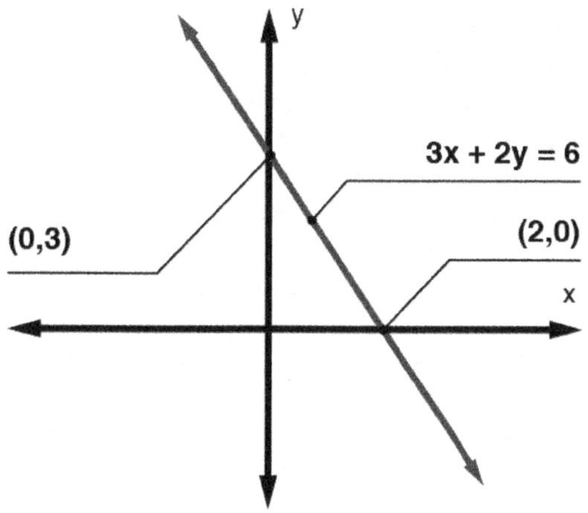

Writing the Equation of a Line Given its Graph

Given the graph of a line, its equation can be written in two ways. If the *y*-intercept is easily identified (is an integer), it and another point can be used to determine the slope. When determining $\frac{change\ in\ y}{change\ in\ x}$ from one point to another on the graph, the distance for $\frac{rise}{run}$ is being figured. The equation should be written in slope-intercept form, $y = mx + b$, with *m* representing the slope and *b* representing the *y*-intercept.

The equation of a line can also be written by identifying two points on the graph of the line. To do so, the slope is calculated and then the values are substituted for the slope and either of the ordered pairs into the point-slope form of an equation.

Vertical, Horizontal, Parallel, and Perpendicular Lines

For a vertical line, the value of *x* remains constant (for all ordered pairs (*x*, *y*) on the line, the value of *x* is the same); therefore, the equations for all vertical lines are written in the form $x = number$. For example, a vertical line that crosses the *x*-axis at -2 would have an equation of $x = -2$. For a horizontal line, the value of *y* remains constant; therefore, the equations for all horizontal lines are written in the form $y = number$.

Parallel lines extend in the same exact direction without ever meeting. Their equations have the same slopes and different *y*-intercepts. For example, given a line with an equation of $y = -3x + 2$, a parallel line would have a slope of -3 and a *y*-intercept of any value other than 2. Perpendicular lines intersect to form a right angle. Their equations have slopes that are opposite reciprocal (the sign is changed and the fraction is flipped; for example, $-\frac{2}{3}$ and $\frac{3}{2}$) and *y*-intercepts that may or may not be the same. For example, given a line with an equation of $y = \frac{1}{2}x + 7$, a perpendicular line would have a slope of $-\frac{2}{1}$ and any value for its *y*-intercept.

Functions

A **function** is defined as a relationship between inputs and outputs where there is only one output value for a given input. As an example, the following function is in function notation: $f(x) = 3x - 4$. The $f(x)$ represents the output value for an input of x. If $x = 2$, the equation becomes:

$$f(2) = 3(2) - 4 = 6 - 4 = 2$$

The input of 2 yields an output of 2, forming the ordered pair $(2, 2)$. The following set of ordered pairs corresponds to the given function: $(2, 2), (0, -4), (-2, -10)$. The set of all possible inputs of a function is its **domain**, and all possible outputs is called the **range**. By definition, each member of the domain is paired with only one member of the range.

Functions can also be defined recursively. In this form, they are not defined explicitly in terms of variables. Instead, they are defined using previously-evaluated function outputs, starting with either $f(0)$ or $f(1)$. An example of a recursively-defined function is:

$$f(1) = 2, f(n) = 2f(n - 1) + 2n, n > 1$$

The domain of this function is the set of all integers.

Interpreting Functions

A **function** is defined as a relationship between inputs and outputs where there is only one output value for a given input. As an example, the following function is in function notation: $f(x) = 3x - 4$. The $f(x)$ represents the output value for an input of x. If $x = 2$, the equation becomes $f(2) = 3(2) - 4 = 6 - 4 = 2$. The input of 2 yields an output of 2, forming the ordered pair $(2, 2)$. The following set of ordered pairs corresponds to the given function: $(2,2),(0,-4),(-2,-10)$. The set of all possible inputs of a function is its **domain**, and all possible outputs is called the **range**. By definition, each member of the domain is paired with only one member of the range.

Functions can also be defined recursively. In this form, they are not defined explicitly in terms of variables. Instead, they are defined using previously-evaluated function outputs, starting with either $f(0)$ or $f(1)$. An example of a recursively-defined function is $f(1)=2, f(n)=2f(n-1)+2n, n>1$. The domain of this function is the set of all integers.

A function $f(x)$ is a mathematical object which takes one number, *x*, as an input and gives a number in return. The input is called the **independent variable**. If the variable is set equal to the output, as in $y = f(x)$, then this is called the **dependent variable**. To indicate the dependent value a function, y, gives for a specific independent variable, x, the notation y = $f(x)$ is used.

The **domain** of a function is the set of values that the independent variable is allowed to take. Unless otherwise specified, the domain is any value for which the function is well defined. The **range** of the function is the set of possible outputs for the function.

In many cases, a function can be defined by giving an equation. For instance, $f(x)=x^2$ indicates that given a value for *x*, the output of *f* is found by squaring *x*.

Not all equations in *x* and *y* can be written in the form $y=f(x)$. An equation can be written in such a form if it satisfies the **vertical line test**: no vertical line meets the graph of the equation at more than a single point. In this case, *y* is said to be a *function of x*. If a vertical line meets the graph in two places, then this equation cannot be written in the form $y=f(x)$.

The graph of a function $f(x)$ is the graph of the equation $y=f(x)$. Thus, it is the set of all pairs (x,y) where $y=f(x)$. In other words, it is all pairs $(x,f(x))$. The *x*-intercepts are called the **zeros** of the function. The *y*-intercept is given by $f(0)$.

If, for a given function f, the only way to get $f(a)=f(b)$ is for $a=b$, then *f* is *one-to-one*. Often, even if a function is not one-to-one on its entire domain, it is one-to-one by considering a restricted portion of the domain.

A function $f(x)=k$ for some number *k* is called a **constant function**. The graph of a constant function is a horizontal line.

The function $f(x)=x$ is called the **identity function**. The graph of the identity function is the diagonal line pointing to the upper right at 45 degrees, $y=x$.

A function is called **monotone** if it is either always increasing or always decreasing. For example, the functions $f(x)=3x$ and $f(x)=-x^5$ are monotone.

An **even function** looks the same when flipped over the *y*-axis: $f(x) = f(-x)$. The following image shows a graphic representation of an even function.

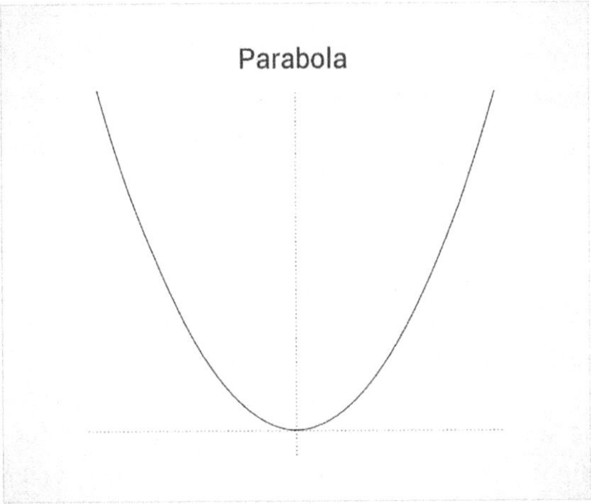

An **odd function** looks the same when flipped over the *y*-axis and then flipped over the *x*-axis: $f(x) = -f(-x)$. The following image shows an example of an odd function.

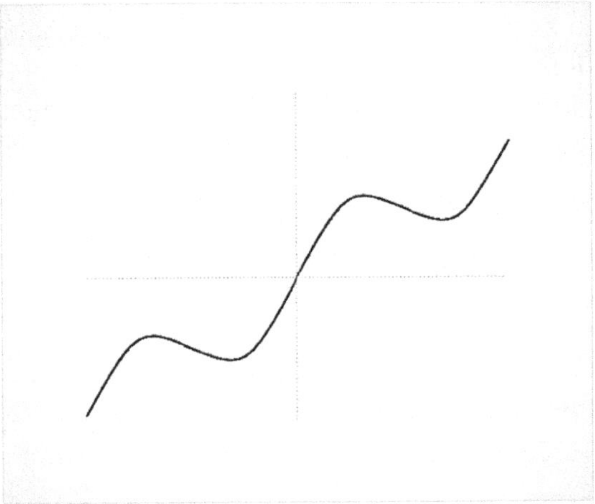

<u>Domain and Range</u>

The domain and range of a function can be found visually by its plot on the coordinate plane. In the function $f(x) = x^2 - 3$, for example, the domain is all real numbers because the parabola stretches as far left and as far right as it can go, with no restrictions. This means that any input value from the real number system will yield an answer in the real number system. For the range, the inequality $y \geq -3$ would be used to describe the possible output values because the parabola has a minimum at $y = -3$. This means there will not be any real output values less than -3 because -3 is the lowest value it reaches on the y-axis.

These same answers for domain and range can be found by observing a table. The table below shows that from input values $x = -1$ to $x = 1$, the output results in a minimum of -3. On each side of $x = 0$, the numbers increase, showing that the range is all real numbers greater than or equal to -3.

x (domain/input)	**y (range/output)**
-2	1
-1	-2
0	-3
-1	-2
2	1

<u>Function Behavior</u>

Different types of functions behave in different ways. A function is defined to be increasing over a subset of its domain if for all $x_1 \geq x_2$ in that interval, $f(x_1) \geq f(x_2)$. Also, a function is decreasing over an interval if for all $x_1 \geq x_2$ in that interval, $f(x_1) \leq f(x_2)$. A point in which a function changes from increasing to decreasing can also be labeled as the **maximum value** of a function if it is the largest point the graph reaches on the y-axis. A point in which a function changes from decreasing to increasing can be labeled as the minimum value of a function if it is the smallest point the graph reaches on the y-axis. Maximum values are also known as **extreme values**. The graph of a continuous function does not have any breaks or jumps in the graph. This description is not true of all functions. A radical function, for example, $f(x) = \sqrt{x}$, has a restriction for the domain and range because there are no real negative inputs or outputs for this function. The domain can be stated as $x \geq 0$, and the range is $y \geq 0$.

A piecewise-defined function also has a different appearance on the graph. In the following function, there are three equations defined over different intervals. It is a function because there is only one y-value for each x-value, passing the Vertical Line Test. The domain is all real numbers less than or equal to 6. The range is all real numbers greater than zero. From left to right, the graph decreases to zero, then increases to almost 4, and then jumps to 6.

From input values greater than 2, the input decreases just below 8 to 4, and then stops.

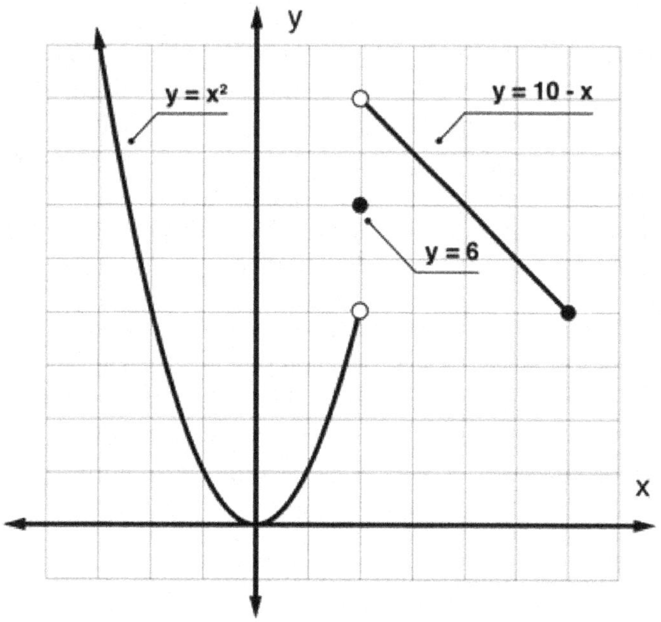

Logarithmic and exponential functions also have different behavior than other functions. These two types of functions are inverses of each other. The **inverse** of a function can be found by switching the place of x and y, and solving for y. When this is done for the exponential equation, $y = 2^x$, the function $y = \log_2 x$ is found. The general form of a **logarithmic function** is $y = log_b x$, which says b raised to the y power equals x.

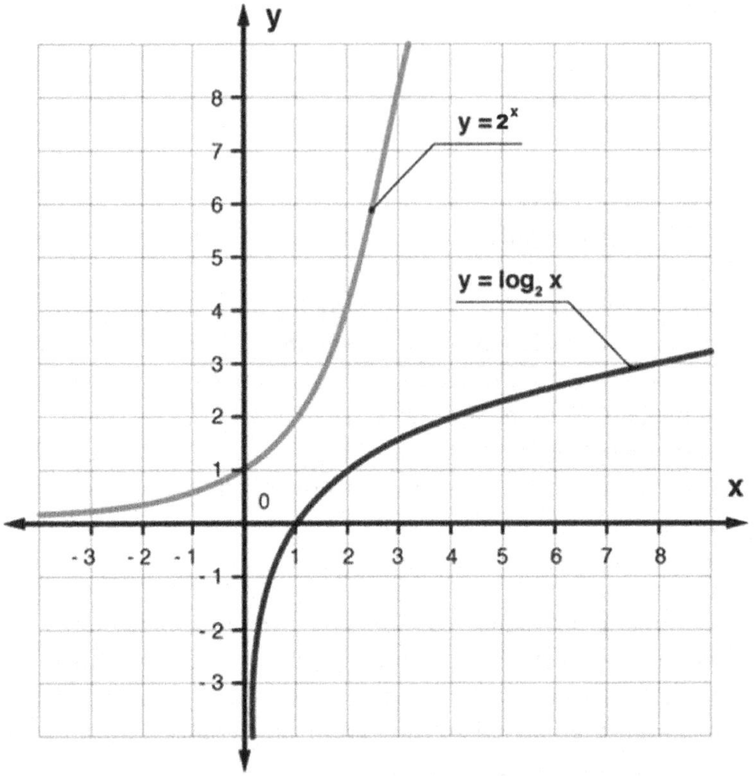

The thick black line on the graph above represents the logarithmic function $y = \log_2 x$. This curve passes through the point $(1, 0)$, just as all log functions do, because any value $b^0 = 1$. The graph of this logarithmic function starts very close to zero but does not touch the y-axis. The output value will never be zero by the definition of logarithms. The thinner gray line seen above represents the exponential function $y = 2^x$. The behavior of this function is opposite the logarithmic function because the graph of an inverse function is the graph of the original function flipped over the line $y = x$. The curve passes through the point $(0, 1)$ because any number raised to the zero power is one. This curve also gets very close to the x-axis but never touches it because an exponential expression never has an output of zero. The x-axis on this graph is called a horizontal asymptote. An **asymptote** is a line that represents a boundary for a function. It shows a value that the function will get close to, but never reach.

Functions can also be described as being even, odd, or neither. If $f(-x) = f(x)$, the function is even. For example, the function $f(x) = x^2 - 2$ is even. Plugging in $x = 2$ yields an output of $y = 2$. After changing the input to $x = -2$, the output is still $y = 2$. The output is the same for opposite inputs. Another way to observe an even function is by the symmetry of the graph. If the graph is symmetrical about the axis, then the function is even. If the graph is symmetric about the origin, then the function is odd. Algebraically, if $f(-x) = -f(x)$, the function is odd.

Also, a function can be described as **periodic** if it repeats itself in regular intervals. Common periodic functions are trigonometric functions. For example, $y = \sin x$ is a periodic function with period 2π because it repeats itself every 2π units along the x-axis.

Common Functions

Three common functions used to model different relationships between quantities are linear, quadratic, and exponential functions. **Linear functions** are the simplest of the three, and the independent variable x has an exponent of 1. Written in the most common form, $y = mx + b$, the coefficient of x tells how fast the function grows at a constant rate, and the b-value tells the starting point. A **quadratic** function has an exponent of 2 on the independent variable x. Standard form for this type of function is $y = ax^2 + bx + c$, and the graph is a parabola. These type functions grow at a changing rate. An **exponential** function has an independent variable in the exponent $y = ab^x$. The graph of these types of functions is described as **growth** or **decay**, based on whether the base, b, is greater than or less than 1. These functions are different from quadratic functions because the base stays constant. A common base is base e.

The following three functions model a linear, quadratic, and exponential function respectively: $y = 2x$, $y = x^2$, and $y = 2^x$. Their graphs are shown below. The first graph, modeling the linear function, shows that the growth is constant over each interval. With a horizontal change of 1, the vertical change is 2. It models a constant positive growth. The second graph shows the quadratic function, which is a curve that is symmetric across the y-axis. The growth is not constant, but the change is mirrored over the axis. The last graph models the exponential function, where the horizontal change of 1 yields a vertical change that increases more and more. The exponential graph gets very close to the x-axis, but never touches it, meaning there is an asymptote there. The y-value can never be zero because the base of 2 can never be raised to an input value that yields an output of zero.

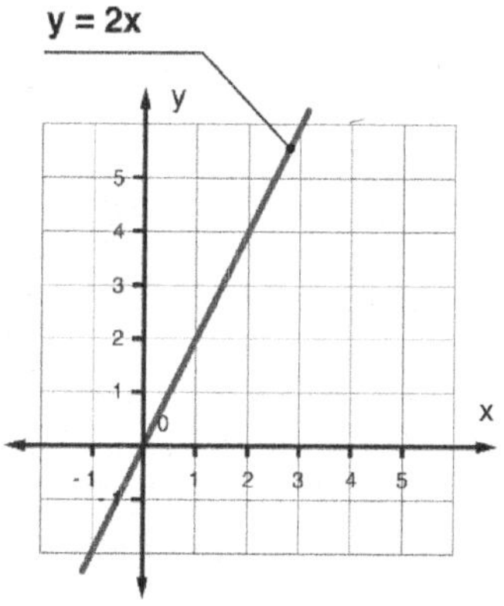

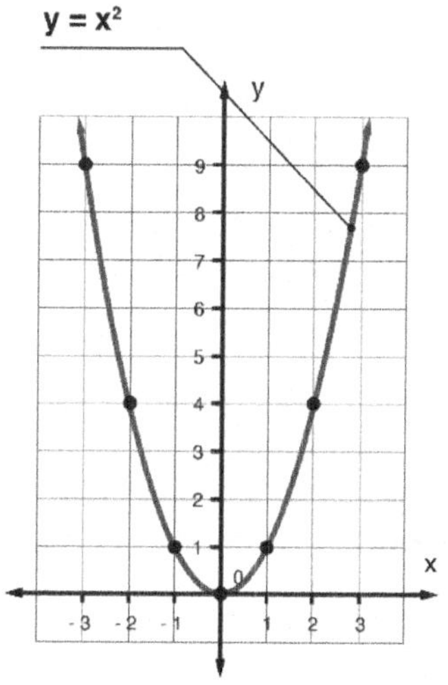

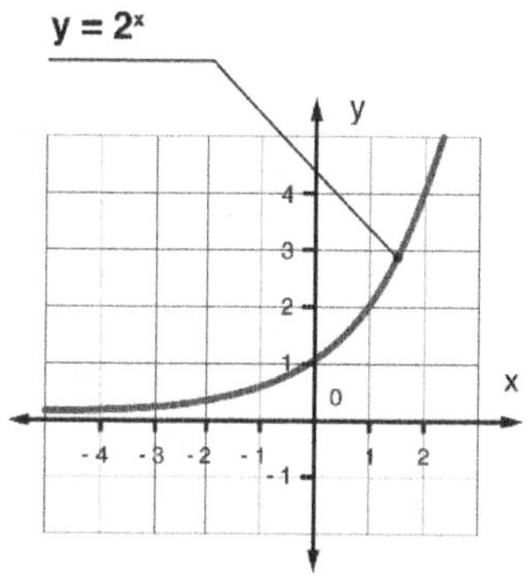

The three tables below show specific values for three types of functions. The third column in each table shows the change in the y-values for each interval. The first table shows a constant change of 2 for each equal interval, which matches the slope in the equation $y = 2x$. The second table shows an increasing change, but it also has a pattern. The increase is changing by 2 more each time, so the change is quadratic. The third table shows the change as factors of the base, 2. It shows a continuing pattern of factors of the base.

y = 2x		
x	y	Δy
1	2	
2	4	2
3	6	2
4	8	2
5	10	2

y = x²		
x	y	Δy
1	1	
2	4	3
3	9	5
4	16	7
5	25	9

$y = 2^x$		
x	y	Δy
1	2	
2	4	2
3	8	4
4	16	8
5	32	16

Given a table of values, the type of function can be determined by observing the change in y over equal intervals. For example, the tables below model two functions. The changes in interval for the x-values is 1 for both tables. For the first table, the y-values increase by 5 for each interval. Since the change is constant, the situation can be described as a linear function. The equation would be $y = 5x + 3$. For the second table, the change for y is 5, 20, 100, and 500, respectively. The increases are multiples of 5, meaning the situation can be modeled by an exponential function. The equation $y = 5^x + 3$ models this situation.

x	y
0	3
1	8
2	13
3	18
4	23

x	y
0	3
1	8
2	28
3	128
4	628

Quadratic equations can be used to model real-world area problems. For example, a farmer may have a rectangular field that he needs to sow with seed. The field has length $x + 8$ and width $2x$. The formula for area should be used: $A = lw$. Therefore:

$$A = (x + 8) \times 2x = 2x^2 + 16x$$

The possible values for the length and width can be shown in a table, with input x and output A. If the equation was graphed, the possible area values can be seen on the y-axis for given x-values.

Exponential growth and decay can be found in real-world situations. For example, if a piece of notebook paper is folded 25 times, the thickness of the paper can be found. To model this situation, a table can be used. The initial point is one-fold, which yields a thickness of 2 papers. For the second fold, the thickness is 4. Since the thickness doubles each time, the table below shows the thickness for the next few folds. Notice the thickness changes by the same factor each time. Since this change for a constant interval of folds is a factor of 2, the function is exponential. The equation for this is $y = 2^x$. For twenty-five folds, the thickness would be 33,554,432 papers.

x (folds)	y (paper thickness)
0	1
1	2
2	4
3	8
4	16
5	32

One exponential formula that is commonly used is the **interest formula**: $A = Pe^{rt}$. In this formula, interest is compounded continuously. A is the value of the investment after the time, t, in years. P is the initial amount of the investment, r is the interest rate, and e is the constant equal to approximately 2.718. Given an initial amount of $200 and a time of 3 years, if interest is compounded continuously at a rate of 6%, the total investment value can be found by plugging each value into the formula. The invested value at the end is $239.44. In more complex problems, the final investment may be given, and the rate may be the unknown. In this case, the formula becomes $239.44 = 200e^{r3}$. Solving for r requires isolating the exponential expression on one side by dividing by 200, yielding the equation $1.20 = e^{r3}$. Taking the natural log of both sides results in $\ln(1.2) = r3$. Using a calculator to evaluate the logarithmic expression, $r = 0.06 = 6\%$.

When working with logarithms and exponential expressions, it is important to remember the relationship between the two. In general, the logarithmic form is $y = log_b x$ for an exponential form $b^y = x$. Logarithms and exponential functions are inverses of each other.

Building a Function

Functions can be built out of the context of a situation. For example, the relationship between the money paid for a gym membership and the months that someone has been a member can be described through a function. If the one-time membership fee is $40 and the monthly fee is $30, then the function can be written $f(x) = 30x + 40$. The x-value represents the number of months the person has been part of the gym, while the output is the total money paid for the membership. The table below shows this relationship. It is a representation of the function because the initial cost is $40 and the cost increases each month by $30.

x (months)	y (money paid to gym)
0	40
1	70
2	100
3	130

Functions can also be built from existing functions. For example, a given function $f(x)$ can be transformed by adding a constant, multiplying by a constant, or changing the input value by a constant. The new function $g(x) = f(x) + k$ represents a vertical shift of the original function. In $f(x) = 3x - 2$, a vertical shift 4 units up would be:

$$g(x) = 3x - 2 + 4 = 3x + 2$$

Multiplying the function times a constant k represents a vertical stretch, based on whether the constant is greater than or less than 1. The function

$$g(x) = kf(x) = 4(3x - 2) = 12x - 8$$

represents a stretch. Changing the input x by a constant forms the function:

$$g(x) = f(x + k) = 3(x + 4) - 2 = 3x + 12 - 2 = 3x + 10$$

and this represents a horizontal shift to the left 4 units. If $(x - 4)$ was plugged into the function, it would represent a vertical shift.

A composition function can also be formed by plugging one function into another. In function notation, this is written:

$$(f \circ g)(x) = f(g(x))$$

For two functions $f(x) = x^2$ and $g(x) = x - 3$, the composition function becomes:

$$f\big(g(x)\big) = (x - 3)^2 = x^2 - 6x + 9$$

The composition of functions can also be used to verify if two functions are inverses of each other. Given the two functions $f(x) = 2x + 5$ and $g(x) = \frac{x-5}{2}$, the composition function can be found $(f \circ g)(x)$. Solving this equation yields:

$$f\big(g(x)\big) = 2\left(\frac{x - 5}{2}\right) + 5 = x - 5 + 5 = x$$

It also is true that $g\big(f(x)\big) = x$. Since the composition of these two functions gives a simplified answer of x, this verifies that $f(x)$ and $g(x)$ are inverse functions. The domain of $f(g(x))$ is the set of all x-values in the domain of $g(x)$ such that $g(x)$ is in the domain of $f(x)$. Basically, both $f(g(x))$ and $g(x)$ have to be defined.

To build an inverse of a function, $f(x)$ needs to be replaced with y, and the x and y values need to be switched. Then, the equation can be solved for y. For example, given the equation $y = e^{2x}$, the inverse can be found by rewriting the equation $x = e^{2y}$. The natural logarithm of both sides is taken down, and the exponent is brought down to form the equation:

$$\ln(x) = \ln(e)\, 2y$$

$\ln(e)$=1, which yields the equation $\ln(x) = 2y$. Dividing both sides by 2 yields the inverse equation

$$\frac{\ln(x)}{2} = y = f^{-1}(x)$$

The domain of an inverse function is the range of the original function, and the range of an inverse function is the domain of the original function. Therefore, an ordered pair (x, y) on either a graph or a table corresponding to $f(x)$ means that the ordered pair (y, x) exists on the graph of $f^{-1}(x)$. Basically, if $f(x) = y$, then $f^{-1}(y) = x$. For a function to have an inverse, it must be one-to-one. That means it must pass the **Horizontal Line Test**, and if any horizontal line passes through the graph of the function twice, a function is not one-to-one. The domain of a function that is not one-to-one can be restricted to an interval in which the function is one-to-one, to be able to define an inverse function.

Functions can also be formed from combinations of existing functions.

Given $f(x)$ and $g(x)$, the following can be built:

$$f + g$$

$$f - g$$

$$fg$$

$$\frac{f}{g}$$

The domains of $f + g, f - g,$ and fg are the intersection of the domains of f and g. The domain of $\frac{f}{g}$ is the same set, excluding those values that make $g(x) = 0$.

For example, if:

$$f(x) = 2x + 3$$

$$g(x) = x + 1$$

then

$$\frac{f}{g} = \frac{2x + 3}{x + 1}$$

Its domain is all real numbers except -1.

Geometry

Relationships Between Geometric Figures

Sometimes, two figures are similar, meaning they have the same basic shape and the same interior angles, but they have different dimensions. If the ratio of two corresponding sides is known, then that ratio, or scale factor, holds true for all of the dimensions of the new figure.

Here is an example of applying this principle. Suppose that Lara is 5 feet tall and is standing 30 feet from the base of a light pole, and her shadow is 6 feet long. How high is the light on the pole? To figure this, it helps to make a sketch of the situation:

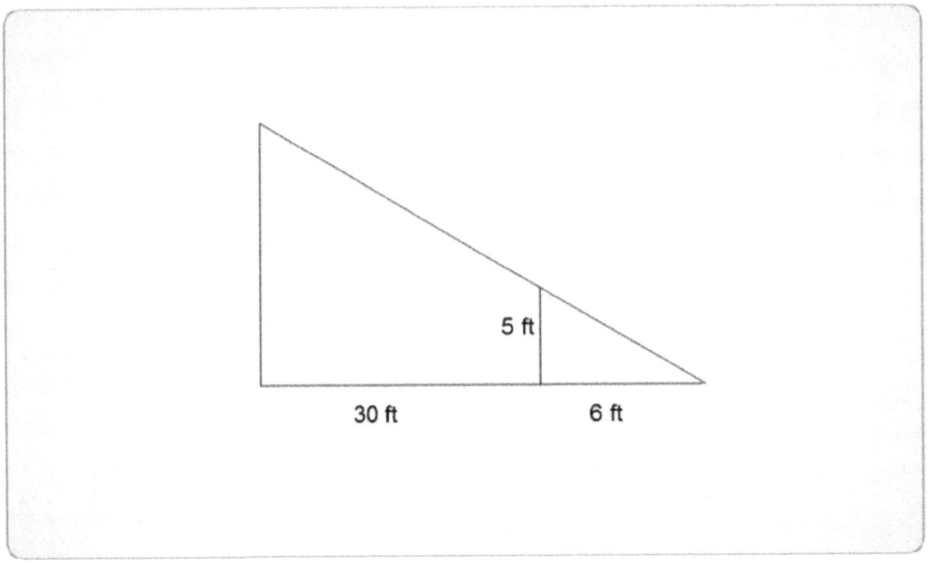

The light pole is the left side of the triangle. Lara is the 5-foot vertical line. Notice that there are two right triangles here, and that they have all the same angles as one another. Therefore, they form similar triangles. So, figure the ratio of proportionality between them.

The bases of these triangles are known. The small triangle, formed by Lara and her shadow, has a base of 6 feet. The large triangle, formed by the light pole along with the line from the base of the pole out to the end of Lara's shadow is $30 + 6 = 36$ feet long. So, the ratio of the big triangle to the little triangle will be $\frac{36}{6} = 6$. The height of the little triangle is 5 feet. Therefore, the height of the big triangle will be $6 \times 5 = 30$ feet, meaning that the light is 30 feet up the pole.

Notice that the perimeter of a figure changes by the ratio of proportionality between two similar figures, but the area changes by the *square* of the ratio. This is because if the length of one side is doubled, the area is quadrupled.

As an example, suppose two rectangles are similar, but the edges of the second rectangle are three times longer than the edges of the first rectangle. The area of the first rectangle is 10 square inches. How much more area does the second rectangle have than the first?

To answer this, note that the area of the second rectangle is $3^2 = 9$ times the area of the first rectangle, which is 10 square inches. Therefore, the area of the second rectangle is going to be $9 \times 10 = 90$ square inches. This means it has $90 - 10 = 80$ square inches more area than the first rectangle.

As a second example, suppose *X* and *Y* are similar right triangles. The hypotenuse of *X* is 4 inches. The area of *Y* is $\frac{1}{4}$ the area of *X*. What is the hypotenuse of *Y*?

First, realize the area has changed by a factor of $\frac{1}{4}$. The area changes by a factor that is the *square* of the ratio of changes in lengths, so the ratio of the lengths is the square root of the ratio of areas. That means that the ratio of lengths must be is $\sqrt{\frac{1}{4}} = \frac{1}{2}$, and the hypotenuse of *Y* must be $\frac{1}{2} \times 4 = 2$ inches.

Volumes between similar solids change like the cube of the change in the lengths of their edges. Likewise, if the ratio of the volumes between similar solids is known, the ratio between their lengths is known by finding the cube root of the ratio of their volumes.

For example, suppose there are two similar rectangular pyramids *X* and *Y*. The base of *X* is 1 inch by 2 inches, and the volume of *X* is 8 inches. The volume of *Y* is 64 inches. What are the dimensions of the base of *Y*?

To answer this, first find the ratio of the volume of *Y* to the volume of *X*. This will be given by $\frac{64}{8} = 8$. Now the ratio of lengths is the cube root of the ratio of volumes, or $\sqrt[3]{8} = 2$. So, the dimensions of the base of *Y* must be 2 inches by 4 inches.

Cross Sections and Rotations

Two-dimensional objects are formed when three-dimensional objects are "sliced" in various ways. For example, any cross section of a sphere is a circle. Some three-dimensional objects have different cross sections depending on how the object is sliced. For example, the cross section of a cylinder can be a circle or a rectangle, and the cross section of a pyramid can be a square or a triangle. In addition, three-dimensional objects can be formed by rotating two-dimensional objects. Certain rotations can relate the two-dimensional cross sections back to the original three-dimensional objects. The objects must be rotated around an imaginary line known as the **rotation axis**. For example, a right triangle can be rotated around one of its legs to form a cone. A sphere can be formed by rotating a semicircle around a line segment formed from its diameter. Finally, rotating a square around one of its sides forms a cylinder.

Simplifying Three-Dimensional Objects

Three-dimensional objects can be simplified into related two-dimensional shapes to solve problems. This simplification can make problem-solving a much easier experience. An isometric representation of a three-dimensional object can be completed so that important properties (e.g., shape, relationships of faces and surfaces) are noted. Edges and vertices can be translated into two-dimensional objects as well.

For example, below is a three-dimensional object that's been partitioned into two-dimensional representations of its faces:

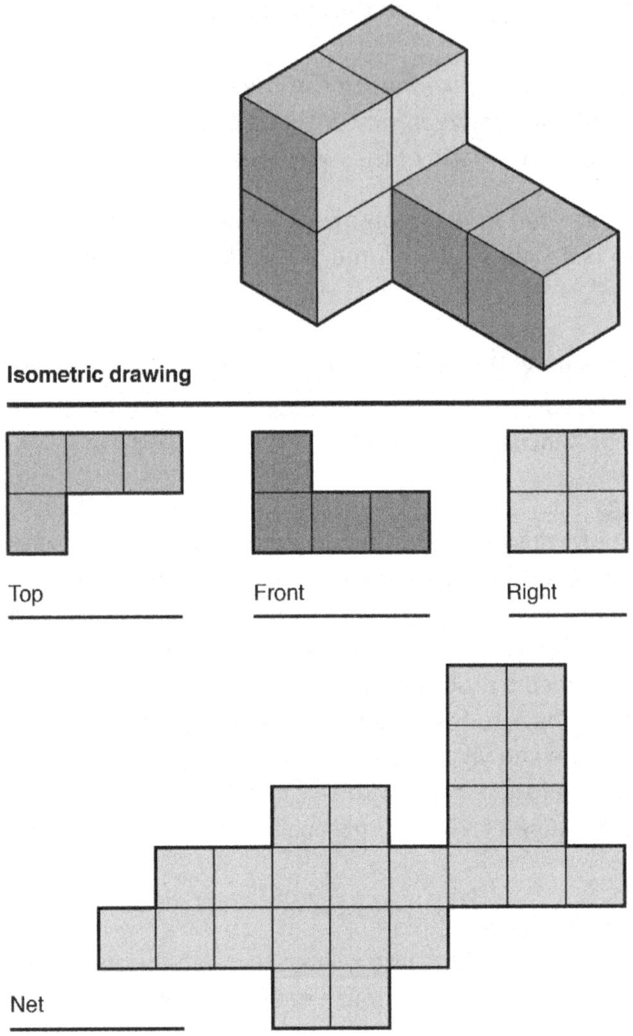

The net represents the sum of the three different faces. Depending on the problem, using a smaller portion of the given shape may be helpful, by simplifying the steps necessary to solve.

Transformations of a Plane

Given a figure drawn on a plane, many changes can be made to that figure, including rotation, translation, and reflection. **Rotations** turn the figure about a point, **translations** slide the figure, and **reflections** flip the figure over a specified line. When performing these transformations, the original figure is called the **pre-image**, and the figure after transformation is called the **image**.

More specifically, **translation** means that all points in the figure are moved in the same direction by the same distance. In other words, the figure is slid in some fixed direction. Of course, while the entire figure is slid by the same distance, this does not change any of the measurements of the figures involved. The result will have the same distances and angles as the original figure.

In terms of Cartesian coordinates, a translation means a shift of each of the original points (x, y) by a fixed amount in the *x* and *y* directions, to become $(x + a, y + b)$.

Another procedure that can be performed is called **reflection**. To do this, a line in the plane is specified, called the **line of reflection**. Then, take each point and flip it over the line so that it is the same distance from the line but on the opposite side of it. This does not change any of the distances or angles involved, but it does reverse the order in which everything appears.

To reflect something over the *x*-axis, the points (x, y) are sent to $(x, -y)$. To reflect something over the *y*-axis, the points (x, y) are sent to the points $(-x, y)$. Flipping over other lines is not something easy to express in Cartesian coordinates. However, by drawing the figure and the line of reflection, the distance to the line and the original points can be used to find the reflected figure.

Example: Reflect this triangle with vertices (-1, 0), (2, 1), and (2, 0) over the *y*-axis. The pre-image is shown below.

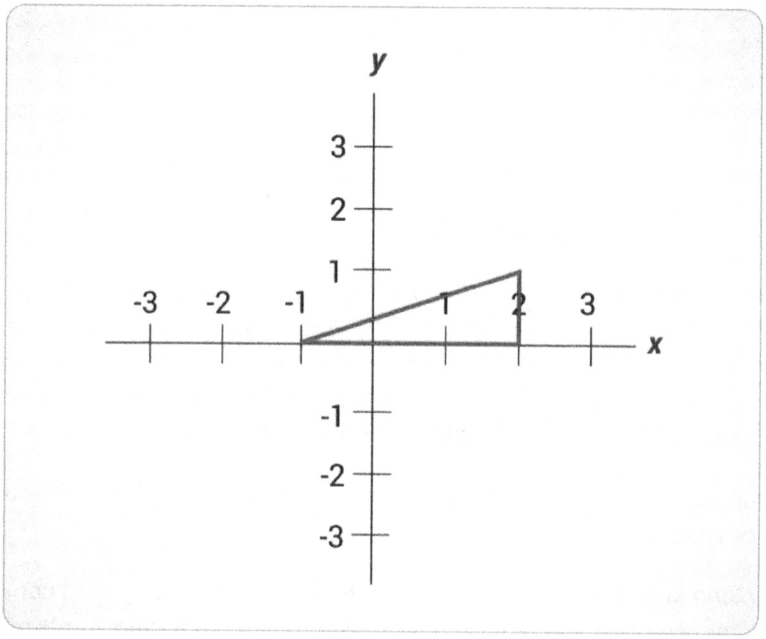

To do this, flip the *x* values of the points involved to the negatives of themselves, while keeping the *y* values the same. The image is shown here.

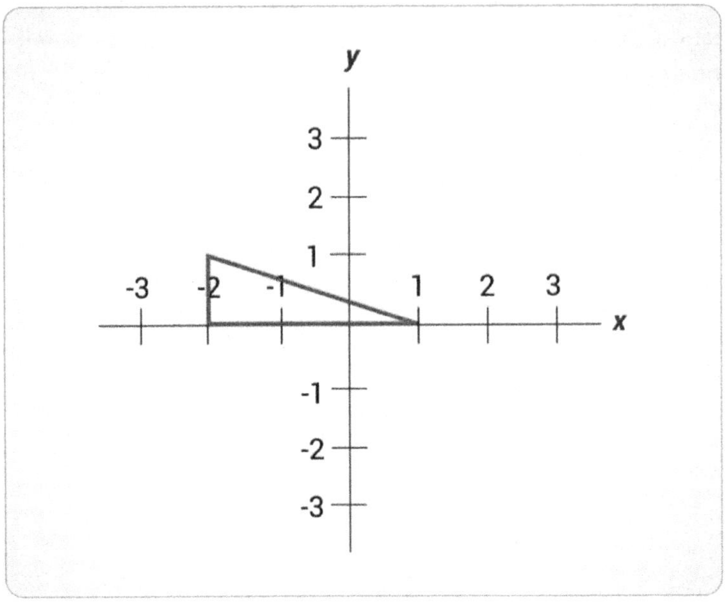

The new vertices will be (1, 0), (-2, 1), and (-2, 0).

Another procedure that does not change the distances and angles in a figure is **rotation**. In this procedure, pick a center point, then rotate every vertex along a circle around that point by the same angle. This procedure is also not easy to express in Cartesian coordinates, and this is not a requirement on this test. However, as with reflections, it's helpful to draw the figures and see what the result of the rotation would look like. This transformation can be performed using a compass and protractor.

Each one of these transformations can be performed on the coordinate plane without changes to the original dimensions or angles.

If two figures in the plane involve the same distances and angles, they are called **congruent figures**. In other words, two figures are congruent when they go from one form to another through reflection, rotation, and translation, or a combination of these.

Remember that rotation and translation will give back a new figure that is identical to the original figure, but reflection will give back a mirror image of it.

To recognize that a figure has undergone a rotation, check to see that the figure has not been changed into a mirror image, but that its orientation has changed (that is, whether the parts of the figure now form different angles with the *x* and *y* axes).

To recognize that a figure has undergone a translation, check to see that the figure has not been changed into a mirror image, and that the orientation remains the same.

To recognize that a figure has undergone a reflection, check to see that the new figure is a mirror image of the old figure.

Keep in mind that sometimes a combination of translations, reflections, and rotations may be performed on a figure.

Dilation

A **dilation** is a transformation that preserves angles, but not distances. This can be thought of as stretching or shrinking a figure. If a dilation makes figures larger, it is called an **enlargement**. If a dilation makes figures smaller, it is called a **reduction**. The easiest example is to dilate around the origin. In this case, multiply the *x* and *y* coordinates by a **scale factor**, k, sending points (x, y) to (kx, ky).

As an example, draw a dilation of the following triangle, whose vertices will be the points (-1, 0), (1, 0), and (1, 1).

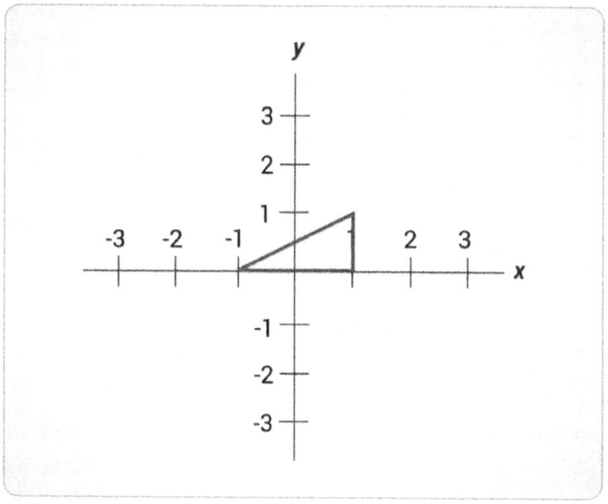

For this problem, dilate by a scale factor of 2, so the new vertices will be (-2, 0), (2, 0), and (2, 2).

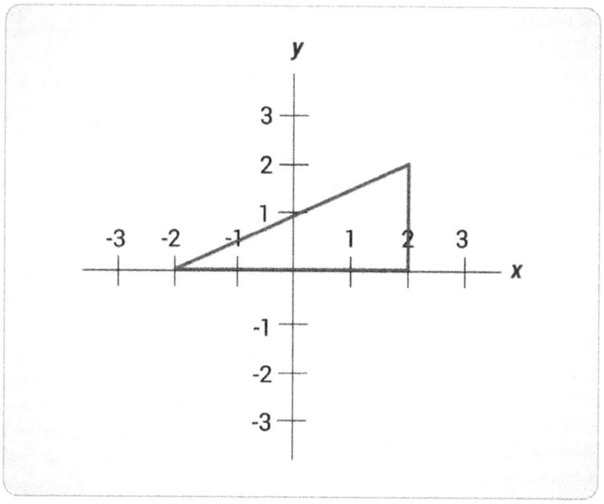

Note that after a dilation, the distances between the vertices of the figure will have changed, but the angles remain the same. The two figures that are obtained by dilation, along with possibly translation, rotation, and reflection, are all *similar* to one another. Another way to think of this is that similar figures have the same number of vertices and edges, and their angles are all the same. Similar figures have the same basic shape but are different in size.

Symmetry

Using the types of transformations above, if an object can undergo these changes and not appear to have changed, then the figure is symmetrical. If an object can be split in half by a line and flipped over that line to lie directly on top of itself, it is said to have **line symmetry**. An example of both types of figures is seen below.

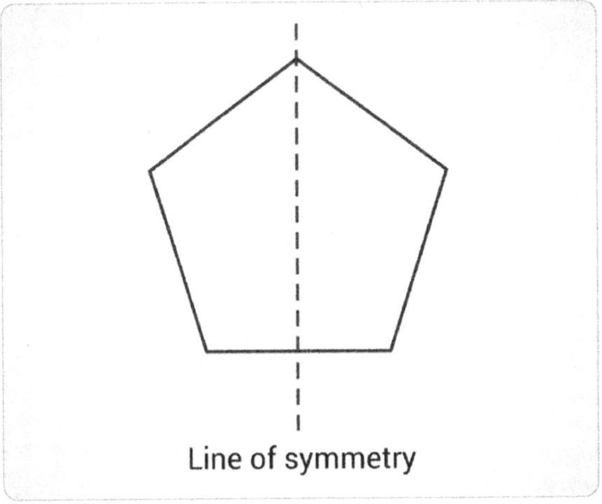

If an object can be rotated about its center to any degree smaller than 360, and it lies directly on top of itself, the object is said to have **rotational symmetry**. An example of this type of symmetry is shown below. The pentagon has an order of 5.

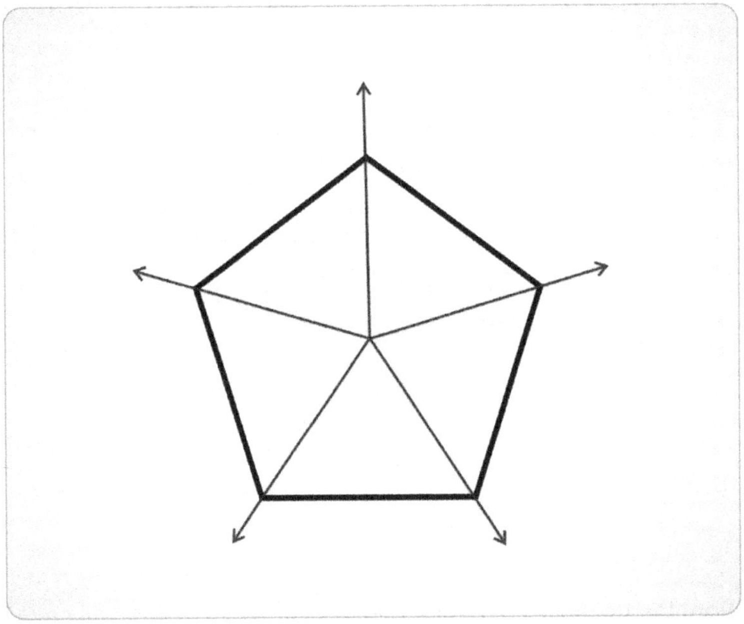

The rotational symmetry lines in the figure above can be used to find the angles formed at the center of the pentagon. Knowing that all of the angles together form a full circle, at 360 degrees, the figure can be split into 5 angles equally. By dividing the 360° by 5, each angle is 72°.

Given the length of one side of the figure, the perimeter of the pentagon can also be found using rotational symmetry. If one side length was 3 cm, that side length can be rotated onto each other side length four times. This would give a total of 5 side lengths equal to 3 cm. To find the perimeter, or distance around the figure, multiply 3 by 5. The perimeter of the figure would be 15 cm.

If a line cannot be drawn anywhere on the object to flip the figure onto itself or rotated less than or equal to 180 degrees to lay on top of itself, the object is asymmetrical. Examples of these types of figures are shown below.

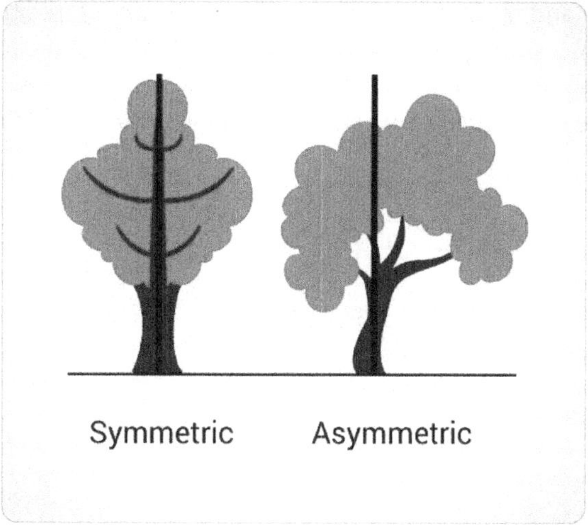

Right Triangles

The Pythagorean Theorem and Right Triangles

<u>Trigonometric Functions</u>

Within similar triangles, corresponding sides are proportional, and angles are congruent. In addition, within similar triangles, the ratio of the side lengths is the same. This property is true even if side lengths are different. Within right triangles, trigonometric ratios can be defined for the acute angle within the triangle. The functions are defined through ratios in a right triangle. Sine of acute angle, A, is opposite over hypotenuse, cosine is adjacent over hypotenuse, and tangent is opposite over adjacent. Note that expanding or shrinking the triangle won't change the ratios. However, changing the angle measurements will alter the calculations.

Complementary Angles

Angles that add up to 90 degrees are **complementary**. Within a right triangle, two complementary angles exist because the third angle is always 90 degrees. In this scenario, the **sine** of one of the complementary angles is equal to the **cosine** of the other angle. The opposite is also true. This relationship exists because sine and cosine will be calculated as the ratios of the same side lengths.

The Pythagorean Theorem

The Pythagorean theorem is an important result in geometry. It states that for right triangles, the sum of the squares of the two shorter sides will be equal to the square of the longest side (also called the **hypotenuse**). The longest side will always be the side opposite to the 90° angle. If this side is called *c*, and the other two sides are *a* and *b*, then the Pythagorean theorem states that $c^2 = a^2 + b^2$. Since lengths are always positive, this also can be written as $c = \sqrt{a^2 + b^2}$.

A diagram to show the parts of a triangle using the Pythagorean theorem is below.

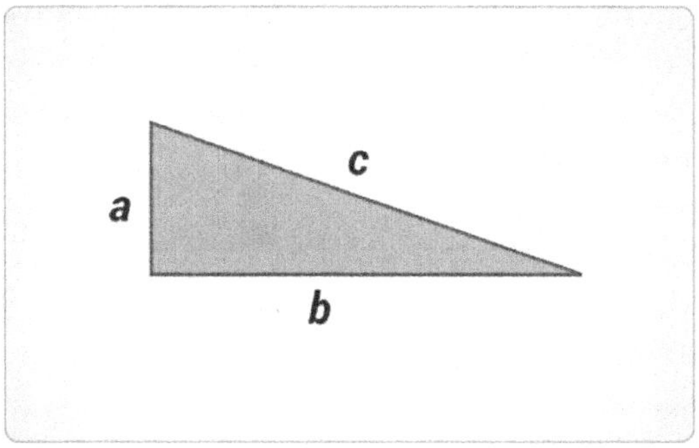

As an example of the theorem, suppose that Shirley has a rectangular field that is 5 feet wide and 12 feet long, and she wants to split it in half using a fence that goes from one corner to the opposite corner. How long will this fence need to be? To figure this out, note that this makes the field into two right triangles, whose hypotenuse will be the fence dividing it in half. Therefore, the fence length will be given by $\sqrt{5^2 + 12^2} = \sqrt{169} = 13$ feet long.

Circle Theorems

Circle Angles

The **radius** of a circle is the distance from the center of the circle to any point on the circle. A **chord** of a circle is a straight line formed when its endpoints are allowed to be any two points on the circle. Many angles exist within a circle. A **central angle** is formed by using two radii as its rays and the center of the circle as its vertex. An inscribed angle is formed by using two chords as its rays, and its vertex is a point on the circle itself. Finally, a **circumscribed angle** has a vertex that is a point outside the circle and rays that intersect with the circle. Some relationships exist between these types of angles, and, in order to define these relationships, arc measure must be understood. An **arc** of a circle is a portion of the circumference. Finding the **arc measure** is the same as finding the degree measure of the central angle that intersects the circle to form the arc. The measure of an inscribed angle is half the measure of its intercepted arc. It's also true that the measure of a circumscribed angle is equal to 180 degrees minus the measure of the central angle that forms the arc in the angle.

Quadrilateral Angles

If a quadrilateral is inscribed in a circle, the sum of its opposite angles is 180 degrees. Consider the quadrilateral ABCD centered at the point O:

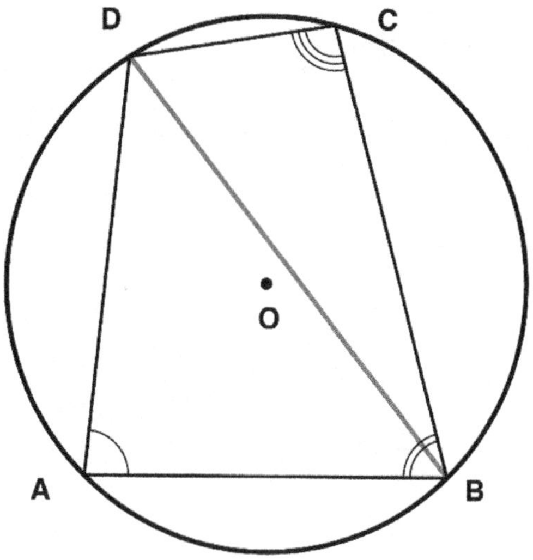

Each of the four-line segments within the quadrilateral is a chord of the circle. Consider the diagonal DB. Angle DAB is an inscribed angle leaning on the arc DCB. Therefore, angle DAB is half the measure of the arc DCB. Conversely, angle DCB is an inscribed angle leaning on the arc DAB. Therefore, angle DCB is half the measure of the arc DAB. The sum of arcs DCB and DAB is 360 degrees because they make up the entire circle. Therefore, the sum of angles DAB and DCB equals half of 360 degrees, which is 180 degrees.

Circle Lines

A **tangent line** is a line that touches a curve at a single point without going through it. A **compass** and a **straight edge** are the tools necessary to construct a tangent line from a point *P* outside the circle to the circle. A tangent line is constructed by drawing a line segment from the center of the circle *O* to the point *P*, and then finding its midpoint *M* by bisecting the line segment. By using *M* as the center, a compass is used to draw a circle through points *O* and *P*. *N* is defined as the intersection of the two circles. Finally, a line segment is drawn through *P* and *N*. This is the tangent line. Each point on a circle has only one tangent line, which is perpendicular to the radius at that point. A line similar to a tangent line is a **secant line**. Instead of intersecting the circle at one point, a secant line intersects the circle at two points. A **chord** is a smaller portion of a secant line.

Here's an example:

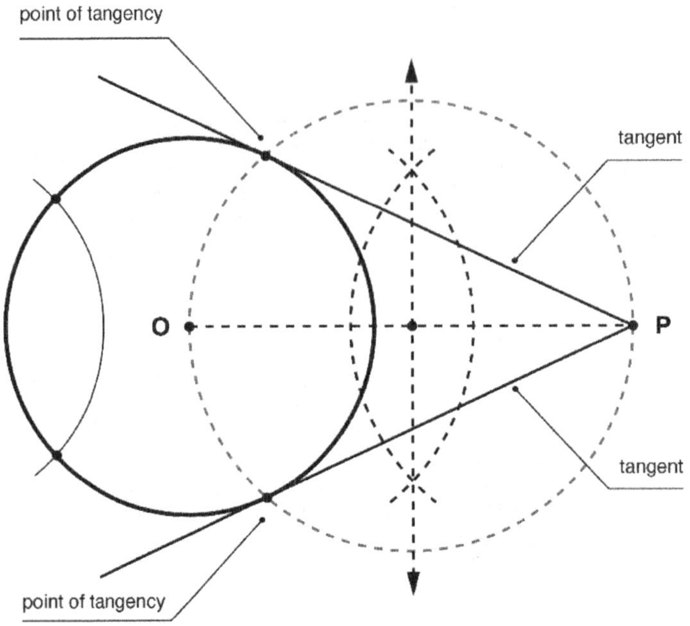

Problems Involving Angle Measure, Area, Perimeter, Surface Area, and Volume

Classification of Angles

An angle consists of two rays that have a common endpoint. This common endpoint is called the vertex of the angle. The two rays can be called sides of the angle. The angle below has a vertex at point *B* and the sides consist of ray *BA* and ray *BC*. An angle can be named in three ways:

1. Using the vertex and a point from each side, with the vertex letter in the middle.
2. Using only the vertex. This can only be used if it is the only angle with that vertex.
3. Using a number that is written inside the angle.

The angle below can be written $\angle ABC$ (read angle *ABC*), $\angle CBA$, $\angle B$, or $\angle 1$.

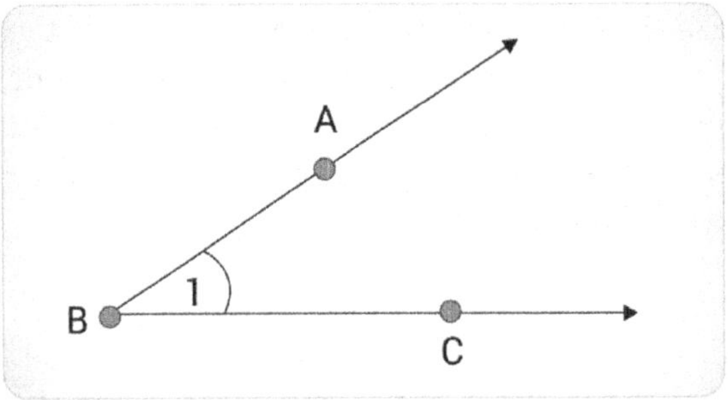

An angle divides a plane, or flat surface, into three parts: the angle itself, the interior (inside) of the angle, and the exterior (outside) of the angle. The figure below shows point *M* on the interior of the angle and point *N* on the exterior of the angle.

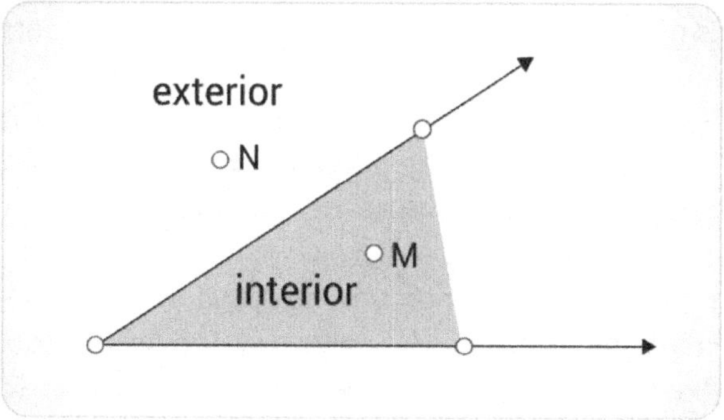

Angles can be measured in units called degrees, with the symbol °. The degree measure of an angle is between 0° and 180° and can be obtained by using a protractor.

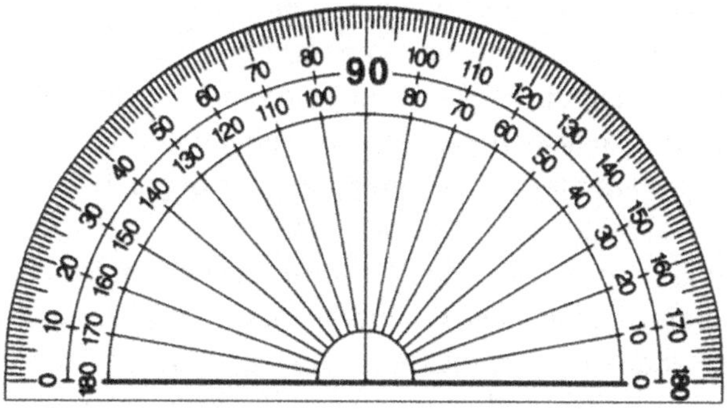

A straight angle (or simply a line) measures exactly 180°. A right angle's sides meet at the vertex to create a square corner. A right angle measures exactly 90° and is typically indicated by a box drawn in the interior of the angle. An acute angle has an interior that is narrower than a right angle. The measure of an acute angle is any value less than 90° and greater than 0°. For example, 89.9°, 47°, 12°, and 1°. An obtuse angle has an interior that is wider than a right angle. The measure of an obtuse angle is any value greater than 90° but less than 180°. For example, 90.1°, 110°, 150°, and 179.9°.

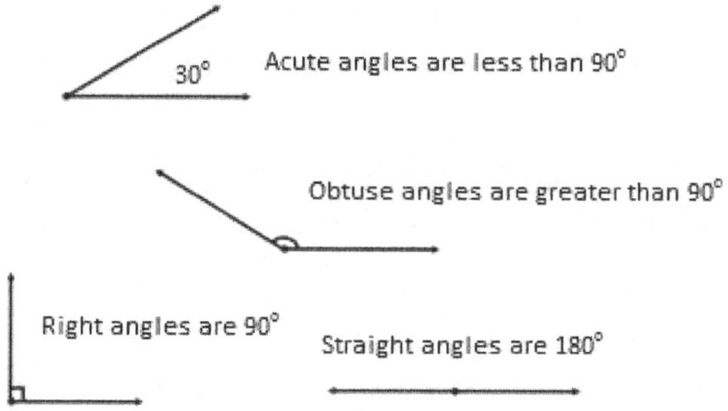

Solving Line Problems

Two lines are parallel if they have the same slope and different intercept. Two lines are perpendicular if the product of their slope equals -1. Parallel lines never intersect unless they are the same line, and perpendicular lines intersect at a right angle. If two lines aren't parallel, they must intersect at one point. Determining equations of lines based on properties of parallel and perpendicular lines appears in word problems. To find an equation of a line, both the slope and a point the line goes through are necessary. Therefore, if an equation of a line is needed that's parallel to a given line and runs through a specified point, the slope of the given line and the point are plugged into the point-slope form of an equation of a line. Secondly, if an equation of a line is needed that's perpendicular to a given line running through a specified point, the negative reciprocal of the slope of the given line and the point are plugged into the point-slope form. Also, if the point of intersection of two lines is known, that point will be used to solve the set of equations. Therefore, to solve a system of equations, the point of intersection must be found. If a set of two equations with two unknown variables has no solution, the lines are parallel.

Angles, Circles, Line Segments, Perpendicular Lines, and Parallel Lines

In geometry, a **line** connects two points, has no thickness, and extends indefinitely in both directions beyond each point. If the length is finite, it's known as a **line segment** and has two **endpoints**. A **ray** is the straight portion of a line that has one endpoint and extends indefinitely in the other direction. An **angle** is formed when two rays begin at the same endpoint and extend indefinitely. The endpoint of an angle is called a **vertex**. **Adjacent angles** are two side-by-side angles formed from the same ray that have the same endpoint. Angles are measured in **degrees** or **radians**, which is a measure of **rotation**. A **full rotation** equals 360 degrees or 2π radians, which represents a circle. Half a rotation equals 180 degrees or π radians and represents a half-circle. Angle measurement is additive. When an angle is broken into two non-overlapping angles, the total measure of the larger angle equals the sum of the two smaller angles. Lines are **coplanar** if they're located in the same plane. Two lines are **parallel** if they are coplanar, extend in the same direction, and never cross. If lines do cross, they're labeled as **intersecting lines** because they "intersect" at one point. If they intersect at more than one point, they're the same line. **Perpendicular lines** are coplanar lines that form a right angle at their point of intersection.

Perimeter and Area

Perimeter is the measurement of a distance around something or the sum of all sides of a polygon. Think of perimeter as the length of the boundary, like a fence. In contrast, **area** is the space occupied by a defined enclosure, like a field enclosed by a fence.

When thinking about perimeter, think about walking around the outside of something. When thinking about area, think about the amount of space or **surface area** something takes up.

Square

The perimeter of a square is measured by adding together all of the sides. Since a square has four equal sides, its perimeter can be calculated by multiplying the length of one side by 4. Thus, the formula is $P = 4 \times s$, where s equals one side. For example, the following square has side lengths of 5 meters:

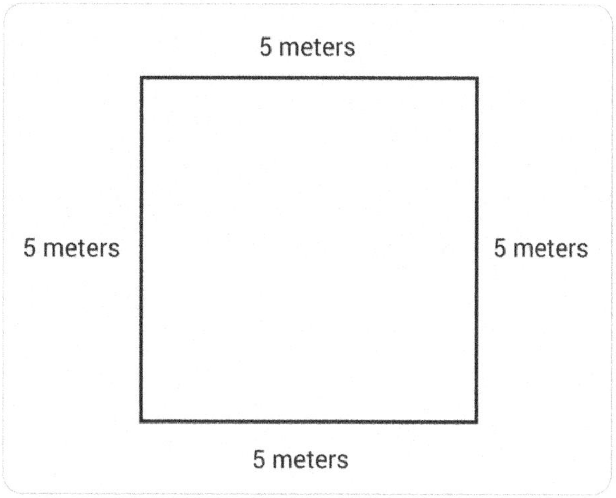

The perimeter is 20 meters because 4 times 5 is 20.

The area of a square is the length of a side squared, and the area of a rectangle is length multiplied by the width. For example, if the length of the square is 7 centimeters, then the area is 49 square centimeters. The formula for this example is $A = s^2 = 7^2 = 49$ square centimeters. An example is if the rectangle has a length of 6 inches and a width of 7 inches, then the area is 42 square inches:

$$A = lw = 6(7) = 42 \text{ square inches}$$

Rectangle

Like a square, a rectangle's perimeter is measured by adding together all of the sides. But as the sides are unequal, the formula is different. A rectangle has equal values for its lengths (long sides) and equal values for its widths (short sides), so the perimeter formula for a rectangle is:

$$P = l + l + w + w = 2l + 2w$$

l equals length
w equals width

The area is found by multiplying the length by the width, so the formula is $A = l \times w$.

For example, if the length of a rectangle is 10 inches and the width 8 inches, then the perimeter is 36 inches because:

$$P = 2l + 2w = 2(10) + 2(8) = 20 + 16 = 36 \text{ inches}$$

Triangle

A triangle's perimeter is measured by adding together the three sides, so the formula is $P = a + b + c$, where a, b, and c are the values of the three sides. The area is the product of one-half the base and height so the formula is:

$$A = \frac{1}{2} \times b \times h$$

It can be simplified to:

$$A = \frac{bh}{2}$$

The base is the bottom of the triangle, and the height is the distance from the base to the peak. If a problem asks to calculate the area of a triangle, it will provide the base and height.

For example, if the base of the triangle is 2 feet and the height 4 feet, then the area is 4 square feet. The following equation shows the formula used to calculate the area of the triangle:

$$\mathrm{A} = \frac{1}{2}\mathrm{bh} = \frac{1}{2}(2)(4) = 4 \text{ square feet}$$

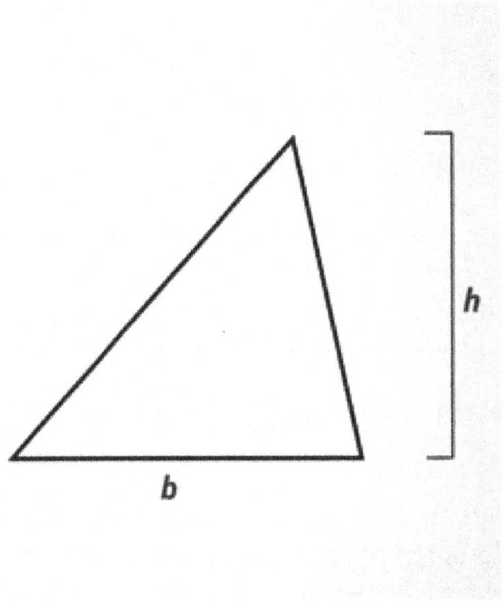

Circle
A circle's perimeter—also known as its circumference—is measured by multiplying the diameter by π.

Diameter is the straight line measured from one end to the direct opposite end of the circle.

π is referred to as pi and is equal to 3.14 (with rounding).

So the formula is $\pi \times d$.

This is sometimes expressed by the formula $C = 2 \times \pi \times r$, where r is the radius of the circle. These formulas are equivalent, as the radius equals half of the diameter.

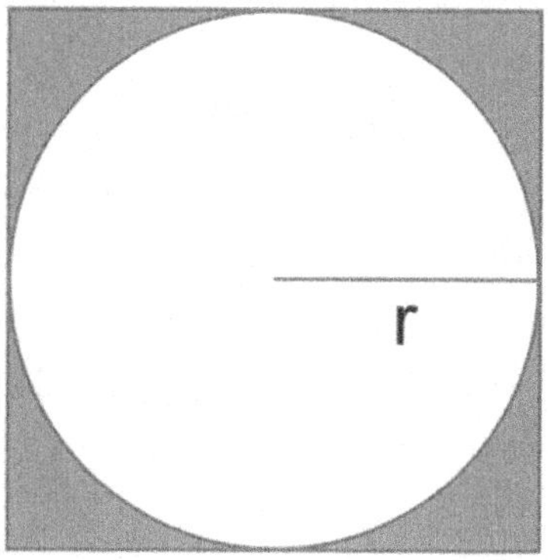

The area of a circle is calculated through the formula $A = \pi \times r^2$. The test will indicate either to leave the answer with π attached or to calculate to the nearest decimal place, which means multiplying by 3.14 for π.

Arc

The **arc of a circle** is the distance between two points on the circle. The length of the arc of a circle in terms of **degrees** is easily determined if the value of the central angle is known. The length of the arc is simply the value of the central angle. In this example, the length of the arc of the circle in degrees is 75°.

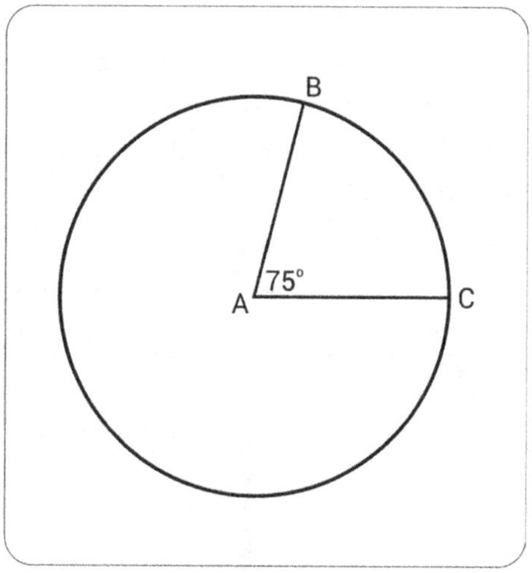

To determine the length of the arc of a circle in **distance**, the student will need to know the values for both the central angle and the radius. This formula is:

$$\frac{central\ angle}{360°} = \frac{arc\ length}{2\pi r}$$

The equation is simplified by cross-multiplying to solve for the arc length.

In the following example, the student should substitute the values of the central angle (75°) and the radius (10 inches) into the equation above to solve for the arc length.

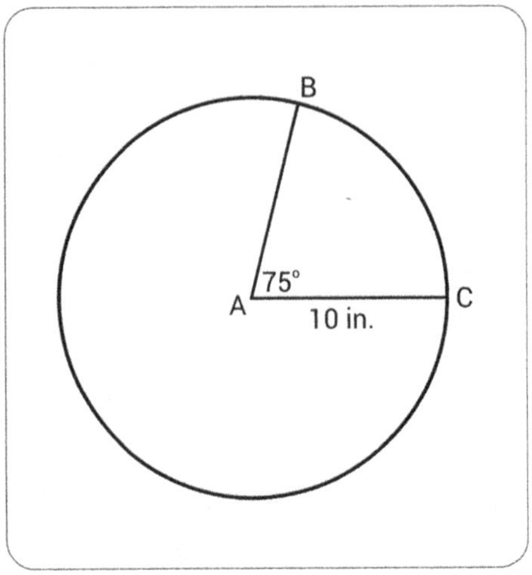

$$\frac{75°}{360°} = \frac{\text{arc length}}{2(3.14)(10\text{in.})}$$

To solve the equation, first cross-multiply: 4710 = 360(arc length). Next, divide each side of the equation by 360. The result of the formula is that the arc length is 13.1 (rounded).

Irregular Shapes

The perimeter of an irregular polygon is found by adding the lengths of all of the sides. In cases where all of the sides are given, this will be very straightforward, as it will simply involve finding the sum of the provided lengths. Other times, a side length may be missing and must be determined before the perimeter can be calculated. Consider the example below:

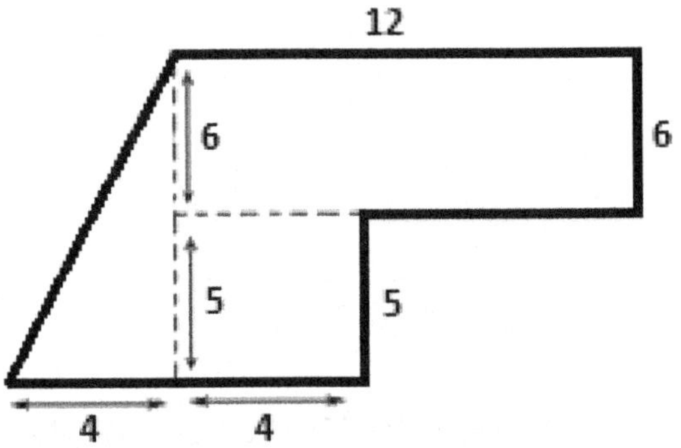

All of the side lengths are provided except for the angled side on the left. Test takers should notice that this is the hypotenuse of a right triangle. The other two sides of the triangle are provided (the base is 4 and the height is 6 + 5 = 11). The Pythagorean Theorem can be used to find the length of the hypotenuse, remembering that $a^2 + b^2 = c^2$.

Substituting the side values provided yields $(4)^2 + (11)^2 = c^2$.

Therefore, $c = \sqrt{16 + 121} = 11.7$

Finally, the perimeter can be found by adding this new side length with the other provided lengths to get the total length around the figure: 4+4+5+8+6+12+11.7=50.7. Although units are not provided in this figure, remember that reporting units with a measurement is important.

The area of an irregular polygon is found by decomposing, or breaking apart, the figure into smaller shapes. When the area of the smaller shapes is determined, these areas are added together to produce the total area of the area of the original figure. Consider the same example provided before:

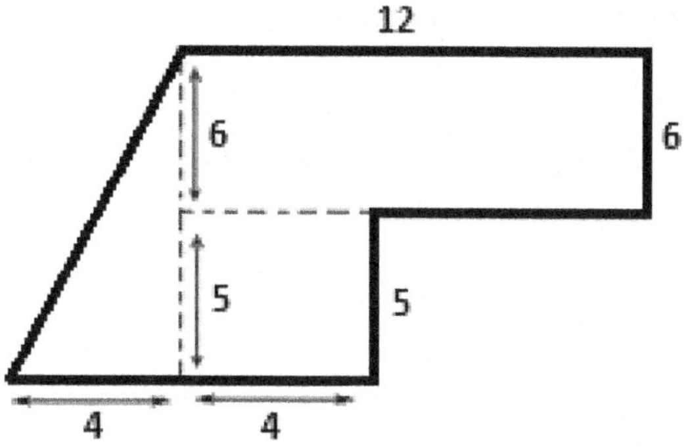

The irregular polygon is decomposed into two rectangles and a triangle. The area of the large rectangles ($A = l \times w \rightarrow A = 12 \times 6$) is 72 square units. The area of the small rectangle is 20 square units ($A = 4 \times 5$). The area of the triangle ($A = \frac{1}{2} \times b \times h \rightarrow A = \frac{1}{2} \times 4 \times 11$) is 22 square units. The sum of the areas of these figures produces the total area of the original polygon: $A = 72 + 20 + 22 \rightarrow A$ = 114 square units.

Surface Area of Three-Dimensional Figures

The area of a two-dimensional figure refers to the number of square units needed to cover the interior region of the figure. This concept is similar to wallpaper covering the flat surface of a wall. For example, if a rectangle has an area of 8 square inches (written 8 in^2), it will take 8 squares, each with sides one inch in length, to cover the interior region of the rectangle. Note that area is measured in square units such as: square feet or ft^2; square yards or yd^2; square miles or mi^2.

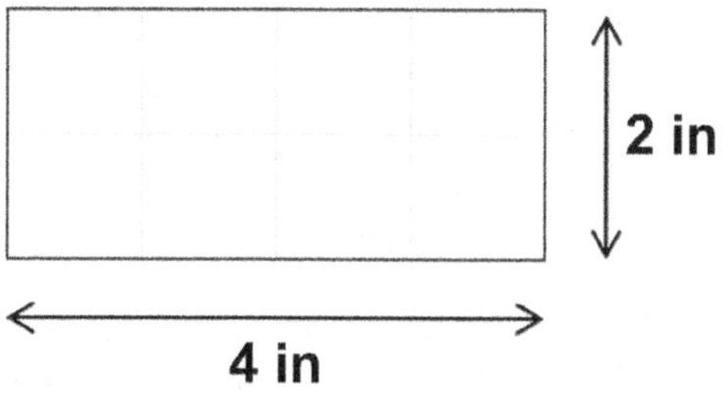

The surface area of a three-dimensional figure refers to the number of square units needed to cover the entire surface of the figure. This concept is similar to using wrapping paper to completely cover the outside of a box. For example, if a triangular pyramid has a surface area of 17 square inches (written $17in^2$), it will take 17 squares, each with sides one inch in length, to cover the entire surface of the pyramid. Surface area is also measured in square units.

Many three-dimensional figures (solid figures) can be represented by nets consisting of rectangles and triangles. The surface area of such solids can be determined by adding the areas of each of its faces and bases. Finding the surface area using this method requires calculating the areas of rectangles and triangles. To find the area (*A*) of a rectangle, the length (*l*) is multiplied by the width $(w) \rightarrow A = l \times w$. The area of a rectangle with a length of 8cm and a width of 4cm is calculated: $A = (8cm) \times (4cm) \rightarrow A = 32cm^2$.

To calculate the area (*A*) of a triangle, the product of $\frac{1}{2}$, the base (*b*), and the height (*h*) is found $\rightarrow A = \frac{1}{2} \times b \times h$. Note that the height of a triangle is measured from the base to the vertex opposite of it forming a right angle with the base. The area of a triangle with a base of 11cm and a height of 6cm is calculated: $A = \frac{1}{2} \times (11cm) \times (6cm) \rightarrow A = 33cm^2$.

Consider the following triangular prism, which is represented by a net consisting of two triangles and three rectangles.

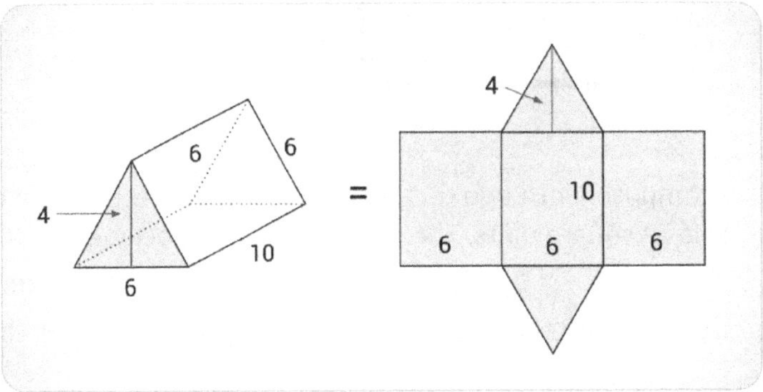

The surface area of the prism can be determined by adding the areas of each of its faces and bases. The surface area (*SA*) = area of triangle + area of triangle + area of rectangle + area of rectangle + area of rectangle.

$$SA = \left(\frac{1}{2} \times b \times h\right) + \left(\frac{1}{2} \times b \times h\right) + (l \times w) + (l \times w) + (l \times w)$$

$$SA = \left(\frac{1}{2} \times 6 \times 4\right) + \left(\frac{1}{2} \times 6 \times 4\right) + (6 \times 10) + (6 \times 10) + (6 \times 10)$$

$$SA = (12) + (12) + (60) + (60) + (60)$$

$$SA = 204 \textit{ square units}$$

Volume is the measurement of how much space an object occupies, like how much space is in the cube. Volume questions will ask how much of something is needed to completely fill the object. The most common surface area and volume questions deal with spheres, cubes, and rectangular prisms.

The **volume** of a cylinder is then found by adding a third dimension onto the circle. Volume of a cylinder is calculated by multiplying the area of the base (which is a circle) by the height of the cylinder. Doing so results in the equation $V = \pi r^2 h$. Next, consider the volume of a rectangular box $= lwh$, where l is length, w is width, and h is height. This can be simplified into $V = Ah$, where A is the area of the base. The **volume** of a pyramid with the same dimensions is $\frac{1}{3}$ of this quantity because it fills up $\frac{1}{3}$ of the space.

Therefore, the volume of a pyramid is $V = \frac{1}{3}Ah$. In a similar fashion, the volume of a cone is $\frac{1}{3}$ of the volume of a cylinder. Therefore, the formula for the volume of a cylinder is $\frac{1}{3}\pi r^2 h$.

Surface Area and Volume

Many real-world objects are a combination of prisms, cylinders, pyramids, and spheres. **Surface area** problems relate to quantifying the outside area of such a three-dimensional object, and **volume** problems involve quantifying how much the three-dimensional object can hold. For example, when calculating how much paint is needed to paint an entire house, surface area is used. Conversely, when calculating how much water a cylindrical tank can hold, volume is used. The surface area of a **prism** is the sum of all the areas, which simplifies into $SA = 2A + Bh$ where A is the area of the base, B is the perimeter of the base, and h is the height of the prism. The volume of the same prism is $V = Ah$. The surface area of a **cylinder** is the sum of the areas of both ends and the side, which is $SA = 2\pi rh + 2\pi r^2$. The surface area of a **pyramid** is calculated by adding known area formulas. It is equal to the area of the base (which is rectangular) plus the area of the four triangles that form the sides. The surface area of a **cone** is equal to the area of the base plus the area of the top, which is $SA = \pi r^2 + \pi\pi r\sqrt{h^2 + r^2}$. Finally, the formula for surface area of a sphere is $SA = 4\pi r^2$ and its volume is $V = \frac{4}{3}\pi r^3$.

Volume Formulas

Cube

The cube is the simplest figure for which volume can be determined because all dimensions in a cube are equal. In the following figure, the length, width, and height of the cube are all represented by the variable *a* because these measurements are equal lengths.

The volume of any rectangular, three-dimensional object is found by multiplying its length by its width by its height. In the case of a cube, the length, width, and height are all equal lengths, represented by the variable *a*. Therefore, the equation used to calculate the volume is $(a \times a \times a)$ or a^3. In a real-world example of this situation, if the length of a side of the cube is 3 centimeters, the volume is calculated by utilizing the formula $(3 \times 3 \times 3) = 9$ cm³.

Rectangular Prism

The dimensions of a rectangular prism are not necessarily equal as those of a cube. Therefore, the formula for a rectangular prism recognizes that the dimensions vary and use different variables to represent these lengths. The length, width, and height of a rectangular prism are represented with the variables *a, b*, and *c*.

The equation used to calculate volume is length times width times height. In a real-world application of this situation, if $a = 3\ cm, b = 4\ cm$, and $c = 5\ cm$, the volume is calculated by utilizing the formula $3 \times 4 \times 5 = 60$ cm³.

Cylinder

Discovering a cylinder's volume requires the measurement of the cylinder's base, length of the radius, and height. The height of the cylinder can be represented with variable *h*, and the radius can be represented with variable *r*.

The formula to find the volume of a cylinder is $\pi r^2 h$. For example, if the radius is 5 feet and the height of the cylinder is 10 feet, the cylinder's volume is calculated by using the following equation: $\pi 5^2 \times 10$. Substituting 3.14 for π, the volume is 785 ft³.

Cone

The formula to calculate the volume of a circular cone is similar to the formula for the volume of a pyramid. The primary difference in determining the area of a cone is that a circle serves as the base of a cone. Therefore, the area of a circle is used for the cone's base.

The variable *r* represents the radius, and the variable *h* represents the height of the cone. The formula used to calculate the volume of a cone is $\frac{1}{3}\pi r^2 h$. In a real-life example where the radius of a cone is 2 meters and the height of a cone is 5 meters, the volume of the cone is calculated by utilizing the formula $\frac{1}{3}\pi 2^2 \times 5 = 21$. After substituting 3.14 for π, the volume is $20.9\ m^3$.

Sphere

The volume of a sphere uses π due to its circular shape. The length of the radius, *r*, is the only variable needed to determine the sphere's volume. The formula to calculate the volume of a sphere is $\frac{4}{3}\pi r^3$. Therefore, if the radius of a sphere is 8 centimeters, the volume of the sphere is calculated by utilizing the formula $\frac{4}{3}\pi(8)^3 = 2{,}143.6\ cm^3$.

Applying Geometric Concepts to Modeling Situations

Real-World Geometry

Many real-world objects can be compared to geometric shapes. Describing certain objects using the measurements and properties of two- and three-dimensional shapes is an important part of geometry. For example, basic ideas such as angles and line segments can be seen in real-world objects. The corner of any room is an angle, and the intersection of a wall with the floor is like a line segment. Building upon this idea, entire objects can be related to both two- and three-dimensional shapes. An entire room can be thought of as square, rectangle, or a sum of a few three-dimensional shapes. Knowing what properties and measures are needed to make decisions in real life is why geometry is such a useful branch of mathematics. One obvious relationship between a real-life situation and geometry exists in construction. For example, to build an addition onto a house, several geometric measurements will be used.

Density

The **density** of a substance is the ratio of mass to area or volume. It's a relationship between the mass and how much space the object actually takes up. Knowing which units to use in each situation is crucial. Population density is an example of a real-life situation that's modeled by using density concepts. It involves calculating the ratio of the number of people to the number of square miles. The amount of material needed per a specific unit of area or volume is another application. For example, estimating the number of BTUs per cubic foot of a home is a measurement that relates to heating or cooling the house based on the desired temperature and the house's size.

Solving Design Problem

Design problems are an important application of geometry (e.g., building structures that satisfy physical constraints and/or minimize costs). These problems involve optimizing a situation based on what's given and required. For example, determining what size barn to build, given certain dimensions and a specific budget, uses both geometric properties and other mathematical concepts. Equations are formed using geometric definitions and the given constraints. In the end, such problems involve solving a system of equations and rely heavily on a strong background in algebra. **Typographic grid systems** also help with such design problems. A grid made up of intersecting straight or curved lines can be used as a visual representation of the structure being designed. This concept is seen in the blueprints used throughout the graphic design process.

Statistics and Probability

Basic Statistics and Probability

The field of statistics describes relationships between quantities that are related, but not necessarily in a deterministic manner. For example, a graduating student's salary will often be higher when the student graduates with a higher GPA, but this is not always the case. Likewise, people who smoke tobacco are more likely to develop lung cancer, but, in fact, it is possible for non-smokers to develop the disease as well. **Statistics** describes these kinds of situations, where the likelihood of some outcome depends on the starting data.

Descriptive statistics involves analyzing a collection of data to describe its broad properties such average (or mean), what percent of the data falls within a given range, and other such properties. An example of this would be taking all of the test scores from a given class and calculating the average test score. **Inferential statistics** attempts to use data about a subset of some population to make inferences about the rest of the population. An example of this would be taking a collection of students who received tutoring and comparing their results to a collection of students who did not receive tutoring, then using that comparison to try to predict whether the tutoring program in question is beneficial.

To be sure that inferences have a high probability of being true for the whole population, the subset that is analyzed needs to resemble a miniature version of the population as closely as possible. For this reason, statisticians like to choose random samples from the population to study, rather than picking a specific group of people based on some similarity. For example, studying the incomes of people who live in Portland does not tell anything useful about the incomes of people who live in Tallahassee.

A statistical question is answered by collecting data with variability. Data consists of facts and/or statistics (numbers), and variability refers to a tendency to shift or change. Data is a broad term, inclusive of things like height, favorite color, name, salary, temperature, gas mileage, and language. Questions requiring data as an answer are not necessarily statistical questions. If there is no variability in the data, then the question is not statistical in nature. Consider the following examples: what is Mary's favorite color? How much money does your mother make? What was the highest temperature last week? How many miles did your car get on its last tank of gas? How much taller than Bob is Ed?

None of the above are statistical questions because each case lacks variability in the data needed to answer the question. The questions on favorite color, salary, and gas mileage each require a single piece of data, whether a fact or statistic. Therefore, variability is absent. Although the temperature question requires multiple pieces of data (the high temperature for each day), a single, distinct number is the answer. The height question requires two pieces of data, Bob's height and Ed's height, but no difference in variability exists between those two values. Therefore, this is not a statistical question. Statistical questions typically require calculations with data.

Consider the following statistical questions:

How many miles per gallon of gas does the 2016 Honda Civic get? To answer this question, data must be collected. This data should include miles driven and gallons used. Different cars, different drivers, and different driving conditions will produce different results. Therefore, variability exists in the data. To answer the question, the mean (average) value could be determined.

Are American men taller than Chinese men? To answer this question, data must be collected. This data should include the heights of American men and the heights of Chinese men. All American men are not the same height and all Chinese men are not the same height. Some American men are taller than some Chinese men and some Chinese men are taller than some American men. Therefore, variability exists in the data. To answer the question, the median values for each group could be determined and compared.

The following are more examples of statistical questions: What proportion of 4th graders have a favorite color of blue? How much money do teachers make? Is it colder in Boston or Chicago?

Describing Distributions

Mean, Median, and Mode

The center of a set of data (statistical values) can be represented by its mean, median, or mode. These are sometimes referred to as measures of central tendency.

Mean

The first property that can be defined for this set of data is the **mean**. This is the same as average. To find the mean, add up all the data points, then divide by the total number of data points. For example, suppose that in a class of 10 students, the scores on a test were 50, 60, 65, 65, 75, 80, 85, 85, 90, 100. Therefore, the average test score will be:

$$\frac{50+60+65+65+75+80+85+85+90+100}{10}=75.5$$

The mean is a useful number if the distribution of data is normal (more on this later), which roughly means that the frequency of different outcomes has a single peak and is roughly equally distributed on both sides of that peak. However, it is less useful in some cases where the data might be split or where there are some outliers. **Outliers** are data points that are far from the rest of the data. For example, suppose there are 10 executives and 90 employees at a company. The executives make $1000 per hour, and the employees make $10 per hour.

Therefore, the average pay rate will be:

$$\frac{\$1000\times 10+\$10\times 90}{100}=\$109\ per\ hour$$

In this case, this average is not very descriptive since it's not close to the actual pay of the executives *or* the employees.

Median

Another useful measurement is the **median**. In a data set, the median is the point in the middle. The middle refers to the point where half the data comes before it and half comes after, when the data is recorded in numerical order. For instance, these are the speeds of the fastball of a pitcher during the last inning that he pitched (in order from least to greatest):

90, 92, 93, 93, 95, 96, 97, 97, 97

There are nine total numbers, so the middle or *median* number in the 5th one, which is 95.

In cases where the number of data points is an even number, then the average of the two middle points is taken. In the previous example of test scores, the two middle points are 75 and 80. Since there is no single point, the average of these two scores needs to be found. The average is:

$$\frac{75+80}{2} = 77.5$$

The median is generally a good value to use if there are a few outliers in the data. It prevents those outliers from affecting the "middle" value as much as when using the mean.

Since an outlier is a data point that is far from most of the other data points in a data set, this means an outlier also is any point that is far from the median of the data set. The outliers can have a substantial effect on the mean of a data set, but usually do not change the median or mode, or do not change them by a large quantity. For example, consider the data set (3, 5, 6, 6, 6, 8). This has a median of 6 and a mode of 6, with a mean of $\frac{34}{6} \approx 5.67$. Now, suppose a new data point of 1000 is added so that the data set is now (3, 5, 6, 6, 6, 8, 1000). This does not change the median or mode, which are both still 6. However, the average is now $\frac{1034}{7}$, which is approximately 147.7. In this case, the median and mode will be better descriptions for most of the data points.

The reason for outliers in a given data set is a complicated problem. It is sometimes the result of an error by the experimenter, but often they are perfectly valid data points that must be taken into consideration.

Mode
One additional measure to define for *X* is the **mode**. This is the data point that appears most frequently. If two or more data points all tie for the most frequent appearance, then each of them is considered a mode. In the case of the test scores, where the numbers were 50, 60, 65, 65, 75, 80, 85, 85, 90, 100, there are two modes: 65 and 85.

Quartiles and Percentiles
The **first quartile** of a set of data *X* refers to the largest value from the first ¼ of the data points. In practice, there are sometimes slightly different definitions that can be used, such as the median of the first half of the data points (excluding the median itself if there are an odd number of data points). The term also has a slightly different use: when it is said that a data point lies *in the first quartile*, it means it is less than or equal to the median of the first half of the data points. Conversely, if it lies *at* the first quartile, then it is equal to the first quartile.

When it is said that a data point lies in the **second quartile**, it means it is between the first quartile and the median.

The **third quartile** refers to data that lies between ½ and ¾ of the way through the data set. Again, there are various methods for defining this precisely, but the simplest way is to include all of the data that lie between the median and the median of the top half of the data.

Data that lies in the **fourth quartile** refers to all of the data above the third quartile.

Percentiles may be defined in a similar manner to quartiles. Generally, this is defined in the following manner:

If a data point lies **in the n-th percentile**, this means it lies in the range of the first *n*% of the data.

If a data point lies **at the n-th percentile**, then it means that *n*% of the data lies below this data point.

Standard Deviation

Given a data set *X* consisting of data points $(x_1, x_2, x_3, \dots x_n)$, the **variance** of *X* is defined to be:

$$\frac{\sum_{i=1}^{n}(x_i - \bar{X})^2}{n}$$

This means that the variance of *X* is the average of the squares of the differences between each data point and the mean of *X*.

Given a data set *X* consisting of data points $(x_1, x_2, x_3, \dots x_n)$, the **standard deviation** of *X* is defined to be:

$$s_x = \sqrt{\frac{\sum_{i=1}^{n}(x_i - \bar{X})^2}{n}}$$

In other words, the standard deviation is the square root of the variance.

Both the variance and the standard deviation are measures of how much the data tend to be spread out. When the standard deviation is low, the data points are mostly clustered around the mean. When the standard deviation is high, this generally indicates that the data are quite spread out, or else that there are a few substantial outliers.

As a simple example, compute the standard deviation for the data set (1, 3, 3, 5). First, compute the mean, which will be $\frac{1+3+3+5}{4} = \frac{12}{4} = 3$. Now, find the variance of *X* with the formula:

$$\sum_{i=1}^{4}(x_i - \bar{X})^2 = (1-3)^2 + (3-3)^2 + (3-3)^2 + (5-3)^2 = -2^2 + 0^2 + 0^2 + 2^2 = 8$$

Therefore, the variance is $\frac{8}{4} = 2$. Taking the square root, the standard deviation will be $\sqrt{2}$.

Note that the standard deviation only depends upon the mean, not upon the median or mode(s). Generally, if there are multiple modes that are far apart from one another, the standard deviation will be high. A high standard deviation does not always mean there are multiple modes, however.

Describing a Set of Data

A set of data can be described in terms of its center, spread, shape and any unusual features. The center of a data set can be measured by its mean, median, or mode. The spread of a data set refers to how far the data points are from the center (mean or median). A data set with data points clustered around the center will have a small spread. A data set covering a wide range will have a large spread.

When a data set is displayed as a graph like the one below, the shape indicates if a sample is normally distributed, symmetrical, or has measures of skewness. When graphed, a data set with a normal distribution will resemble a bell curve.

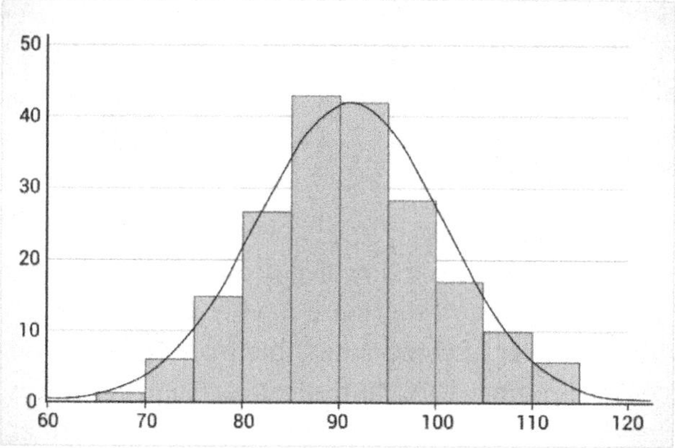

If the data set is symmetrical, each half of the graph when divided at the center is a mirror image of the other. If the graph has fewer data points to the right, the data is skewed right. If it has fewer data points to the left, the data is skewed left.

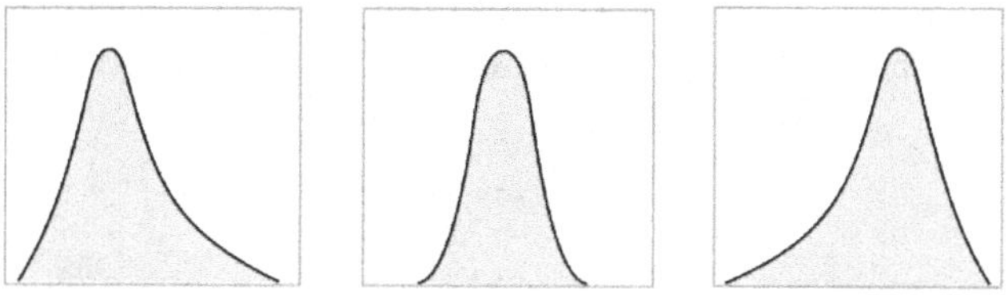

A description of a data set should include any unusual features such as gaps or outliers. A gap is a span within the range of the data set containing no data points. An outlier is a data point with a value either extremely large or extremely small when compared to the other values in the set.

The graphs above can be referred to as **unimodal** since they all have a single peak. This is contrast to **bimodal** graph that have multiple peaks.

Random Sampling

An **experiment** is the method in which a hypothesis is tested using a trial-and-error process. A cause and the effect of that cause are measured, and the hypothesis is accepted or rejected. Experiments are usually completed in a controlled environment where the results of a control population are compared to the results of a test population. The groups are selected using a randomization process in which each group has a representative mix of the population being tested. Finally, an **observational study** is similar to an experiment. However, this design is used when there cannot be a designed control and test population because of circumstances (e.g., lack of funding or unrealistic expectations). Instead, existing control and test populations must be used, so this method has a lack of randomization.

Samples and Populations

Statistics involves making decisions and predictions about larger data sets based on smaller data sets. Basically, the information from one part or subset can help predict what happens in the entire data set or population at large. The entire process involves guessing, and the predictions and decisions may not be 100 percent correct all of the time; however, there is some truth to these predictions, and the decisions do have mathematical support. The smaller data set is called a **sample** and the larger data set (in which the decision is being made) is called a **population**. A **random sample** is used as the sample, which is an unbiased collection of data points that represents the population as well as it can. There are many methods of forming a random sample, and all adhere to the fact that every potential data point has a predetermined probability of being chosen.

Chance Processes and Probability Models

Counting Techniques

There are many counting techniques that can help solve problems involving counting possibilities. For example, the **Addition Principle** states that if there are m choices from Group 1 and n choices from Group 2, then $n + m$ is the total number of choices possible from Groups 1 and 2. For this to be true, the groups can't have any choices in common. The **Multiplication Principle** states that if Process 1 can be completed n ways and Process 2 can be completed m ways, the total number of ways to complete both Process 1 and Process 2 is $n \times m$. For this rule to be used, both processes must be independent of each other. Counting techniques also involve permutations. A **permutation** is an arrangement of elements in a set for which order must be considered. For example, if three letters from the alphabet are chosen, ABC and BAC are two different permutations. The multiplication rule can be used to determine the total number of possibilities. If each letter can't be selected twice, the total number of possibilities is $26 \times 25 \times 24 = 15{,}600$. A formula can also be used to calculate this total. In general, the notation $P(n, r)$ represents the number of ways to arrange r objects from a set of n and, the formula is:

$$P(n,r) = \frac{n!}{(n-r)!}$$

In the previous example, $P(26, 3) = \frac{26!}{23!} = 15{,}600$. Contrasting permutations, a **combination** is an arrangement of elements in which order doesn't matter. In this case, ABC and BAC are the same combination. In the previous scenario, there are six permutations that represent each single combination. Therefore, the total number of possible combinations is $15{,}600 \div 6 = 2{,}600$. In general, $C(n, r)$ represents the total number of combinations of n items selected r at a time where order doesn't matter, and the formula is:

$$C(n,r) = \frac{n!}{(n-r)!\ r!}$$

Therefore, the following relationship exists between permutations and combinations:

$$C(n,r) = \frac{P(n,r)}{n!} = \frac{P(n,r)}{P(r,r)}$$

Fundamental Counting Principle

The **fundamental counting principle** states that if there are *m* possible ways for an event to occur, and *n* possible ways for a second event to occur, there are $m \cdot n$ possible ways for both events to occur. For example, there are two events that can occur after flipping a coin and six events that can occur after rolling a die, so there are $2 \times 6 = 12$ total possible event scenarios if both are done simultaneously. This principle can be used to find probabilities involving finite sample spaces and independent trials because it calculates the total number of possible outcomes. For this principle to work, the events must be independent of each other.

Independence and Conditional Probability

Sample Subsets

A sample can be broken up into subsets that are smaller parts of the whole. For example, consider a sample population of females. The sample can be divided into smaller subsets based on the characteristics of each female. There can be a group of females with brown hair and a group of females that wear glasses. There also can be a group of females that have brown hair *and* wear glasses. This "and" relates to the **intersection** of the two separate groups of brunettes and those with glasses. Every female in that intersection group has both characteristics. Similarly, there also can be a group of females that either have brown hair *or* wear glasses. The "or" relates to the union of the two separate groups of brunettes and glasses. Every female in this group has at least one of the characteristics. Finally, the group of females who do not wear glasses can be discussed. This "not" relates to the **complement** of the glass-wearing group. No one in the complement has glasses. **Venn diagrams** are useful in highlighting these ideas. When discussing statistical experiments, this idea can also relate to events instead of characteristics.

Verifying Independent Events

Two events aren't always independent. For example, females with glasses and brown hair aren't independent characteristics. There definitely can be overlap because females with brown hair can wear glasses. Also, two events that exist at the same time don't have to have a relationship. For example, even if all females in a given sample are wearing glasses, the characteristics aren't related. In this case, the probability of a brunette wearing glasses is equal to the probability of a female being a brunette multiplied by the probability of a female wearing glasses. This mathematical test of $P(A \cap B) = P(A)P(B)$ verifies that two events are independent.

Conditional Probability

Conditional probability is the probability that event A will happen given that event B has already occurred. An example of this is calculating the probability that a person will eat dessert once they have eaten dinner. This is different than calculating the probability of a person just eating dessert. The formula for the conditional probability of event A occurring given B is $P(A|B) = \frac{P\text{ (}A\text{ and }B\text{)}}{P(B)}$, and it's defined to be the probability of both A and B occurring divided by the probability of event B occurring. If A and B are independent, then the probability of both A and B occurring is equal to $P(A)P(B)$, so $P(A|B)$ reduces to just $P(A)$. This means that A and B have no relationship, and the probability of A occurring is the same as the conditional probability of A occurring given B. Similarly, $P(B|A) = \frac{P\text{ (}B\text{ and A)}}{P(A)} = P(B)$ if A and B are independent.

Independent Versus Related Events

To summarize, conditional probability is the probability that an event occurs given that another event has happened. If the two events are related, the probability that the second event will occur changes if the other event has happened. However, if the two events aren't related and are therefore independent, the first event to occur won't impact the probability of the second event occurring.

Measuring Probabilities with Two-Way Frequency Tables

When measuring event probabilities, two-way frequency tables can be used to report the raw data and then used to calculate probabilities. If the frequency tables are translated into relative frequency tables, the probabilities presented in the table can be plugged directly into the formulas for conditional probabilities. By plugging in the correct frequencies, the data from the table can be used to determine if events are independent or dependent.

Differing Probabilities

The probability that event A occurs differs from the probability that event A occurs given B. When working within a given model, it's important to note the difference. $P(A|B)$ is determined using the formula $P(A|B) = \frac{P\text{ (A and B)}}{P(B)}$ and represents the total number of A's outcomes left that could occur after B occurs. $P(A)$ can be calculated without any regard for B. For example, the probability of a student finding a parking spot on a busy campus is different once class is in session.

The Addition Rule

The probability of event A or B occurring isn't equal to the sum of each individual probability. The probability that both events can occur at the same time must be subtracted from this total. This idea is shown in the **addition rule**: $P(A \text{ or } B) = P(A) + P(B) - P(A \text{ and } B)$. The addition rule is another way to determine the probability of compound events that aren't mutually exclusive. If the events are mutually exclusive, the probability of both A and B occurring at the same time is 0.

<u>Computing Probabilities</u>

Simple and Compound Events

A **simple event** consists of only one outcome. The most popular simple event is flipping a coin, which results in either heads or tails. A **compound event** results in more than one outcome and consists of more than one simple event. An example of a compound event is flipping a coin while tossing a die. The result is either heads or tails on the coin and a number from one to six on the die. The probability of a simple event is calculated by dividing the number of possible outcomes by the total number of outcomes. Therefore, the probability of obtaining heads on a coin is $\frac{1}{2}$, and the probability of rolling a 6 on a die is $\frac{1}{6}$. The probability of compound events is calculated using the basic idea of the probability of simple events. If the two events are independent, the probability of one outcome is equal to the product of the probabilities of each simple event. For example, the probability of obtaining heads on a coin and rolling a 6 is equal to $\frac{1}{2} \times \frac{1}{6} = \frac{1}{12}$. The probability of either A or B occurring is equal to the sum of the probabilities minus the probability that both A and B will occur. Therefore, the probability of obtaining either heads on a coin or rolling a 6 on a die is $\frac{1}{2} + \frac{1}{6} - \frac{1}{12} = \frac{7}{12}$. The two events aren't mutually exclusive because they can happen at the same time. If two events are mutually exclusive, and the probability of both events occurring at the same time is zero, the probability of event A or B occurring equals the sum of both probabilities. An example of calculating the probability of two mutually exclusive events is determining the probability of pulling a king or a queen from a deck of cards. The two events cannot occur at the same time.

Uniform and Non-Uniform Probability Models

A **uniform probability model** is one where each outcome has an equal chance of occurring, such as the probabilities of rolling each side of a die. A **non-uniform probability model** is one where each outcome has an unequal chance of occurring. In a uniform probability model, the conditional probability formulas for $P(B|A)$ and $P(A|B)$ can be multiplied by their respective denominators to obtain two formulas for $P(A \text{ and } B)$. Therefore, the multiplication rule is derived as $P(A \text{ and } B) = P(A)P(B|A) = P(B)P(A|B)$. In a model, if the probability of either individual event is known and the corresponding conditional probability is known, the multiplication rule allows the probability of the joint occurrence of A and B to be calculated.

Patterns of Association in Bivariate Data

In an experiment, variables are the key to analyzing data, especially when data is in a graph or table. Variables can represent anything, including objects, conditions, events, and amounts of time.

Covariance is a general term referring to how two variables move in relation to each other. Take for example an employee that gets paid by the hour. For them, hours worked and total pay have a positive covariance. As hours worked increases, so does pay.

Constant variables remain unchanged by the scientist across all trials. Because they are held constant for all groups in an experiment, they aren't being measured in the experiment, and they are usually ignored. Constants can either be controlled by the scientist directly like the nutrition, water, and sunlight given to plants, or they can be selected by the scientist specifically for an experiment like using a certain animal species or choosing to investigate only people of a certain age group.

Independent variables are also controlled by the scientist, but they are the same only for each group or trial in the experiment. Each group might be composed of students that all have the same color of car or each trial may be run on different soda brands. The independent variable of an experiment is what is being indirectly tested because it causes change in the dependent variables.

Dependent variables experience change caused by the independent variable and are what is being measured or observed. For example, college acceptance rates could be a dependent variable of an experiment that sorted a large sample of high school students by an independent variable such as test scores. In this experiment, the scientist groups the high school students by the independent variable (test scores) to see how it affects the dependent variable (their college acceptance rates).

Note that most variables can be held constant in one experiment but independent or dependent in another. For example, when testing how well a fertilizer aids plant growth, its amount of sunlight should be held constant for each group of plants, but if the experiment is being done to determine the proper amount of sunlight a plant should have, the amount of sunlight is an independent variable because it is necessarily changed for each group of plants.

Correlation

An **X-Y diagram**, also known as a scatter diagram, visually displays the relationship between two variables. The independent variable is placed on the **x-axis**, or horizontal axis, and the dependent variable is placed on the **y-axis**, or vertical axis.

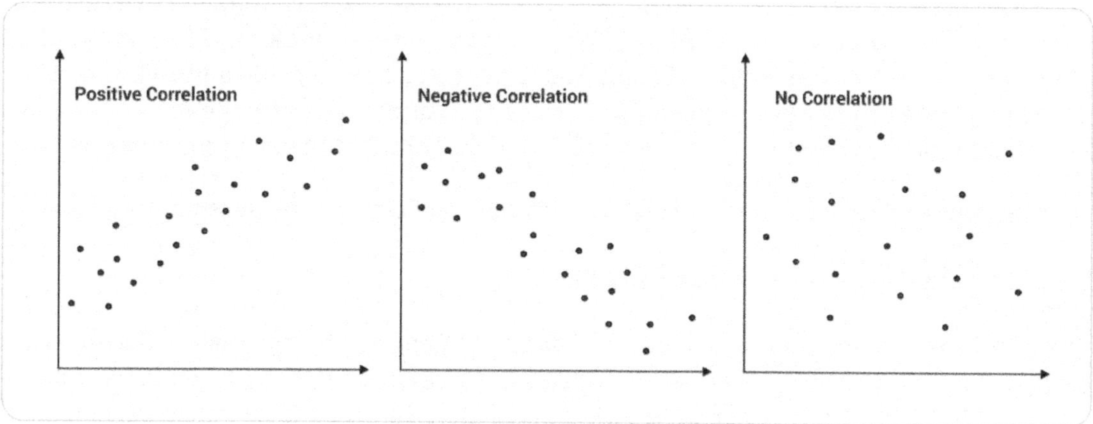

As shown in the figures above, an X-Y diagram may result in positive, negative, or no correlation between the two variables. So, in the first scatter plot as the Y factor increases the X factor increases as well. The opposite is true as well: as the X factor increases the Y factor also increases. Thus, there is a positive correlation because one factor appears to positively affect the other factor.

It's important to note, however, that a positive correlation between two variables doesn't equate to a cause-and-effect relationship. For example, a positive correlation between labor hours and units produced may not equate to a cause and effect relationship between the two. Any instance of correlation only indicates how likely the presence of one variable is in the instance of another. The variables should be further analyzed to determine which, if any, other variables (i.e. quality of employee work) may contribute to the positive correlation.

A box plot, also called a box-and-whisker plot, divides the data points into four groups and displays the five-number summary for the set, as well as any outliers. The five-number summary consists of:

- The lower extreme: the lowest value that is not an outlier
- The higher extreme: the highest value that is not an outlier
- The median of the set: also referred to as the second quartile or Q_2
- The first quartile or Q_1: the median of values below Q_2
- The third quartile or Q_3: the median of values above Q_2

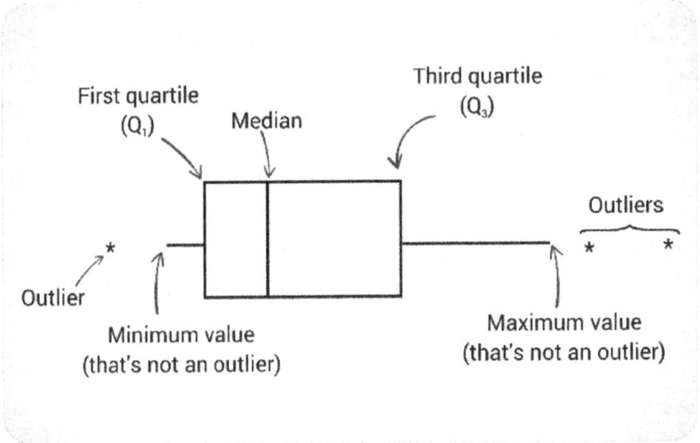

Suppose the box plot displays IQ scores for 12th grade students at a given school. The five-number summary of the data consists of: lower extreme (67); upper extreme (127); Q_2 or median (100); Q_1 (91); Q_3 (108); and outliers (135 and 140). Although all data points are not known from the plot, the points are divided into four quartiles each, including 25% of the data points. Therefore, 25% of students scored between 67 and 91, 25% scored between 91 and 100, 25% scored between 100 and 108, and 25% scored between 108 and 127. These percentages include the normal values for the set and exclude the outliers. This information is useful when comparing a given score with the rest of the scores in the set.

Summarizing, Representing, and Interpreting Data on a Single Count or Measurement Variable

Data Collection from Measurements on a Single Variable

Representing Data

Most statistics involve collecting a large amount of data, analyzing it, and then making decisions based on previously known information. These decisions also can be measured through additional data collection and then analyzed. Therefore, the cycle can repeat itself over and over. Representing the data visually is a large part of the process, and many plots on the real number line exist that allow this to be done. For example, a **dot plot** uses dots to represent data points above the number line. Also, a **histogram** represents a data set as a collection of rectangles, which illustrate the frequency distribution of the data. Finally, a **box plot** (also known as a **box and whisker plot**) plots a data set on the number line by segmenting the distribution into four quartiles that are divided equally in half by the median. Here's an example of a box plot, a histogram, and a dot plot for the same data set:

Box Plot

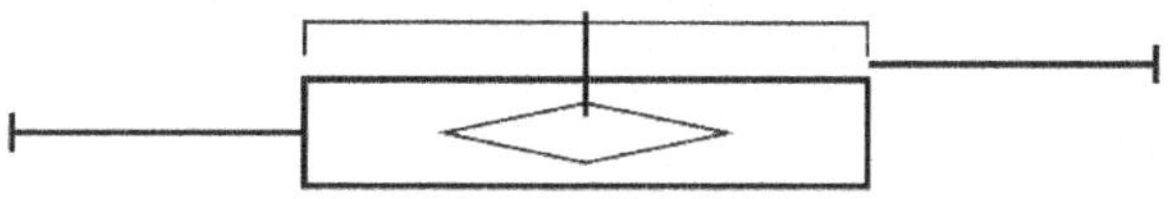

Histogram

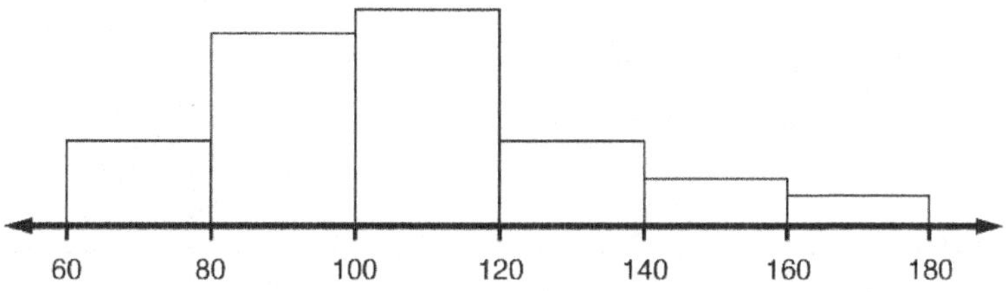

Dot Plot

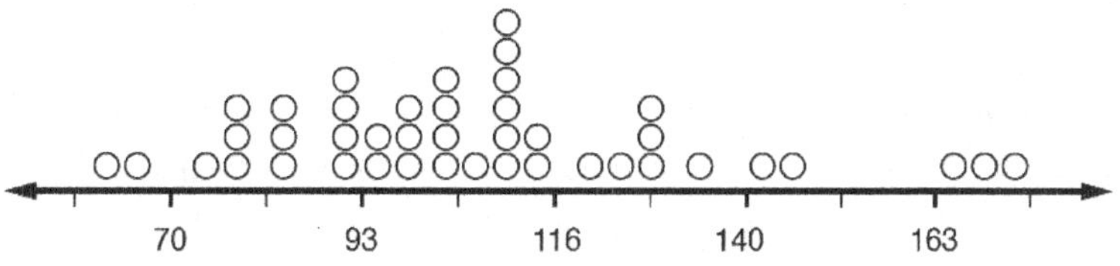

Normal Distribution

A **normal distribution** of data follows the shape of a bell curve and the data set's median, mean, and mode are equal. Therefore, 50 percent of its values are less than the mean and 50 percent are greater than the mean. Data sets that follow this shape can be generalized using normal distributions. Normal distributions are described as **frequency distributions** in which the data set is plotted as percentages rather than true data points. A **relative frequency distribution** is one where the y-axis is between zero and 1, which is the same as 0% to 100%. Within a standard deviation, 68 percent of the values are within

1 standard deviation of the mean, 95 percent of the values are within 2 standard deviations of the mean, and 99.7 percent of the values are within 3 standard deviations of the mean. The number of standard deviations that a data point falls from the mean is called the **z-score**. The formula for the z-score is $Z = \frac{x-\mu}{\sigma}$, where μ is the mean, σ is the standard deviation, and x is the data point. This formula is used to fit any data set that resembles a normal distribution to a standard normal distribution, in a process known as **standardizing**.

Here is a normal distribution with labelled z-scores:

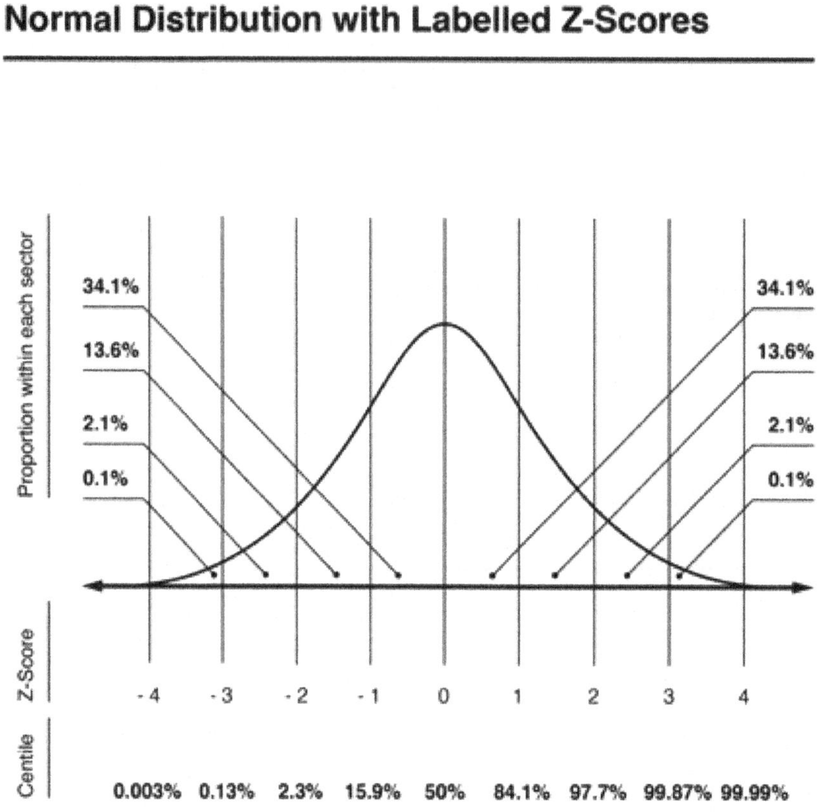

Population percentages can be estimated using normal distributions. For example, the probability that a data point will be less than the mean, or that the z-score will be less than 0, is 50%. Similarly, the probability that a data point will be within 1 standard deviation of the mean, or that the z-score will be between -1 and 1, is about 68.2%. When using a table, the left column states how many standard deviations (to one decimal place) away from the mean the point is, and the row heading states the second decimal place. The entries in the table corresponding to each column and row give the probability, which is equal to the area.

Areas Under the Curve

The area under the curve of a standard normal distribution is equal to 1. Areas under the curve can be estimated using the z-score and a table. The area is equal to the probability that a data point lies in that region in decimal form. For example, the area under the curve from $z = -1$ to $z = 1$ is 0.682.

Data Collection from Measurements on Two Variables

Two-Way Frequency Tables

Data that isn't described using numbers is known as **categorical data**. For example, age is numerical data but hair color is categorical data. Categorical data is summarized using two-way frequency tables. A **two-way frequency table** counts the relationship between two sets of categorical data. There are rows and columns for each category, and each cell represents frequency information that shows the actual data count between each combination.

For example, the graphic on the left-side below is a two-way frequency table showing the number of girls and boys taking language classes in school. Entries in the middle of the table are known as the **joint frequencies**. For example, the number of girls taking French class is 12, which is a joint frequency. The totals are the **marginal frequencies**. For example, the total number of boys is 20, which is a marginal frequency. If the frequencies are changed into percentages based on totals, the table is known as a **two-way relative frequency table**. Percentages can be calculated using the table total, the row totals, or the column totals. Here's the process of obtaining the two-way relative frequency table using the table total:

Two-Way Frequency Table

	Spanish	French	German	Total
Boys	10	2	8	**20**
Girls	15	12	3	**30**
Total	**25**	**14**	**11**	**50**

Joint frequencies

Marginal frequencies

Divide all tables entries by the table total (50)

Two-Way Relative Frequency Table (with respect to table total)

	Spanish	French	German	Total
Boys	0.2	0.04	0.16	**0.40**
Girls	0.3	0.24	0.06	**0.60**
Total	**0.5**	**0.28**	**0.22**	**1.00**

The middle entries are known as **joint probabilities** and the totals are **marginal probabilities**. In this data set, it appears that more girls than boys take Spanish class. However, that might not be the case because more girls than boys were surveyed, and the results might be misleading. To avoid such errors, **conditional relative frequencies** are used. The relative frequencies are calculated based on a row or column.

Here are the conditional relative frequencies using column totals:

Two-Way Frequency Table

	Spanish	French	German	Total
Boys	10	2	8	**20**
Girls	15	12	3	**30**
Total	**25**	**14**	**11**	**50**

Divide each column entry by that column's total →

Two-Way Relative Frequency Table (with respect to table total)

	Spanish	French	German	Total
Boys	0.4	0.14	0.73	**0.4**
Girls	0.6	0.86	0.27	**0.6**
Total	**1.00**	**1.00**	**1.00**	**1.00**

Data Conclusions

Two-way frequency tables can help in making many conclusions about the data. If either the row or column of conditional relative frequencies differs between each row or column of the table, then an association exists between the two categories. If the frequencies are equal across the rows, there is no association and the variables are labelled as independent. It's important to note that the association does exist in the above scenario, though these results may not occur the next semester when students are surveyed.

Plotting Variables

A **scatter plot** is a way to visually represent the relationship between two variables. Each variable has its own axis, and usually the independent variable is plotted on the horizontal axis while the dependent variable is plotted on the vertical axis. Data points are plotted in a process that's similar to how ordered pairs are plotted on an *xy*-plane. Once all points from the data set are plotted, the scatter plot is finished. Below is an example of a scatter plot that's plotting the quality and price of an item. Note that price is the independent variable and quality is the dependent variable:

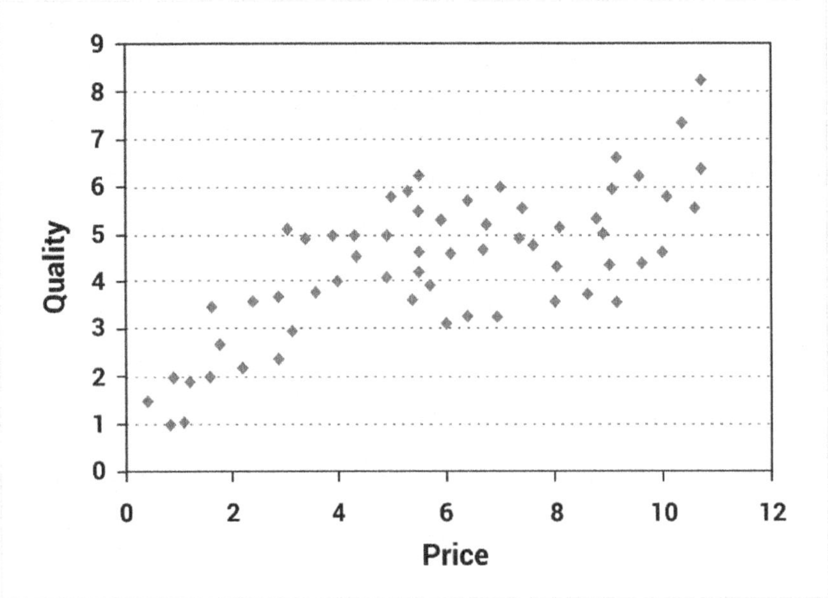

In this example, the quality of the item increases as the price increases.

Linear Regression Models

Linear Regression

Regression lines are a way to calculate a relationship between the independent variable and the dependent variable. A straight line means that there's a linear trend in the data. Technology can be used to find the equation of this line (e.g., a graphing calculator or Microsoft Excel®). In either case, all of the data points are entered, and a line is "fit" that best represents the shape of the data. Other functions used to model data sets include quadratic and exponential models.

Estimating Data Points

Regression lines can be used to estimate data points not already given. For example, if an equation of a line is found that fit the temperature and beach visitor data set, its input is the average daily temperature and its output is the projected number of visitors. Thus, the number of beach visitors on a 100-degree day can be estimated. The output is a data point on the regression line, and the number of daily visitors is expected to be greater than on a 96-degree day because the regression line has a positive slope.

Plotting and Analyzing Residuals

Once the function is found that fits the data, its accuracy can be calculated. Therefore, how well the line fits the data can be determined. The difference between the actual dependent variable from the data set and the estimated value located on the regression line is known as a **residual**. Therefore, the residual is known as the predicted value $\hat{y}$ minus the actual value y. A residual is calculated for each data point and can be plotted on the scatterplot. If all the residuals appear to be approximately the same distance from the regression line, the line is a good fit. If the residuals seem to differ greatly across the board, the line isn't a good fit.

Interpreting the Regression Line

The formula for a regression line is $y = mx + b$, where m is the slope and b is the *y*-intercept. Both the slope and *y*-intercept are found in the **Method of Least Squares**, which is the process of finding the equation of the line through minimizing residuals. The slope represents the rate of change in *y* as x gets larger. Therefore, because *y* is the dependent variable, the slope actually provides the predicted values given the independent variable. The *y*-intercept is the predicted value for when the independent variable equals zero. In the temperature example, the y-intercept is the expected number of beach visitors for a very cold average daily temperature of zero degrees.

Correlation Coefficient

The **correlation coefficient** (r) measures the association between two variables. Its value is between -1 and 1, where -1 represents a perfect negative linear relationship, 0 represents no relationship, and 1 represents a perfect positive linear relationship. A **negative linear relationship** means that as x values increase, *y* values decrease. A **positive linear relationship** means that as *x* values increase, *y* values increase. The formula for computing the correlation coefficient is:

$$r = \frac{n(\sum xy) - (\sum x)(\sum y)}{\sqrt{n(\sum x^2) - (\sum x)^2}\sqrt{n(\sum y^2) - (\Sigma y)^2}}$$

n is the number of data points.

Both Microsoft Excel® and a graphing calculator can evaluate this easily once the data points are entered. A correlation greater than 0.8 or less than -0.8 is classified as "strong" while a correlation between -0.5 and 0.5 is classified as "weak."

Correlation Versus Causation

Correlation and causation have two different meanings. If two values are correlated, there is an association between them. However, correlation doesn't necessarily mean that one variable causes the other. **Causation** (or "cause and effect") occurs when one variable causes the other. Average daily temperature and number of beachgoers are correlated and have causation. If the temperature increases, the change in weather causes more people to go to the beach. However, alcoholism and smoking are correlated but don't have causation. The more someone drinks the more likely they are to smoke, but drinking alcohol doesn't cause someone to smoke.

The Processes Underlying Statistical Experiments

Data Gathering Techniques

The three most common types of data gathering techniques are sample surveys, experiments, and observational studies. **Sample surveys** involve collecting data from a random sample of people from a desired population. The measurement of the variable is only performed on this set of people. To have accurate data, the sampling must be unbiased and random. For example, surveying students in an advanced calculus class on how much they enjoy math classes is not a useful sample if the population should be all college students based on the research question. An **experiment** is the method in which a hypothesis is tested using a trial-and-error process. A cause and the effect of that cause are measured, and the hypothesis is accepted or rejected. Experiments are usually completed in a controlled environment where the results of a control population are compared to the results of a test population. The groups are selected using a randomization process in which each group has a representative mix of the population being tested. Finally, an **observational study** is similar to an experiment. However, this design is used when there cannot be a designed control and test population because of circumstances (e.g., lack of funding or unrealistic expectations). Instead, existing control and test populations must be used, so this method has a lack of randomization.

Population Mean and Proportion

Both the population mean and proportion can be calculated using data from a sample. The **population mean** (μ) is the average value of the parameter for the entire population. Due to size constraints, finding the exact value of μ is impossible, so the mean of the sample population is used as an estimate instead. The larger the sample size, the closer the sample mean gets to the population mean. An alternative to finding μ is to find the **proportion** of the population, which is the part of the population with the given characteristic. The proportion can be expressed as a decimal, a fraction, or a percentage, and can be given as a single value or a range of values. Because the population mean and proportion are both estimates, there's a **margin of error**, which is the difference between the actual value and the expected value.

T-Tests

A **randomized experiment** is used to compare two treatments by using statistics involving a *t-test,* which tests whether two data sets are significantly different from one another. To use a t-test, the test statistic must follow a normal distribution. The first step of the test involves calculating the *t* value, which is given as:

$$t = \frac{\overline{x_1} - \overline{x_2}}{s_{\bar{x}_1 - \bar{x}_2}}$$

where $\bar{x}_1$ and $\bar{x}_2$ are the averages of the two samples. Also,

$$s_{\bar{x}_1 - \bar{x}_2} = \sqrt{\frac{s_1^2}{n_1} + \frac{s_2^2}{n_2}}$$

where $s_1$and s_2 are the standard deviations of each sample and $n_1$and n_2 are their respective sample sizes. The **degrees of freedom** for two samples are calculated as the following (rounded to the lowest whole number).

$$df = \frac{(n_1 - 1) + (n_2 - 1)}{2}$$

Also, a significance level α must be chosen, where a typical value is $\alpha = 0.05$. Once everything is compiled, the decision is made to use either a **one-tailed test** or a **two-tailed test**. If there's an assumed difference between the two treatments, a one-tailed test is used. If no difference is assumed, a two-tailed test is used.

Analyzing Test Results

Once the type of test is determined, the t-value, significance level, and degrees of freedom are applied to the published table showing the *t* distribution. The row is associated with degrees of freedom and each column corresponds to the probability. The t-value can be exactly equal to one entry or lie between two entries in a row. For example, consider a t-value of 1.7 with degrees of freedom equal to 30. This **test statistic** falls between the *p* values of 0.05 and 0.025. For a one-tailed test, the corresponding *p* value lies between 0.05 and 0.025. For a two-tailed test, the *p* values need to be doubled so the corresponding *p* value falls between 0.1 and 0.05. Once the probability is known, this range is compared to α. If $p < \alpha$, the hypothesis is rejected. If $p > \alpha$, the hypothesis isn't rejected. In a two-tailed test, this scenario means the hypothesis is accepted that there's no difference in the two treatments. In a one-tailed test, the hypothesis is accepted, indicating that there's a difference in the two treatments.

Evaluating Completed Tests

In addition to applying statistical techniques to actual testing, evaluating completed tests is another important aspect of statistics. Reports can be read that already have conclusions, and the process can be evaluated using learned concepts. For example, deciding if a sample being used is appropriate. Other things that can be evaluated include determining if the samples are randomized or the results are significant. Once statistical concepts are understood, the knowledge can be applied to many applications.

Making Informed Decisions Using Probabilities and Expected Values

Graphical Displays

Graphical displays are used to visually represent probability distributions in statistical experiments. Specific displays representing probability distributions illustrate the probability of each event. Histograms are typically used to represent probability distributions, and the actual probability can be thought of as $P(x)$, where x is the independent variable.

Expected Value

The **expected value** of a random variable represents the mean value in either a large sample size or after a large number of trials. According to the law of large numbers, after a large number of trials, the actual mean (and that of the probability distribution) is approximately equal to the expected value. The expected value is a weighted average and is calculated as $E(X) = \sum x_i p_i$, where x_i represents the value of each outcome and p_i represents the probability of each outcome. If all probabilities are equal, the expected value is:

$$E(X) = \frac{x_1 + x_2 + \cdots + x_n}{n}$$

Expected value is often called the **mean of the random variable** and is also a measure of central tendency.

Calculating Theoretical Probabilities

Given a statistical experiment, a theoretical probability distribution can be calculated if the theoretical probabilities are known. The theoretical probabilities are plugged into the formula for both the binomial probability and the expected value. An example of this is any scenario involving rolls of a die or flips of a coin. The theoretical probabilities are known without any observed experiments. Another example of this is finding the theoretical probability distribution for the number of correct answers obtained by guessing a specific number of multiple choice questions on a class exam.

Determining Unknown Probabilities

Empirical data is defined as real data. If real data is known, approximations concerning samples and populations can be obtained by working backwards. This scenario is the case where theoretical probabilities are unknown, and experimental data must be used to make decisions. The sample data (including actual probabilities) must be plugged into the formulas for both binomial probability and the expected value. The actual probabilities are obtained using observation and can be seen in a probability distribution. An example of this scenario is determining a probability distribution for the number of televisions per household in the United States and determining the expected number of televisions per household as well.

Weighing Outcomes

Calculating if it's worth it to play a game or make a decision is a critical part of probability theory. Expected values can be calculated in terms of payoff values, and deciding whether to make a decision or play a game can be done based on the actual expected value. Applying this theory to gambling and card games is fairly typical. The payoff values in these instances are the actual monetary totals.

Fairness

Fairness can be used when making decisions given different scenarios. For example, a game of chance can be deemed fair if every outcome has an equal probability of occurring. Also, a decision or choice can be labeled as fair if each possible option has an equal probability of being chosen. Using basic probability knowledge allows one to make decisions based on fairness. Fairness helps determine if an event's outcome is truly random and no bias is involved in the results. Random number generators are a good way to ensure fairness. An example of an event that isn't fair is the rolling of a weighted die.

Simulations

Simulations are experiments where devices such as coins, cards, and dice are used to generate results representing real outcomes. The simulations are used to estimate probabilities that replace theoretical probabilities in cases where collecting empirical data or using theoretical probability models is improbable or even impossible. Simulation allows experiments to be performed that closely resemble a real scenario. An example of this is determining how likely it is for a family with four children to have all girls. A coin toss can simulate this probability distribution, where heads means having a girl and tails means having a boy. Dice also can be used to simulate this process and calculate a similar experimental probability distribution by assigning even-numbered rolls to girls and odd-numbered rolls to boys. Performing either simulation would be a much less expensive process than surveying a large number of families with four children.

Statistical Inferences

Statistical inference is defined as the process in which properties are deduced involving data analysis completed on a given probability distribution. If completed simulations can estimate theoretical probability distributions, that data can be used in the decision-making process. The process of defining hypotheses and deriving estimates can be applied to the data stemming from the simulation. The assumed population is a data set that's larger than the simulation's data set. Therefore, the sample data can be used to make informal inferences about the larger population without 100% certainty.

Practice Questions

1. Which of the following is the result of simplifying the expression:

$$\frac{4a^{-1}b^3}{a^4b^{-2}} * \frac{3a}{b}$$

a. $12a^3b^5$

b. $12\frac{b^4}{a^4}$

c. $\frac{12}{a^4}$

d. $7\frac{b^4}{a}$

2. What is the product of two irrational numbers?

a. Irrational
b. Rational
c. Irrational or rational
d. Complex and imaginary

3. The graph shows the position of a car over a 10-second time interval. Which of the following is the correct interpretation of the graph for the interval 1 to 3 seconds?

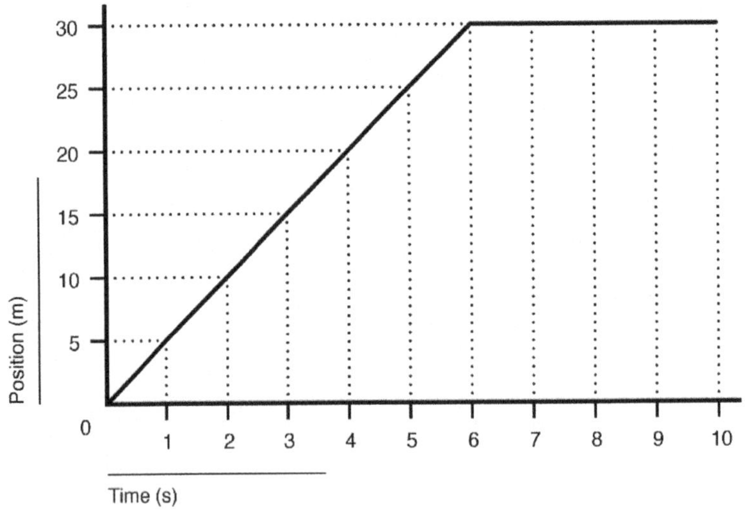

a. The car remains in the same position.
b. The car is traveling at a speed of 5m/s.
c. The car is traveling up a hill.
d. The car is traveling at 5mph.

4. How is the number -4 classified?

a. Real, rational, integer, whole, natural
b. Real, rational, integer, natural
c. Real, rational, integer
d. Real, irrational

5. Which of the following is NOT a way to write 40 percent of *N*?

a. $(0.4)N$
b. $\frac{2}{5}N$
c. $40N$
d. $\frac{4N}{10}$

6. A student gets an 85% on a test with 20 questions. How many answers did the student solve correctly?

a. 15
b. 16
c. 17
d. 18

7. Four people split a bill. The first person pays for $\frac{1}{5}$, the second person pays for $\frac{1}{4}$, and the third person pays for $\frac{1}{3}$. What fraction of the bill does the fourth person pay?

a. $\frac{13}{60}$
b. $\frac{47}{60}$
c. $\frac{1}{4}$
d. $\frac{4}{15}$

8. What is the solution to the following system of equations?

$$x^2 - 2x + y = 8$$
$$x - y = -2$$

a. $(-2, 3)$
b. There is no solution.
c. $(-2, 0)\ (1, 3)$
d. $(-2, 0)\ (3, 5)$

9. Which of the following shows the correct result of simplifying the following expression:

$$(7n + 3n^3 + 3) + (8n + 5n^3 + 2n^4)$$

a. $9n^4 + 15n - 2$
b. $2n^4 + 5n^3 + 15n - 2$
c. $9n^4 + 8n^3 + 15n$
d. $2n^4 + 8n^3 + 15n + 3$

10. What is the product of the following expression?

$$(4x - 8)(5x^2 + x + 6)$$

a. $20x^3 - 36x^2 + 16x - 48$
b. $6x^3 - 41x^2 + 12x + 15$
c. $204 + 11x^2 - 37x - 12$
d. $2x^3 - 11x^2 - 32x + 20$

11. How could the following equation be factored to find the zeros?

$$y = x^3 - 3x^2 - 4x$$

a. $0 = x^2(x - 4), x = 0, 4$
b. $0 = 3x(x + 1)(x + 4), x = 0, -1, -4$
c. $0 = x(x + 1)(x + 6), x = 0, -1, -6$
d. $0 = x(x + 1)(x - 4), x = 0, -1, 4$

12. What is the simplified quotient of the following expression?

$$\frac{5x^3}{3x^2y} \div \frac{25}{3y^9}$$

a. $\frac{125x}{9y^{10}}$

b. $\frac{x}{5y^8}$

c. $\frac{5}{xy^8}$

d. $\frac{xy^8}{5}$

13. What is the solution for the following equation?

$$\frac{x^2 + x - 30}{x - 5} = 11$$

a. $x = -6$
b. There is no solution.
c. $x = 16$
d. $x = 5$

14. $3\frac{2}{3} - 1\frac{4}{5} =$

a. $1\frac{13}{15}$
b. $\frac{14}{15}$
c. $2\frac{2}{3}$
d. $\frac{4}{5}$

15. How do you solve $V = lwh$ for h?

a. $lwV = h$
b. $h = \frac{V}{lw}$
c. $h = \frac{Vl}{w}$
d. $h = \frac{Vw}{l}$

16. What is the domain for the function $y = \sqrt{x}$?

a. All real numbers

b. $x \geq 0$

c. $x > 0$

d. $y \geq 0$

17. If Sarah reads at an average rate of 21 pages in four nights, how long will it take her to read 140 pages?

a. 6 nights

b. 26 nights

c. 8 nights

d. 27 nights

18. The phone bill is calculated each month using the equation $c = 50g + 75$. The cost of the phone bill per month is represented by c, and g represents the gigabytes of data used that month. What is the value and interpretation of the slope of this equation?

a. 75 dollars per day

b. 75 gigabytes per day

c. 50 dollars per day

d. 50 dollars per gigabyte

19. If $\frac{5}{2} \div \frac{1}{3} = n$, then n is between:

a. 5 and 7

b. 7 and 9

c. 9 and 11

d. 3 and 5

20. A closet is filled with red, blue, and green shirts. If $\frac{1}{3}$ of the shirts are green and $\frac{2}{5}$ are red, what fraction of the shirts are blue?

a. $\frac{4}{15}$

b. $\frac{1}{5}$

c. $\frac{7}{15}$

d. $\frac{1}{2}$

21. Shawna buys $2\frac{1}{2}$ gallons of paint. If she uses $\frac{1}{3}$ of it on the first day, how much does she have left?

a. $1\frac{5}{6}$ gallons

b. $1\frac{1}{2}$ gallons

c. $1\frac{2}{3}$gallons

d. 2 gallons

22. What are all the factors of 12?
   a. 12, 24, 36
   b. 1, 2, 4, 6, 12
   c. 12, 24, 36, 48
   d. 1, 2, 3, 4, 6, 12

23. Twenty is 40% of what number?
   a. 50
   b. 8
   c. 200
   d. 5000

24. Divide and reduce $4/13 \div 27/169$.
   a. 52/27
   b. 51/27
   c. 52/29
   d. 51/29

25. You measure the width of your door to be 36 inches. The true width of the door is 35.75 inches. What is the relative error in your measurement?
   a. 0.7%
   b. 0.007%
   c. 0.99%
   d. 0.1%

26. What are the y-intercept(s) for $y = x^2 + 3x - 4$?
   a. $y = 1$
   b. $y = -4$
   c. $y = 3$
   d. $y = 4$

27. Is the following function even, odd, neither, or both?

$$y = \frac{1}{2}x^4 + 2x^2 - 6$$

   a. Even
   b. Odd
   c. Neither
   d. Both

28. Which equation is not a function?
   a. $y = |x|$
   b. $y = \sqrt{x}$
   c. $x = 3$
   d. $y = 4$

29. What type of function is modeled by the values in the following table?

X	f(x)
1	2
2	4
3	8
4	16
5	32

a. Linear
b. Exponential
c. Quadratic
d. Cubic

30. If $a \neq b$, solve for x if $\frac{1}{x} + \frac{2}{a} = \frac{2}{b}$

a. $\frac{a-b}{ab}$

b. $\frac{ab}{2(a-b)}$

c. $\frac{2(a-b)}{ab}$

d. $\frac{a-b}{2ab}$

31. If $x^2 + x - 3 = 0$, then $\left(x - \frac{1}{2}\right)^2 =$

a. $\frac{11}{2}$

b. $\frac{11}{4}$

c. 11

d. $\frac{121}{4}$

32. An equation for the line passing through the origin and the point $(2, 1)$ is
a. $y = 2x$
b. $y = \frac{1}{2}x$
c. $y = x - 2$
d. $2y = x + 1$

33. Jessica buys 10 cans of paint. Red paint costs $1 per can and blue paint costs $2 per can. In total, she spends $16. How many red cans did she buy?
a. 2
b. 3
c. 4
d. 5

34. A farmer owns two (non-adjacent) square plots of land, which he wishes to fence. The area of one is 1000 square feet, while the area of the other is 10 square feet. How much fencing does he need, in feet?

a. 44

b. $40\sqrt{10}$

c. $440\sqrt{10}$

d. $44\sqrt{10}$

35. $2x(3x + 1) - 5(3x + 1) =$

a. $10x(3x + 1)$

b. $10x^2(3x + 1)$

c. $(2x - 5)(3x + 1)$

d. $(2x + 1)(3x - 5)$

36. For which real numbers *x* is $-3x^2 + x - 8 > 0$?

a. All real numbers *x*

b. $-2\sqrt{\frac{2}{3}} < x < 2\sqrt{\frac{2}{3}}$

c. $1 - 2\sqrt{\frac{2}{3}} < x < 1 + 2\sqrt{\frac{2}{3}}$

d. For no real numbers *x*

37. A root of $x^2 - 2x - 2$ is

a. $1 + \sqrt{3}$

b. $1 + 2\sqrt{2}$

c. $2 + 2\sqrt{3}$

d. $2 - 2\sqrt{3}$

38. In the *xy*-plane, the graph of $y = x^2 + 2$ and the circle with center $(0,1)$ and radius 1 have how many points of intersection?

a. 0

b. 1

c. 2

d. 3

39. A line goes through the point (-4, 0) and the point (0,2). What is the slope of the line?

a. 2

b. 4

c. $\frac{3}{2}$

d. $\frac{1}{2}$

40. Six people apply to work for Janice's company, but she only needs four workers. How many different groups of four employees can Janice choose?

a. 6

b. 10

c. 15

d. 36

41. Which of the following shows a line of symmetry?

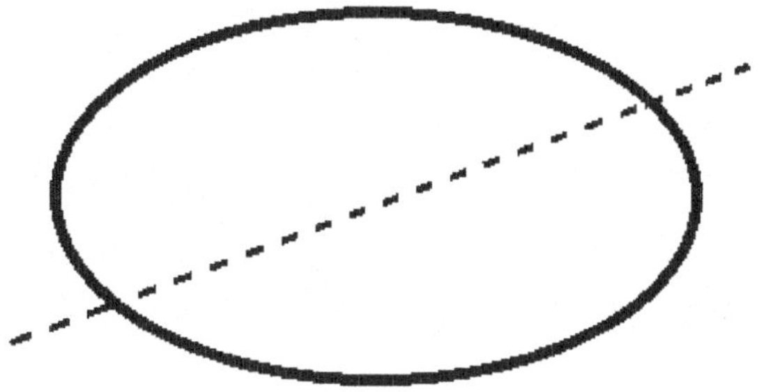

a.

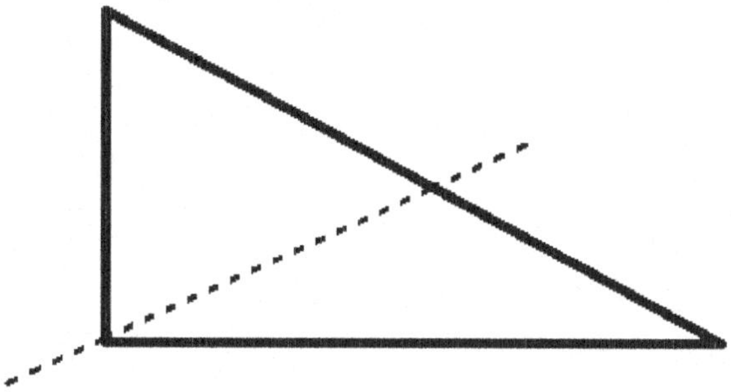

b.

c.

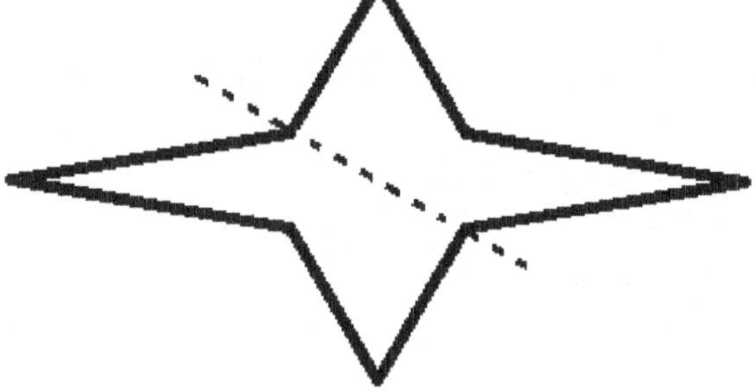

d.

42. If $4x - 3 = 5$, then $x =$

a. 1

b. 2

c. 3

d. 4

43. A ball is drawn at random from a ball pit containing 8 red balls, 7 yellow balls, 6 green balls, and 5 purple balls. What's the probability that the ball drawn is yellow?

a. $\frac{1}{26}$

b. $\frac{19}{26}$

c. $\frac{7}{26}$

d. 1

44. Two cards are drawn from a shuffled deck of 52 cards. What's the probability that both cards are Kings if the first card isn't replaced after it's drawn and is a King?

a. $\frac{1}{169}$

b. $\frac{1}{221}$

c. $\frac{1}{13}$

d. $\frac{4}{13}$

45. What's the probability of rolling a 6 at least once in two rolls of a die?

a. $\frac{1}{3}$

b. $\frac{1}{36}$

c. $\frac{1}{6}$

d. $\frac{11}{36}$

46. For a group of 20 men, the median weight is 180 pounds and the range is 30 pounds. If each man gains 10 pounds, which of the following would be true?

a. The median weight will increase, and the range will remain the same.

b. The median weight and range will both remain the same.

c. The median weight will stay the same, and the range will increase.

d. The median weight and range will both increase.

47. For the following similar triangles, what are the values of x and y (rounded to one decimal place)?

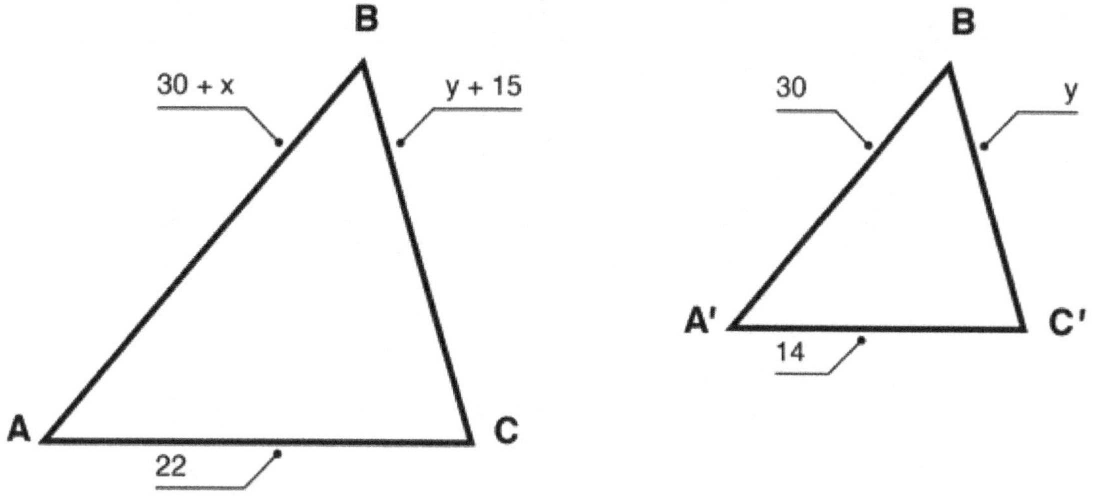

a. $x = 16.5, y = 25.1$
b. $x = 19.5, y = 24.1$
c. $x = 17.1, y = 26.3$
d. $x = 26.3, y = 17.1$

48. What are the center and radius of a circle with equation $4x^2 + 4y^2 - 16x - 24y + 51 = 0$?
a. Center (3, 2) and radius ½
b. Center (2, 3) and radius ½
c. Center (3, 2) and radius ¼
d. Center (2, 3) and radius ¼

49. If the ordered pair $(-3, -4)$ is reflected over the *x*-axis, what's the new ordered pair?
a. $(-3, -4)$
b. $(3, -4)$
c. $(3, 4)$
d. $(-3, 4)$

50. If the volume of a sphere is 288π cubic meters, what are the radius and surface area of the same sphere?
a. Radius 6 meters and surface area 144π square meters
b. Radius 36 meters and surface area 144π square meters
c. Radius 6 meters and surface area 12π square meters
d. Radius 36 meters and surface area 12π square meters

51. The triangle shown below is a right triangle. What's the value of x?

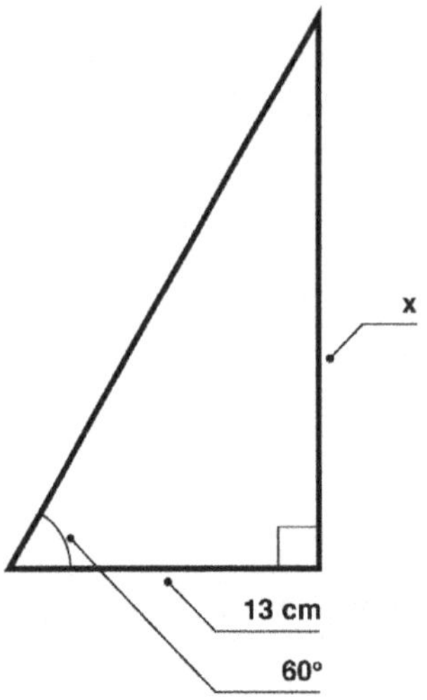

a. $x = 1.73$
b. $x = 0.57$
c. $x = 13$
d. $x = 22.49$

52. What's the midpoint of a line segment with endpoints $(-1, 2)$ and $(3, -6)$?
a. $(1, 2)$
b. $(1, 0)$
c. $(-1, 2)$
d. $(1, -2)$

53. A sample data set contains the following values: 1, 3, 5, 7. What's the standard deviation of the set?
a. 2.58
b. 4
c. 6.23
d. 1.1

54. A pair of dice is thrown, and the sum of the two scores is calculated. What's the expected value of the roll?
a. 5
b. 6
c. 7
d. 8

55. In a statistical experiment, 29 college students are given an exam during week 11 of the semester, and 30 college students are given an exam during week 12 of the semester. Both groups are being tested to determine which exam week might result in a higher grade. What's the degree of freedom in this experiment?

a. 29
b. 30
c. 59
d. 28

56. What is the sum of $(2.6 \times 10^5) + (1.3 \times 10^4)$? Enter your answer in the answer box below.

57. What would the equation be for the following problem? Enter your answer in the answer box below.
3 times the sum of a number and 7 is greater than or equal to 32.

58. What are the zeros of the function: $x^3 + 2x^2 - 15x$? Select all that apply.

a. 0
b. -3
c. -5
d. 3

Answer Explanations

1. B: To simplify the given equation, the first step is to make all exponents positive by moving them to the opposite place in the fraction. This expression becomes:

$$\frac{4b^3b^2}{a^1a^4} * \frac{3a}{b}$$

Then the rules for exponents can be used to simplify. Multiplying the same bases means the exponents can be added. Dividing the same bases means the exponents are subtracted.

2. C: The product of two irrational numbers can be rational or irrational. Sometimes, the irrational parts of the two numbers cancel each other out, leaving a rational number. For example, $\sqrt{2} * \sqrt{2} = 2$ because the roots cancel each other out. Technically, the product of two irrational numbers can be complex because complex numbers can have either the real or imaginary part (in this case, the imaginary part) equal zero and still be considered a complex number. However, Choice *D* is incorrect because the product of two irrational numbers is not an imaginary number so saying the product is complex *and* imaginary is incorrect.

3. B: The car is traveling at a speed of five meters per second. On the interval from one to three seconds, the position changes by fifteen meters. By making this change in position over time into a rate, the speed becomes ten meters in two seconds or five meters in one second.

4. C: The number negative four is classified as a real number because it exists and is not imaginary. It is rational because it does not have a decimal that never ends. It is an integer because it does not have a fractional component. The next classification would be whole numbers, for which negative four does not qualify because it is negative. Although -4 could technically be considered a complex number because complex numbers can have either the real or imaginary part equal zero and still be considered a complex number, Choice *D* is wrong because -4 is not considered an irrational number because it does not have a never-ending decimal component.

5. C: 40*N* would be 4000% of *N*. It's possible to check that each of the others is actually 40% of *N*.

6. C: 85% of a number means multiplying that number by 0.85. So, $0.85 \times 20 = \frac{85}{100} \times \frac{20}{1}$, which can be simplified to $\frac{17}{20} \times \frac{20}{1} = 17$.

7. A: To find the fraction of the bill that the first three people pay, the fractions need to be added, which means finding common denominator. The common denominator will be 60. $\frac{1}{5} + \frac{1}{4} + \frac{1}{3} = \frac{12}{60} + \frac{15}{60} + \frac{20}{60} = \frac{47}{60}$. The remainder of the bill is $1 - \frac{47}{60} = \frac{60}{60} - \frac{47}{60} = \frac{13}{60}$.

8. D: This system of equations involves one quadratic function and one linear function, as seen from the degree of each equation. One way to solve this is through substitution. Solving for y in the second equation yields $y = x + 2$. Plugging this equation in for the y of the quadratic equation yields $x^2 - 2x + x + 2 = 8$. Simplifying the equation, it becomes $x^2 - x + 2 = 8$. Setting this equal to zero and factoring, it becomes $x^2 - x - 6 = 0 = (x - 3)(x + 2)$. Solving these two factors for x gives the zeros $x = 3, -2$. To find the y-value for the point, each number can be plugged in to either original equation. Solving each one for y yields the points $(3, 5)$ and $(-2, 0)$.

9. D: The expression is simplified by collecting like terms. Terms with the same variable and exponent are like terms, and their coefficients can be added.

10. A: Finding the product means distributing one polynomial to the other so that each term in the first is multiplied by each term in the second. Then, like terms can be collected. Multiplying the factors yields the expression $20x^3 + 4x^2 + 24x - 40x^2 - 8x - 48$. Collecting like terms means adding the x^2 terms and adding the x terms. The final answer after simplifying the expression is $20x^3 - 36x^2 + 16x - 48$.

11. D: Finding the zeros for a function by factoring is done by setting the equation equal to zero, then completely factoring. Since there was a common x for each term in the provided equation, that is factored out first. Then the quadratic that is left can be factored into two binomials: $(x + 1)(x - 4)$. Setting each factor equation equal to zero and solving for x yields three zeros.

12. D: Dividing rational expressions follows the same rule as dividing fractions. The division is changed to multiplication, and the reciprocal is found in the second fraction. This turns the expression into:

$$\frac{5x^3}{3x^2} * \frac{3y^9}{25}$$

Multiplying across and simplifying, the final expression is $\frac{xy^8}{5}$.

13. B: The equation can be solved by factoring the numerator into $(x + 6)(x - 5)$. Since that same factor $(x - 5)$ exists on top and bottom, that factor cancels. This leaves the equation $x + 6 = 11$. Solving the equation gives the answer $x = 5$. When this value is plugged into the equation, it yields a zero in the denominator of the fraction. Since this is undefined, there is no solution.

14. A: These numbers to improper fractions: $\frac{11}{3} - \frac{9}{5}$. Take 15 as a common denominator: $\frac{11}{3} - \frac{9}{5} =: \frac{55}{15} - \frac{27}{15} = \frac{28}{15} = 1\frac{13}{15}$ (when rewritten to get rid of the partial fraction).

15. B: The formula can be manipulated by dividing both sides by the length, *l*, and the width, *w*. The length and width will cancel on the right, leaving height by itself.

16. B: The domain is all possible input values, or x-values. For this equation, the domain is every number greater than or equal to zero. There are no negative numbers in the domain because taking the square root of a negative number results in an imaginary number.

17. D: This problem can be solved by setting up a proportion involving the given information and the unknown value. The proportion is: $\frac{21\ pages}{4\ nights} = \frac{140\ pages}{x\ nights}$

Solving the proportion by cross-multiplying, the equation becomes $21x = 4 * 140$, where $x = 26.67$. Since it is not an exact number of nights, the answer is rounded up to 27 nights. Twenty-six nights would not give Sarah enough time.

18. D: The slope from this equation is 50, and it is interpreted as the cost per gigabyte used. Since the g-value represents number of gigabytes and the equation is set equal to the cost in dollars, the slope relates these two values. For every gigabyte used on the phone, the bill goes up 50 dollars.

19. B: $\frac{5}{2} \div \frac{1}{3} = \frac{5}{2} \times \frac{3}{1} = \frac{15}{2} = 7.5$.

20. A: The total fraction taken up by green and red shirts will be $\frac{1}{3}+\frac{2}{5}=\frac{5}{15}+\frac{6}{15}=\frac{11}{15}$. The remaining fraction is $1-\frac{11}{15}=\frac{15}{15}-\frac{11}{15}=\frac{4}{15}$.

21. C: If she has used 1/3 of the paint, she has 2/3 remaining. $2\frac{1}{2}$ gallons are the same as $\frac{5}{2}$ gallons. The calculation is $\frac{2}{3}\times\frac{5}{2}=\frac{5}{3}=1\frac{2}{3}$ gallons.

22. D: 1, 2, 3, 4, 6, 12. A given number divides evenly by each of its factors to produce an integer (no decimals). The number 5, 7, 8, 9, 10, 11 (and their opposites) do not divide evenly into 12. Therefore, these numbers are not factors.

23. A: Setting up a proportion is the easiest way to represent this situation. The proportion becomes $\frac{20}{x}=\frac{40}{100}$, where cross-multiplication can be used to solve for x. The answer can also be found by observing the two fractions as equivalent, knowing that twenty is half of forty, and fifty is half of one-hundred.

24. A: 52/27

Set up the division problem.

$$\frac{4}{13}\div\frac{27}{169}$$

Flip the second fraction and multiply.

$$\frac{4}{13}\times\frac{169}{27}$$

Simplify and reduce with cross multiplication.

$$\frac{4}{1}\times\frac{13}{27}$$

Multiply across the top and across the bottom to solve.

$$\frac{4\times 13}{1\times 27}=\frac{52}{27}$$

25. A: The relative error can be found by finding the absolute error and making it a percent of the true value. The absolute value is $36-35.75=0.25$. This error is then divided by 36—the true value—to find 0.7%.

26. B: The y-intercept of an equation is found where the x -value is zero. Plugging zero into the equation for x, the first two terms cancel out, leaving -4.

27. A: The equation is *even* because $f(-x)=f(x)$. Plugging in a negative value will result in the same answer as when plugging in the positive of that same value. The function:

$$f(-2)=\frac{1}{2}(-2)^4+2(-2)^2-6=8+8-6=10$$

yields the same value as:

$$f(2) = \frac{1}{2}(2)^4 + 2(2)^2 - 6 = 8 + 8 - 6 = 10$$

28. C: The equation $x = 3$ is not a function because it does not pass the vertical line test. This test is made from the definition of a function, where each x-value must be mapped to one and only one y-value. This equation is a vertical line, so the x-value of 3 is mapped with an infinite number of y-values.

29. B: The table shows values that are increasing exponentially. The differences between the inputs are the same, while the differences in the outputs are changing by a factor of 2. The values in the table can be modeled by the equation $f(x) = 2^x$.

30. B: $\frac{2}{a}$ must be subtracted from both sides, with a result of $\frac{1}{x} = \frac{2}{b} - \frac{2}{a}$. The reciprocal of both sides needs to be taken, but the right-hand side needs to be written as a single fraction in order to do that. Since the two fractions on the right have denominators that are not equal, a common denominator of *ab* is needed. This leaves $\frac{1}{x} = \frac{2a}{ab} - \frac{2b}{ab} = \frac{2(a-b)}{ab}$. Taking the reciprocals, which can be done since $b - a$ is not zero, with a result of $x = \frac{ab}{2(a-b)}$.

31. B: Plugging into the quadratic formula yields, for solutions:

$$x = \frac{1 \pm \sqrt{-1 + 4 \cdot 1(-3)}}{2} = \frac{1}{2} \pm \frac{\sqrt{11}}{2}$$

Therefore, $x - \frac{1}{2} = \pm\frac{\sqrt{11}}{2}$. Now, if this is squared, then the $\pm$ cancels and left with $\left(\frac{\sqrt{11}}{2}\right)^2 = \frac{11}{4}$.

32. B: The slope will be given by $\frac{1-0}{2-0} = \frac{1}{2}$. The *y*-intercept will be 0, since it passes through the origin. Using slope-intercept form, the equation for this line is $y = \frac{1}{2}x$.

33. C: Let *r* be the number of red cans and *b* be the number of blue cans. One equation is $r + b = 10$. The total price is \$16, and the prices for each can means $1r + 2b = 16$. Multiplying the first equation on both sides by -1 results in $-r - b = -10$. Add this equation to the second equation, leaving $b = 6$. So, she bought 6 *blue* cans. From the first equation, this means *r* = 4; thus, she bought 4 *red* cans.

34. D: The first field has an area of 1000 feet, so the length of one side is $\sqrt{1000} = 10\sqrt{10}$. Since there are four sides to a square, the total perimeter is $40\sqrt{10}$. The second square has an area of 10 square feet, so the length of one side is $\sqrt{10}$, and the total perimeter is $4\sqrt{10}$. Adding these together gives $40\sqrt{10} + 4\sqrt{10} = (40 + 4)\sqrt{10} = 44\sqrt{10}$.

35. C: The $(3x + 1)$ can be factored to get $(2x - 5)(3x + 1)$.

36. D: Because the coefficient of x^2 is negative, this function has a graph that is a parabola that opens downward. Therefore, it will be greater than 0 between its real roots, if it has any. Checking the discriminant, the result is $1^2 - 4(-3)(-8) = 1 - 96 = -95$. Since the discriminant is negative, this equation has no real solutions. Since this has no real roots, it must be always positive or always negative. Its graph opens downward, so it has at least some negative values. That means it is always negative. Thus, it is bigger than zero for no real numbers.

37. A: Check each value, but it is easiest to use the quadratic formula, which gives

$$x = \frac{2 \pm \sqrt{(-2)^2 - 4(1)(-2)}}{2} = 1 \pm \frac{\sqrt{12}}{2} = 1 \pm \frac{2\sqrt{3}}{2} = 1 \pm \sqrt{3}$$

The only one of these which appears as an answer choice is $1 + \sqrt{3}$.

38. B: The *y* coordinate of every point on the graph of $y = x^2 + 2$ has a vertex at (0,2) on the y-axis. The circle with a center at (0,1) also lies on the y-axis. With a radius of 1, the circle touches the parabola at one point. The vertex of the parabola (0,2).

39. D: The slope is given by the change in *y* divided by the change in *x*. The change in *y* is 2-0 = 2, and the change in *x* is 0 – (-4) = 4. The slope is $\frac{2}{4} = \frac{1}{2}$.

40. C: Janice will be choosing 4 employees out of a set of 6 applicants, so this will be given by the choice function. The following equation shows the choice function worked out:

$$\binom{6}{4} = \frac{6!}{4!\,(6-4)!} = \frac{6!}{4!\,(2)!} = \frac{6 \cdot 5 \cdot 4 \cdot 3 \cdot 2 \cdot 1}{4 \cdot 3 \cdot 2 \cdot 1 \cdot 2 \cdot 1} = \frac{6 \cdot 5}{2} = 15$$

41. C: The triangle in Choice B doesn't contain a line of symmetry. The figures in Choices A and D do contain a line of symmetry but it is not the line that is shown here. Choice C is the only one with a correct line of symmetry shown, such that the figure is mirrored on each side of the line.

42. B: Add 3 to both sides to get $4x = 8$. Then divide both sides by 4 to get $x = 2$.

43. C: The sample space is made up of $8 + 7 + 6 + 5 = 26$ balls. The probability of pulling each individual ball is $\frac{1}{26}$. Since there are 7 yellow balls, the probability of pulling a yellow ball is $\frac{7}{26}$.

44. B: For the first card drawn, the probability of a King being pulled is $\frac{4}{52}$. Since this card isn't replaced, if a King is drawn first, the probability of a King being drawn second is $\frac{3}{51}$. The probability of a King being drawn in both the first and second draw is the product of the two probabilities: $\frac{4}{52} \times \frac{3}{51} = \frac{12}{2{,}652}$ which, divided by 12, equals $\frac{1}{221}$.

45. D: The addition rule is necessary to determine the probability because a 6 can be rolled on either roll of the die. The rule used is $P(A \text{ or } B) = P(A) + P(B) - P(A \text{ and } B)$. The probability of a 6 being individually rolled is $\frac{1}{6}$ and the probability of a 6 being rolled twice is $\frac{1}{6} \cdot \frac{1}{6} = \frac{1}{36}$. Therefore, the probability that a 6 is rolled at least once is $\frac{1}{6} + \frac{1}{6} - \frac{1}{36} = \frac{11}{36}$.

46. A: If each man gains 10 pounds, every original data point will increase by 10 pounds. Therefore, the man with the original median will still have the median value, but that value will increase by 10. The smallest value and largest value will also increase by 10 and, therefore, the difference between the two won't change. The range does not change in value and, thus, remains the same.

47. C: Because the triangles are similar, the lengths of the corresponding sides are proportional. Therefore:

$$\frac{30+x}{30}=\frac{22}{14}=\frac{y+15}{y}$$

This results in the equation $14(30+x)=22\cdot 30$ which, when solved, gives $x=17.1$. The proportion also results in the equation $14(y+15)=22y$ which, when solved, gives $y=26.3$.

48. B: The technique of completing the square must be used to change $4x^2+4y^2-16x-24y+51=0$ into the standard equation of a circle. First, the constant must be moved to the right-hand side of the equals sign, and each term must be divided by the coefficient of the x^2 term (which is 4). The x and y terms must be grouped together to obtain:

$$x^2-4x+y^2-6y=-\frac{51}{4}$$

Then, the process of completing the square must be completed for each variable. This gives:

$$(x^2-4x+4)+(y^2-6y+9)=-\frac{51}{4}+4+9$$

The equation can be written as:

$$(x-2)^2+(y-3)^2=\frac{1}{4}$$

Therefore, the center of the circle is (2, 3) and the radius is:

$$\sqrt{\frac{1}{4}}=\frac{1}{2}$$

49. D: When an ordered pair is reflected over an axis, the sign of one of the coordinates must change. When it's reflected over the x-axis, the sign of the x coordinate must change. The y value remains the same. Therefore, the new ordered pair is $(-3,4)$.

50. A: Because the volume of the given sphere is 288π cubic meters, this means ${}^4\!/_3\,\pi r^3=288\pi$. This equation is solved for r to obtain a radius of 6 meters. The formula for the surface area of a sphere is $4\pi r^2$, so if $r=6$ in this formula, the surface area is 144π square meters.

51. D: SOHCAHTOA is used to find the missing side length. Because the angle and adjacent side are known, $\tan 60=\frac{\mathrm{x}}{13}$. Making sure to evaluate tangent with an argument in degrees, this equation gives:

$$x=13\tan 60=13\cdot 1.73=22.49$$

52. D: The midpoint formula should be used.

$$M=\left(\frac{x_1+x_2}{2},\frac{y_1+y_2}{2}\right)=\left(\frac{-1+3}{2},\frac{2+(-6)}{2}\right)=(1,-2)$$

53. A: First, the sample mean must be calculated:

$$\bar{x} = \frac{1}{4}(1 + 3 + 5 + 7) = 4$$

The standard deviation of the data set is $\sigma = \sqrt{\frac{\sum(x-\bar{x})^2}{n-1}}$, and $n = 4$ represents the number of data points. Therefore,

$$\sigma = \sqrt{\frac{1}{3}[(1-4)^2 + (3-4)^2 + (5-4)^2 + (7-4)^2]} = \sqrt{\frac{1}{3}(9 + 1 + 1 + 9)} = 2.58$$

54. C: The expected value is equal to the total sum of each product of individual score and probability. There are 36 possible rolls. The probability of rolling a 2 is $\frac{1}{36}$. The probability of rolling a 3 is $\frac{2}{36}$. The probability of rolling a 4 is $\frac{3}{36}$. The probability of rolling a 5 is $\frac{4}{36}$. The probability of rolling a 6 is $\frac{5}{36}$. The probability of rolling a 7 is $\frac{6}{36}$. The probability of rolling an 8 is $\frac{5}{36}$. The probability of rolling a 9 is $\frac{4}{36}$. The probability of rolling a 10 is $\frac{3}{36}$. The probability of rolling an 11 is $\frac{2}{36}$. Finally, the probability of rolling a 12 is $\frac{1}{36}$.

Each possible outcome is multiplied by the probability of it occurring. Like this:

$$2 \times \frac{1}{36} = a$$

$$3 \times \frac{2}{36} = b$$

$$4 \times \frac{3}{36} = c$$

And so forth.

Then all of those results are added together:

$$a + b + c \ldots = expected\ value$$

In this case, it equals 7.

55. D: The degree of freedom for two samples is calculated as:

$$df = \frac{(n_1 - 1) + (n_2 - 1)}{2}$$

(rounded to the lowest whole number)

For this example:

$$df = \frac{(29 - 1) + (30 - 1)}{2} = \frac{28 + 29}{2} = 28.5$$

which, rounded to the lowest whole number, is 28.

56. $\mathbf{2.73 \times 10^5}$**:** The exponent of the ten must be the same before any operations are performed on the numbers. So, $(2.6 * 10^5) + (1.3 * 10^4)$ cannot be added until one of the exponents on the ten is changed. The $1.3 * 10^4$ can be changed to $0.13 * 10^5$, then the 2.6 and 0.13 can be added. The answer comes out to be $2.73 * 10^5$.

57. $\mathbf{3(n + 7) \geq 32}$**:** 3 times the sum of a number and 7 is greater than or equal to 32 can be translated into equation form utilizing mathematical operators and numbers.

58. A, C, and D: There are three zeros for the given function. They are $x = 0, 3, -5$. The zeros can be found a number of ways, but this particular equation can be factored into:

$$f(x) = x(x^2 + 2x - 15) = x(x - 3)(x + 5)$$

By setting each factor equal to zero and solving for x, there are three solutions. On a graph, these zeros can be seen where the line crosses the x-axis.

Dear Praxis Core Test Taker,

We would like to start by thanking you for purchasing this study guide. We hope that we exceeded your expectations.

Our goal in creating this study guide was to cover all of the topics that you will see on the test. We also strove to make our practice questions as similar as possible to what you will encounter on test day. With that being said, if you found something that you feel was not up to your standards, please send us an email and let us know.

We would also like to let you know about other books in our catalog that may interest you, all of which can be found on Amazon.

Praxis Elementary Education Multiple Subjects Exam

amzn.com/1628454326

Praxis English Language Arts Content Knowledge Exam

amzn.com/1628454105

Praxis General Science Content Knowledge Exam

amzn.com/1628454385

Praxis Mathematics Content Knowledge Exam

amzn.com/1628454261

Praxis Social Studies Content Knowledge Exam

amzn.com/1628454210

We have study guides in a wide variety of fields. If the one you are looking for isn't listed above, then try searching for it on Amazon or send us an email.

Thanks Again and Happy Testing!
Product Development Team
info@studyguideteam.com

Interested in buying more than 10 copies of our product? Contact us about bulk discounts:

bulkorders@studyguideteam.com

FREE Test Taking Tips DVD Offer

To help us better serve you, we have developed a Test Taking Tips DVD that we would like to give you for FREE. **This DVD covers world-class test taking tips that you can use to be even more successful when you are taking your test.**

All that we ask is that you email us your feedback about your study guide. Please let us know what you thought about it – whether that is good, bad or indifferent.

To get your **FREE Test Taking Tips DVD**, email freedvd@studyguideteam.com with "FREE DVD" in the subject line and the following information in the body of the email:

a. The title of your study guide.

b. Your product rating on a scale of 1-5, with 5 being the highest rating.

c. Your feedback about the study guide. What did you think of it?

d. Your full name and shipping address to send your free DVD.

If you have any questions or concerns, please don't hesitate to contact us at freedvd@studyguideteam.com.

Thanks again!

37059402R00137

Made in the USA
Middletown, DE
21 February 2019